12139355

GW00497812

MA

~~DELAYED~~

UNIVERSITY COLLEGE DUBLIN

Patrick Modiano

New Directions in European Writing

....

Editor: John Flower, Professor of French, University of Exeter.

As the twentieth century draws to a close we are witnessing profound and significant changes across the new Europe. The past is being reassessed; the millennium is awaited with interest. Some, pessimistically, have predicted the death of literature; others see important developments within national literature and in movements cutting across frontiers. This enterprising series focuses on these developments through the study either of individual writers or of groups or movements. There are no definitive statements. By definition they are introductory and set out to assess and explore the full spectrum of modern European writing on the threshold of a new age.

ISBN 1350-9217

Patrick Modiano

Alan Morris

BERG
Oxford • Washington, D.C.

First published in 1996 by
Berg
Editorial offices:
150 Cowley Road, Oxford, OX4 1JJ, UK
13950 Park Center Road, Herndon, VA 22071, USA

Berg is the imprint of Oxford International Publishers Ltd.

Library of Congress Cataloging-in-Publication Data

A catalogue record for this book is available from the Library of
Congress.

British Library Cataloguing-in-Publication Data

A catalogue record for this book is available from the British Library.

Cover photograph: by Jacques Robert. © Gallimard.

ISBN 1 85973 098 1 (Cloth)
      1 85973 004 3 (Paper)

Typeset by JS Typesetting, Wellingborough, Northants.
Printed in the United Kingdom by WBC Bookbinders, Bridgend,
Mid Glamorgan.

For Sandra and Amanda

A chaque être, plusieurs autres vies me semblaient dues.

Arthur Rimbaud

Le Roman! mais c'est l'histoire, toujours, plus ou moins, des faits souvenus, agrandis, modifiés, arrangés selon l'imagination.

Jules Barbey d'Aurevilly

J'aimerais avoir vingt ans éternellement.

Patrick Modiano

Contents

Acknowledgements

A number of people have assisted me considerably in bringing this project to fruition: Professor J. E. Flower and Berg Publishers Ltd, whose encouragement and patience have been essential; my colleagues at the University of Strathclyde, who, for the second semester of 1993, took over all my teaching duties and allowed me to depart on study leave; the various students with whom, over the years, I have discussed Modiano's novels in tutorials; and last but not least, my wife Sandra, whose support and forbearance have been almost limitless. I gratefully record my thanks to them all, and hope that the work which follows is worthy of the interest they have taken in it.

Finally, thanks are also due to the University of Strathclyde and to the Carnegie Trust for the Universities of Scotland; without the financial assistance of these two institutions, the research expounded by this book could never have been pursued.

Introduction

Of all the novelists who have emerged in France in the course of the last twenty-five years or so, one of the most consistently applauded – by critics and by general public alike – has visibly proved to be Patrick Modiano. Prix Fénéon, Prix Roger Nimier, Prix de la Plume de Diamant, Grand Prix du roman de l'Académie française, Prix des Libraires, Prix Goncourt, Prix Pierre de Monaco, Prix relais H du roman d'évasion, Chevalier des Arts et des Lettres, regular listings in the bestseller charts – the *palmarès modianesque* is a list of virtually every honour open to the writer of modern French fiction. And such is the author's abiding appeal that his run of success looks set to continue.

Despite this outstanding achievement, however, Modiano remains relatively obscure outside his native France. He is, it is true, appearing on more and more syllabuses as the years go by, and his works have, admittedly, been translated into a number of foreign languages, but he is still far from an international household name. Perhaps because of this, critics have, somewhat unjustly, tended to neglect him. Apart from two invaluable, but partial, monographs in French,[1] interest has been limited to the occasional article or interview, supported by a series of perfunctory book reviews. As far as I know, there is, at present, no complete, up-to-date published study of the *œuvre* in existence anywhere, with nothing longer than chapter length available in English.

So, there is clearly a gap which needs to be filled, and this, precisely, is what the pages which follow will endeavour to do. Not that the gap can be filled in completely. Such is the extent and the variety of Modiano's output (which includes *romans, récits*, short stories, children's books, prefaces, articles, a play, a film script and a book review)[2] that something has to give in a work of this nature, and what has given, except for the odd reference where relevant, is everything other than the texts for which the author is rightly famous – his fifteen major prose works (novels for the most part).

This deliberate selectivity is reflected in the structure of the present survey. After an initial discussion of Modiano's reasons for taking up his pen (Chapter 1), we will progress chronologically, book by book, from *La Place de l'Étoile* in 1968 to *Un cirque passe* in 1992. 'Comment apprécier [. . .] l'œuvre d'un écrivain [. . .] si on ne la prend dès ses débuts, si on ne la suit pas à pas', Joris-Karl Huysmans has said,[3] and while this approach may not be favoured by all, it does help to secure two of the vital objectives of this analysis: first, to examine the fifteen texts individually, and to introduce them both as self-standing entities and as companions to their fellow texts; and second, to build up an overview of the *œuvre* in its entirety, to show (and to try to explain) the developments that have occurred as novel has followed novel, while at the same time stressing what has remained constant.

This pursuit of change-within-continuity has, like the choice of texts before it, had a considerable effect on the structure of the present survey, for associated works have been grouped together into chapters and hence distinguished from their surrounding books. Granted, Modiano has, quite pertinently, insisted that he, along with every other writer, 'fait toujours le même roman';[4] but that said, some of his novels plainly have much more in common than others, and it is this that will allow them, albeit often quite tentatively, to be cut off from their neighbours and viewed in combinations. Thus, Chapter 2 will look at *La Place de l'Étoile, La Ronde de nuit* and *Les Boulevards de ceinture*, focusing on their shared background of the Occupation; Chapter 3 will consider *Villa Triste, Livret de famille* and *Rue des Boutiques Obscures* – as variations on an established theme (that of imaginary autobiography); Chapter 4 will take in *Une jeunesse* and *De si braves garçons*, and stress their (not all too successful) experimentations; Chapter 5 will pair *Quartier perdu* and *Dimanches d'août*, two tales of crime and mystery; Chapter 6 will switch to childhood, and link *Remise de peine* to *Vestiaire de l'enfance*, while Chapter 7 will spotlight exorcism, through the study of *Voyage de noces, Fleurs de ruine* and *Un cirque passe*.

Implicit in this plan of action, of course, is a discussion of the key elements of the *œuvre* at different stages of the survey below, and this is an approach which is very much in tune with

Modiano's own *modus operandi*: he too brings the various aspects
of his universe to the fore at different times, stressing one thing
in one novel, another in the next, and slowly compiling a global
picture as if he were doing a jigsaw – bit by bit, building on the
details he has revealed earlier. And just as this implies a constant
attente for his devoted readers, an awareness that the questions
he raises will not be answered – in full – until his very last book
is written (if then), so will a complete overview of the novelist's
concerns emerge only in retrospect here, once each of the
aforenoted texts has been examined.

For example, we shall discover, as we proceed, that much of
Modiano's fiction is cathartic in impulse, a means of assuaging
the pain caused by the tragic death of his younger brother, Rudy,
the near-total absence of his father, Albert, and the troubling
events of the German Occupation. We shall also see how
the world he creates, for all its apparent *passéisme*, has great
contemporary (and often overtly *fin-de-millénaire*) relevance,
thanks to its fundamental bleakness, its essential uncertainty/
ambiguity, and the specific nature of the problems it exemplifies
(such as those of time, memory, identity and the past; or the
escapist flight from an unfulfilling present; or the extensive
difficulty involved in communicating; or the ins and outs of the
Jewish question). We shall further ascertain that the author is an
eclectic writer, drawing on predecessors as varied as, say, Scott
Fitzgerald (whom he resembles in his focus on transience,
amongst other things) or, much closer to home, the *nouveaux
romanciers* (whose narrative innovations and *série-noire* 'feel' he,
like so many of his *confrères* today, is loath to ignore whatever he
may think of the 'theories' which inform them). Finally, we shall
perceive that, the breadth of these literary borrowings
notwithstanding, Modiano is the complete master of his chosen
medium, the forger of a style so distinctive that it can really only
be summed up as uniquely *modianesque*.[5] However, as already
emphasized, none of these points will emerge *fully* from the
discussion of any one text. It will not, in fact, be until the
Conclusion that the fragments offered are drawn together and
their complete significance highlighted; not until the Conclusion
that the *œuvre* in general is addressed *at length*, and its place in
literary history established.

This mention of literary history leads on – conveniently – to a
question which may have been provoked by some of the earlier

comments above: what is the critical standpoint of this survey? And the answer to this question is: there is not one. Or rather, there are lots of them. Structuralist, psychoanalytical, the Author as source – these are just some of the varied (and conflicting) theoretical methods adopted below, and while some would no doubt prefer a less wide-ranging, and more consistent, line of attack, there is, I believe, strong justification for this diversity: Modiano himself (as has just been suggested, and as we will shortly see) draws on a whole host of (likewise incompatible) models, so his work can really only be explained – in any comprehensive sense – by a similar unboundedness on the part of his commentator.

This is not to imply, though, that the text which follows is full of heavy jargon. On the contrary, clarity is another major aim of this analysis, for without it, I could never achieve my prime objectives: to introduce Modiano to those who do not know him; to refresh the interest of those who already do; and finally, through a combination of the previous concerns, to secure a further, single, all-embracing goal – to make accessible to everyone this 'auteur qui est désormais un classique'.[6]

Notes

1. Nettelbeck and Hueston's *Patrick Modiano: Pièces d'identité: écrire l'entretemps* is a seminal work, but was written in the mid-1980s, and so deals with none of the novels which appeared thereafter. The much more recent *Patrick Modiano*, by Jules Bedner (ed.), is another insightful godsend, but (as is often the case with collections of essays) patchy in its coverage of individual texts. (For full bibliographical details of these two books, and, indeed, of all publications on or by Modiano cited hereafter, see the Select Bibliography.)
2. For a more comprehensive, and more detailed, breakdown here, see the Select Bibliography (the editions of individual texts listed there being the ones to which all references will henceforth relate).
3. *A Rebours* (Paris, Crès, 1929), p.xxii. Note that here, as throughout the book, I have used square brackets around three dots to indicate my own ellipsis, and hence to distinguish it from that already existing in the extracts quoted.

4. Geille, 'Patrick Modiano m'intimide!', p.66.
5. Even before we read Modiano, we can infer the unique and masterful nature of his style from the fact that it has led to an amusing pastiche (probably by Nettelbeck and Hueston) – see Patrick O'Modian, 'Un soir ou un autre', *Australian Journal of French Studies*, XXI, 2 (May–August 1984), p.224.
6. Bona, 'Géographie du passé', p.4.

1

The Birth of a Novelist

Par mon hérédité, qui croise en moi deux systèmes de vie très différents, se peuvent expliquer cette complexité et ces contradictions dont je souffre.

André Gide

J'avais la *manie* de regarder en arrière, toujours ce sentiment de quelque chose de perdu, pas comme le paradis, mais de perdu, oui.

Patrick Modiano

L'imagination lui semblait pouvoir aisément suppléer à la vulgaire réalité des faits.

Joris-Karl Huysmans

Il n'y a rien de plus anachronique aujourd'hui que le roman. [. . .] Faute d'audience, faute de pouvoir s'adapter au rythme du monde moderne, [. . .] le roman ne peut plus, à mon sens, déterminer ou orienter la sensibilité commune, comme il pouvait encore le faire au début de ce siècle. Bousculé par le cinéma et les moyens d'expression modernes, son influence est plus sournoise et réduite qu'au temps où il était interdit dans les pensionnats.[1]

These words, uttered by Patrick Modiano in 1975, come as something of a shock to the unsuspecting critic or reader, not because of what they say, which is scarcely new, but because of the puzzling enigma they seem to embody. How, we may wonder, can one of the greatest French novelists alive today have been drawn into a genre which he considers 'anachronique'? What could have possessed him, at the start of his career, to devote himself to fiction-writing, rather than to one of the numerous other, much more modern forms of artistic creation? What, in short, when everything seemed to militate against it, could have led to the birth of a novelist in him? It is precisely these questions, and others like them, that the present chapter will seek to answer.

To expedite this quest for insights into Modiano's choice of profession, it will be extremely informative (no matter what anti-intentionalists may say) to turn to the author himself, and to let him explain what prompted him to enter the realm of literature.[2] And where better to begin here than by having him rule out a number of motivations which might have applied, but which most definitely did not. For example, globally speaking, he was clearly not led to take up the pen by any determination to join an existing literary school, movement or trend. Not for him a political *engagement* to be expressed in his works: 'Si l'on écrit des romans, il faut gommer les préoccupations politiques. Lorsque les écrivains se mêlent de politique, c'est grotesque.'[3] Nor is he driven by any commitment to extend the formal boundaries of literature, as many of his contemporaries undoubtedly are. 'Les gens de *Tel quel* sont pour moi des Martiens', he openly admits,[4] and he finds little common ground with the *nouveaux romanciers* either: 'Je ne m'intéresse à aucune école expérimentale et je reproche notamment au Nouveau Roman de n'avoir ni ton ni vie. Je suis étranger à la littérature désincarnée.'[5] Finally, the vogue for eroticism in the novel can quickly be dismissed as uninfluential as well, for here too the author makes it perfectly clear that, albeit as a reader, he has very little sympathy for such a concern. 'Pour moi', he insists, 'l'érotisme est quelque chose de tout à fait mineur [. . .]. Je me trompe peut-être, mais je ne vois pas là une grande, une vraie nécessité d'écrire.'[6]

This final reference to 'une grande, une vraie nécessité d'écrire' is obviously important, and it takes us away now from the reasons Modiano did *not* have for turning to fiction-writing, and on, allusively, to the factor which (the danger of reductionism notwithstanding) actually does appear to have spawned his artistic vocation: somē sort of emotional compulsion. And thanks (yet again) to his own revelations on the matter, the exact nature of this compulsion is not especially hard to identify. Still contrasting his position with that of the experimental writers, he discloses: 'La littérature pour la littérature, les recherches sur l'écriture, tout ce byzantinisme pour chaires et colloques, ça ne m'intéresse pas: j'écris pour savoir qui je suis, pour me trouver une identité.'[7] It is, then, self-avowedly, to try to resolve an identity crisis that Modiano first puts pen to paper.

That such an identity crisis should have arisen in him is

scarcely surprising in retrospect, for his family background seems to have been extremely problematic to say the least. And the word 'seems' is not used loosely here, for Modiano has deliberately sought to obscure the precise details of his *état civil* ever since he shot to fame in 1968. Tantalizingly reticent in the interviews he agrees to give, and frequently contradicting himself whenever he does choose to speak, he is a notoriously difficult individual to pin down with any degree of certainty. Indeed, it took years of questioning for him to admit that he was, in fact, born on 30 July 1945, in Boulogne-Billancourt, rather than in 1947 in Pontoise, as he had originally led everyone to believe. Yet in spite of this studied elusiveness, specific aspects of his past *have* slowly emerged into the public domain,[8] and when these facts are added to his pronouncements in interview, and to the evidently autobiographical passages of, say, *Livret de famille*, and, more recently, *Remise de peine* and *Fleurs de ruine*, a relatively consistent (though by no means definitive) account of his life history can tentatively be put forward.

Beyond any doubt at all now is the contradictory, exotic character of the heritage he received at birth from his parents, his mother, Luisa Colpeyn, being a Belgian actress-cum-model-cum-chorus girl (of apparently Hungarian and Flemish stock), and his father, Albert Modiano (1912–78), being a 'juif cosmopolite',[9] whose own roots stretched back to the eastern Mediterranean, and in particular to the *apatride* communities of Thessalonika and Alexandria. Now clearly, anyone with such an inheritance could not fail to suffer from a sense of cultural orphanage, and this was most palpably the case with Modiano: plagued by 'le sentiment de ne pouvoir [se] rattacher à aucune tradition, à aucun passé national ou historique; le sentiment d'être un déraciné',[10] he grew up intensely aware that he was an 'étranger, ou du moins [un] Français de hasard'.[11] And as if this *déracinement* were not enough to colour his future development, the tragic events of his childhood were soon to have a profound and lasting effect on him as well.

From almost the very first, it would appear, Modiano's early years, which he spent in a flat at 15 quai Conti in Paris, were marked by solitude, sadness and emotional upheaval. His father, ever keen to unearth profitable new business ventures for himself, would often be away from home wheeling and dealing in the world of finance, while his mother, in order to pursue her career as an actress, would frequently go off on theatrical tours, and so also entrust her son to the care of others. To offset such parental absence, Modiano did, admittedly, have one slight crumb of comfort to sustain him: his younger brother (and best friend) Rudy. But it was a crumb of comfort which, unfortunately, was destined to vanish just as quickly as his parents did. In circumstances which have not, as yet, been unambiguously established (but which were probably 'une maladie du sang' in 1957),[12] Rudy tragically died, leaving his elder brother afflicted for life. 'De cette absence, il ne s'est jamais remis', Pierre Assouline has rightly observed,[13] and when Albert then walked out on the family, at the start of the 1960s, Modiano's deprivation and loss were complete.

The corollary of this affective vacuum for him was essentially twofold. The more visible consequence, predictably perhaps, was that he displayed a total inability to settle down at school. From Biarritz to Deauville, from Jouy-en-Josas to Haute Savoie, the future novelist was, at one stage or another, a pupil in various institutions throughout the length and breadth of France.[14] No matter where he happened to be enrolled for classes, though, the end result was always the same: 'Je changeais de collège tous les ans. On me renvoyait pour indiscipline.'[15] He eventually returned to Paris to complete his studies, such as they were, at the prestigious Lycée Henri-IV, and the *baccalauréat* he obtained there allowed him to go on to university, his choice of which was the no less prestigious Sorbonne. But the groves of Academe were still unable to retain him for long; at the end of his first year, he effectively dropped out.[16]

The second, less visible consequence of Modiano's deprivation and loss was an awareness that the world around him was sadly lacking in permanence. 'Le temps qui passe, l'érosion des êtres, m'ont toujours fasciné', he avowed in 1974,[17] and then added in explanation a year later: 'Si j'ai senti, très jeune et de façon aiguë, que le temps finissait par tout ronger, par tout dissoudre, par tout détruire, c'est que j'avais moi-même un profond sentiment d'insécurité.'[18]

This 'sentiment d'insécurité', the product, as has just be seen, of his troubled family background, was to haunt him well into his adult life. Little wonder, then, that he should feel driven to concede: 'La vie réelle ne suffit pas [. . .] à me satisfaire.'[19] And little wonder either that, in his imagination, he should seek to make up for this deficiency by creating more appealing, surrogate existences for himself.[20]

It is, of course, only a small step from real-life *rêverie* to the discipline of fiction-writing, and Modiano was not slow to realize this. Constantly fashioning false autobiographies in his mind, he soon found that, in the novel, he had at his disposal the ideal means to make his alternative lives more concrete, and hence more convincing. As he revealed in 1976, following his interview with Emmanuel Berl: 'En face de Berl, je retourne à mes préoccupations: le temps, le passé, la mémoire. Il les ravive, ces préoccupations. Il m'encourage dans mon dessein: me créer un passé et une mémoire avec le passé et la mémoire des autres.'[21] 'Me créer un passé et une mémoire avec le passé et la mémoire des autres' – this final comment says it all: Modiano is, most definitely, using his fiction to palliate his identity crisis. And this, at the end of the day, is why there is no real contradiction in his choice of medium. The novel may very well be 'anachronique', in most respects, when compared, say, to television or the cinema, but it still offers to the budding artist one vitally important possibility: the chance to combine creativity and therapy. As may by now be clear, this was precisely the possibility that mattered most for Modiano. And it was a possibility which, in his coming literary career, he would eagerly and continually exploit.

Notes

1. Ezine, 'Sur la sellette: Patrick Modiano ou le passé antérieur', p.5.
2. For a useful summary of anti-intentionalism, see Catherine Belsey, *Critical Practice* (London/New York, Routledge, 1987), pp.15–16. Whatever the appeal (or otherwise) of this standpoint, it is still *informative* to know what a writer claims to be doing when composing – we do not, after all, have to agree with him or her. (This will be my stance throughout.)
3. Texier, 'Rencontre avec un jeune romancier: Patrick Modiano', p.8. This stance is perhaps all the more surprising in that, as we shall see, Modiano's first novel was published in the spring of 1968 – the very time when the links between politics and literature were being imprinted on everyone's mind.

4. Duranteau, 'L'Obsession de l'anti-héros', p.13.
5. Montalbetti, 'La Haine des professeurs: Instantané Patrick Modiano', p.2.
6. Duranteau, 'L'Obsession de l'anti-héros', p.13.
7. Ezine, 'Sur la sellette', p.5.
8. See e.g. his entry in *Who's Who in France*, published annually by the Éditions Lafitte.
9. Pudlowski, 'Modiano le magnifique', p.28.
10. Malka, 'Patrick Modiano: un homme sur du sable mouvant', p.2.
11. Ezine, 'Sur la sellette', p.5.
12. This explanation is given in Assouline, 'Modiano: lieux de mémoire' (p.36). Earlier (Chalon, 'Patrick Modiano: Le Dernier promeneur solitaire', p.12) the cause of death had been given as a car crash (but at that time Modiano was still covering his tracks, trying to keep his personal life secret).
13. Assouline, 'Lieux de mémoire', p.36.
14. He also had private maths lessons from Raymond Queneau – ibid., p.44.
15. Chalon, 'Le Dernier promeneur', p.10.
16. Using the information available (much of which is the author's own fiction) a very rough (and by no means definitive) dating of Modiano's *scolarité* can be assembled. The story seems to begin at the institut Sainte-Marie in Biarritz, in October 1950, when the young Patrick begins his very first day at school (*Livret de famille*, p.92). Later, he is apparently to be found back in Paris, at the *école communale* in the rue du Pont-de-Lodi (*Fleurs de ruine*, p.38). By the mid-1950s, he is at Jouy-en-Josas and, after the upheaval of Rudy's death in 1957, there again (but at a different school) as the new decade arrives (see Chapters 4 and 6 below). Expelled because of a *fugue* on 18 January 1960 (*Fleurs de ruine*, pp.38, 96, 114–16), he moves on, and can definitely be placed at the collège Saint-Joseph in Thônes in 1961 and 1962 (Morel, 'Une dissertation de Modiano', p.37). Back in Paris afresh, he is at the Lycée Henri-IV at the age of 18 (i.e. from 1963 to 1964 – *Fleurs de ruine*, p.11), which would suggest he stopped going to the Sorbonne in 1965, although he had earlier (Brunn, 'Patrick Modiano: Exilé de quelque chose', p.10) situated this event in 1966 – a timely reminder that most of the above dating is speculative.

17. M., 'Patrick Modiano: "Non, je ne suis pas un auteur rétro"', p.11.
18. Ezine, 'Sur la sellette', p.5.
19. Rambures, 'Comment travaillent les écrivains: Patrick Modiano: "apprendre à mentir"', p.24.
20. See Jamet, 'Patrick Modiano s'explique'. 'Quelle a été votre histoire, votre passé, jusqu'à 18, 20 ans?' Jamet asks him. 'Vous voulez dire, dans la réalité?' he illuminatingly replies (p.29).
21. Berl, *'Interrogatoire par Patrick Modiano' suivi de 'Il fait beau, allons au cimetière'*, p.9.

2

A Novelist's Occupation: 'La Place de l'Étoile', 'La Ronde de nuit' and 'Les Boulevards de ceinture'

Comme tous les gens qui n'ont ni terroir ni racines, je suis obsédé par ma préhistoire. Et ma préhistoire, c'est la période troublé et honteuse de l'Occupation.

Patrick Modiano

N'eus-je pas *une fois* une jeunesse aimable, héroïque, fabuleuse, à écrire sur des feuilles d'or – trop de chance! Par quel crime, par quelle erreur, ai-je mérité ma faiblesse actuelle?

Arthur Rimbaud

One's first influences are largely literary but the point where the personal note emerges *can* come very young.

Scott Fitzgerald

As the preceding pages have endeavoured to establish, Modiano was thrust into novel-writing by emotional necessity. 'Je ne pouvais rien faire d'autre', he helpfully confirms, giving an unwitting *précis* of the argument constructed in Chapter 1. 'J'avais fait des études secondaires chaotiques et il m'était impossible de m'incorporer dans le milieu universitaire. Je n'avais pas d'ancrage familial non plus. Il y avait une espèce d'urgence.'[1] Indeed, so intense was his inner turmoil that, even before he dropped out of university, he had turned to literature as an attractive outlet for his emotions. At the age of about nine or ten he was regularly composing poems, and by the time he was just five years older he was attempting to write whole books, albeit without ever getting past the first forty pages.[2] Nevertheless, the 'urgence' to which he would later refer was already clearly there. It was just that a certain immaturity and the lack of a definite focus prevented him from bringing any of his various projects to fruition. By the mid-1960s, however, things had dramatically changed. Now aged twenty, he had suddenly become a good deal more mature (precociously so), and hence better equipped for the literary career he had chosen to follow. And that was not all; he had also come to discover the focus he had previously – and regretfully – lacked: the *années noires* of 1940–44. In other words, as his majority approached, Modiano was ready to pursue an occupation in two different senses of the word: on the one hand, he was anxious to embark on his professional *vocation*, and on the other he was preparing to evoke the 'dark years' of *the* Occupation. This being the case, it is in the light of its implicit double meaning that the title of the present chapter can best be interpreted. And it is in this selfsame light that, in the pages which follow, we can first approach and then guide ourselves into the first three novels which Modiano produced: *La Place de l'Étoile* (1968), *La Ronde de nuit* (1969) and *Les Boulevards de ceinture* (1972).

Submitted to Gallimard in June 1967, and finally published in the spring of 1968, Modiano's debut novel was rewarded by two literary prizes and a vast amount of critical acclaim. Its title, intriguingly, was *La Place de l'Étoile*, an allusion both to the well-known Parisian landmark and to the place where Jews wore the Star of David during the Occupation (over the heart), which is highly significant, for the book is, precisely, a French Jew's *cri de cœur*, a dazzling – and provocative – examination of Jewish identity.[3] Or to be more exact, in the first instance at least, it is an examination of Modiano's *own* Jewish identity, for as he himself recalls, looking back to the time when he was working on the novel: 'Tout est venu ensemble, le ton, l'axe, le sujet, comme en spirale. A la base, il y avait la volonté d'élucider ma propre origine, une quête de mon identité.'[4]

This authorial quest for an identity informs each and every page of *La Place de l'Étoile*, and the focal point for its expression is the outlandish narrator of the work, who revels in the name of Raphaël Schlemilovitch. A composite of many different, stereotyped (and often contradictory) personalities, Schlemilovitch is the impossible incarnation of *Le Juif* in the abstract, the totemic archetype of his people as a whole, as one early reviewer was quick to notice: 'Tous les juifs de ce monde sont un seul juif, qui s'appelle toujours Raphaël Schlemilovitch – et un seul juif, hélas! porte le poids de tous les autres, présents, passés et à venir.'[5] In short, and to use the novel itself as a basis for comparison, he is just like one of the kaleidoscopes which his father manufactures: 'un visage humain composé de mille facettes lumineuses et qui change sans arrêt de forme...' (pp.109–10).[6]

Needless to say, perhaps, given the example of the *nouveaux romanciers* and other modern-minded writers in France, this fragmentation of the narrative voice in *La Place de l'Étoile* goes hand in hand with a more general, all-embracing *éclatement* of the conventional novel form: geographical locations, historical periods and even a number of characters constantly merge into each other; contradictions do not just occur, they are actively cultivated (Schlemilovitch dies on at least three different occasions); the use of parody, pastiche and quotation ensures that there is no unified – or unifying – style; and this is to mention only the more visible ways in which the classical tradition is challenged in the text.

Yet in spite of this abandonment of the Realist world-view and approach to fiction, it would be wrong to infer that illogicality reigns supreme in *La Place de l'Étoile*. This is not the case at all. There is a logic at work in the text, but it is a logic which does not usually merit the name, a logic which, for Raphaël, represents the only source of certainty in an otherwise troubled and confusing universe: the logic of Jewish precedent. For example, when he works hard to get into the École nationale supérieure, he admits to following in the footsteps of Edmond Fleg, Léon Blum and Henri Franck;[7] when he turns his hand to pimping he has in mind that 'quand Apollinaire parlait du "maquereau juif, roux et rose", il pensait à moi',[8] and when he is afflicted by tuberculosis he confesses, quite openly, that he has simply taken Franz Kafka's disease to be his own.[9] In fact, incongruous as this may appear at first glance, his 'retour à la terre' phase can also be interpreted in this manner, since Pétain's pithy maxim, which he personalizes and adopts – 'Je hais les mensonges qui m'ont fait tant de mal. La terre, elle, ne ment pas' (p.83) – was, in reality, composed by Emmanuel Berl, a Jew.[10]

This flirtation with the man who, during the *années noires*, served as the figurehead of state anti-Semitism is not the only contact that Schlemilovitch has with his nominal enemies. Recalling that Jews like Jean Lévy, Pierre-Marius Zadoc, Raoul-Charles Leman, Marc Boasson, René Riquier, Louis Latzarus and René Gross were all strong supporters of Charles Maurras, he frequents the pre-war milieux of the extreme right, mixes with historical figures such as Maurice Pujo and Maxime Réal del Sarte, and ends up by becoming part of the team of *Je suis partout*.[11] Then a few years later, after the German invasion of 1940, he quickly transforms this persona of 'juif antisémite' (p.25) into the far more topical one (as demonstrated by Maurice Sachs and Joseph Joanovici) of 'juif collaborateur' (p.25),[12] a role which he in turn rapidly discards when he pursues his political journey to its unlikely, yet inevitable, conclusion: reminding himself that Jewish blood was said to flow in the veins of Reinhard Heydrich (and perhaps aware that similar rumours circulated about Adolf Hitler as well), he metamorphoses into a Nazi and takes Eva Braun as his lover.[13]

Raphaël Schlemilovitch, the archetypal Jew, suddenly taking on the form of a Fascist – there seems to be a dire lack of logic here, even allowing for the aforementioned 'law' of Jewish precedent. However, if the matter is approached from a slightly different angle, there would, in actual fact, appear to be quite some method in Raphaël's apparent madness, since by befriending and consorting with renowned Fascists he is able, quite rationally, to kill three additional birds with one stone. First, he can, as it were, conduct a pre-emptive, defensive strike against his persecutors, 'pour court-circuiter la menace', as Modiano himself concurs.[14] Second, he can give free rein to the other side of his schizophrenic character, prove himself to be totally *French*, and embrace the *antidreyfusard* heritage which, historically, this implies. And finally, he can usurp the rabid anti-Semite's perspective on life, and thereby achieve a greater, more revealing insight into the public identity he has as a Jew.

This last concern is arguably the most influential of the three, for Raphaël believes he has a bounden duty to live up to (if not exceed) every anti-Semitic expectation of him, and as early as the opening paragraph he is to be found translating this self-made obligation into practice – his possession of an 'héritage vénézuélien' acknowledges the 'well-known fact' of Jewish internationalism (an allusion echoed later when he refers to his cousins in Cairo, London, Paris, Caracas, Trieste and Budapest), and his very name would strike most readers as being manifestly 'typical' of his race as a whole.[15] Indeed, the farther the novel progresses, the more noticeable it becomes that Schlemilovitch's *raison d'être* and popular prejudice are more or less one and the same thing. 'Oui, je dirige le complot juif mondial à coups de partouzes et de millions,' he willingly agrees. 'Oui, la guerre de 1939 a été déclarée par ma faute. Oui, je suis une sorte de Barbe-Bleue [. . .]. Oui, je rêve de ruiner toute la paysannerie française et d'enjuiver le Cantal' (p.35).[16]

This readiness on Raphaël's part to lay claim to the various roles imposed on him – more obviously seen in comments such as 'Je jouerai à la perfection mon rôle de persécuté' (p.62) – is again brazenly flaunted when he encounters Charles Lévy-Vendôme, who can be viewed as the Jew-as-seen-by-the-anti-Semite *par excellence*. As the tension of his name itself indicates, Lévy-Vendôme embodies the perceived Judaic 'threat' to France, for not only does he seek out young French women as raw material for the white slave trade, he converts the country's literary classics into crude erotica. 'Non content de débaucher les femmes de ce pays', he observes, 'j'ai voulu aussi prostituer toute la littérature française' (p.68). Schlemilovitch, predictably, needs no persuading to emulate this subversive behaviour, and quickly gets involved in *la traite des blanches* himself. Furthermore, he then crowns his antisocial activity by having an affair with a *marquise*, who, by dressing up as a character from history each time they make love, allows him to fulfil his allotted mission in overtly symbolic terms – with her assistance, it is explicitly noted, 'il souilla la France à loisir' (p.95).[17]

Given now, as the above demonstration has endeavoured to show, that Raphaël has a certain existentialist tinge to his nature, an all too visible air of *existence pour autrui*, it is highly appropriate that Jean-Paul Sartre's *Réflexions sur la question juive* (1954) should also have helped to make him into the kind of person(s) he is. Not that the influence of this work is immediately apparent to the naked eye. Quite the opposite – at first sight Sartre (and his argument along with him) is provocatively dismissed out of hand: 'Il affirmait que le juif n'existerait pas si les goyes ne daignaient lui prêter attention. Il faut donc attirer *leurs* regards aux moyens d'étoffes bariolées' (p.48).[18] On a more fundamental level, however, the influence is quite glaring, and relates to one area of the philosophical essay in particular: the mention of the various character traits which, typically, 'la mythologie antisémite' ascribes to its *bête noire*, the Jew – cupidity, constant introspection and an inability to assimilate, among others.[19]

Never one to ignore any facet of his social identity, Raphaël acts on each of these three prescriptions with alacrity. 'Je suis JUIF. Par conséquent, seuls l'argent et la luxure m'intéressent', he avers (p.34), highlighting his love of money with his own provocative brand of logic. Fifty pages further on, it is the assigned tendency towards self-analysis which has now come to engross his thoughts:

> Après avoir été un juif collabo, façon Joanovici-Sachs, Raphaël Schlemilovitch joue la comédie du 'retour à la terre' façon Barrès-Pétain. A quand l'immonde comédie du juif militariste, façon capitaine Dreyfus-Stroheim? Celle du juif honteux façon Simone Weil-Céline? Celle du juif distingué façon Proust-Daniel Halévy-Maurois? Nous voudrions que Raphaël Schlemilovitch se contente d'être un juif tout court . . .. (p.84)[20]

Where Schlemilovitch most palpably draws on Sartre, though, is in his cultural alienation, his total incapacity to put down any permanent roots in France at all. Part of his problem here is his striking failure to construct enduring relationships for himself. He does, admittedly, have a mother and a father to give him certain family ties, and he actually manages to make friends with Frenchmen as varied as Adrien Debigorre (an extreme-right-wing teacher) and Jean-François Des Essarts (an enthusiastic philosemite), but all of these characters quickly disappear from his life, leaving him completely isolated and adrift as he readily – and compositely! – avows: 'Notre mère était morte ou folle. Nous ne connaissions pas l'adresse de notre père à New York. [. . .] Ni celle d'Adrien Debigorre. [. . .] Des Essarts était mort' (p.103). The other cause of his difficulty is no less dramatic, if somewhat more predictable – the sorry awareness that, as he himself confides, 'Je ne suis pas un enfant de ce pays' (p.12), and that this makes him 'une fleur artificielle au milieu de la France' (p.47).

Yet it is not through want of effort that Raphaël finds himself with no deep-set roots to nourish and sustain him. He is constantly doing all he can to integrate himself into French society, employing two strategies in particular to procure the stability that he lacks but so desires. On the one hand: the ploy of marriage. He has fiancées in every province when he works in the white slave trade, and generally seems eager to wed any woman who crosses his path, whether it be Rebecca, the Israeli soldier, or Hilda, whose father is a strict SS disciplinarian. On the other hand, there is his drive to create a whole string of surrogate relatives for himself: he does not hesitate to speak of 'mon père, le vicomte Lévy-Vendôme' (p.85), nor does he fail to give special mentions to 'Des Essarts, mon frère' (p.105), 'mon grand-père, le colonel Aravis' (p.75) and 'mon grand-oncle Adrien Debigorre' (p.75). His comment on Maurras, Pujo and Réal del Sarte further reflects this obsession of his: 'Depuis mon enfance je rêvais à des grands-pères de ce genre. Le mien, juif obscur d'Odessa, ne savait pas parler français' (p.25).

This pursuit of some sort of attachment culminates, naturally, in a visit to Israel, 'la terre ancestrale' (p.122). But no sooner does Raphaël arrive in Tel Aviv than any hopes he may have had of a warm welcome there are irrevocably trampled underfoot. Instead of being met with open arms, as he might have expected, he is made to feel every bit as unwanted and alien as he was in France, for the Israelis, he learns to his cost, are a nation of Fascistic strong men, and totally disdain their lily-livered European counterparts, proclaiming: 'Nous ne voulons plus entendre parler de l'esprit critique juif, de l'intelligence juive, du scepticisme juif, des contorsions juives, de l'humiliation, du malheur juif et patati et patata' (p.133). Such a controversial portrayal of the Jewish homeland derives, no doubt, from the common conviction that Israel is peopled by fervent militarists, all committed to imposing their will and ensuring that they never go like lambs to the slaughter again.[21] Nevertheless, during his stay Raphaël does also discover a nightclub where German uniforms have to be donned, so the stereotyped 'couple éternel du SS et de la juive' (p.22) has by no means been neglected.[22]

On a more general, non-geographical level, there is one final way in which Schlemilovitch endeavours to give himself roots and ties in France – through creative writing, which allows him to graft himself on to a well-embedded cultural tradition, and thereby construct his literary identity (as his Jewish identity) by overt reference to what has gone before. 'La nuit [. . .], j'écris la première partie de mes Mémoires pour me débarrasser d'une jeunesse orageuse', he remarks at one point (p.83), evoking the work of Maurice Sachs,[23] and is soon to be found alluding to the famous novelist Gustave Flaubert as well: 'Je parachèverai en Normandie mon éducation sentimentale' (p.86).[24] Elsewhere, the acknowledgement of previous authors takes on a slightly different form: that of direct quotation, as when André Gide's celebrated dictum, 'Familles, je vous hais!', is recorded (p.75).[25] Elsewhere still, it is through pastiche and parody that the debt to tradition openly manifests itself, with the victims ranging from the right-wing Lucien Rebatet,[26] who is rechristened Léon Rabatête for the occasion, to the left-wing (and aforementioned) Jean-Paul Sartre, who now becomes author of 'Saint Jacob X comédien et martyr'.[27]

Of all the various writers mentioned in *La Place de l'Étoile*, however, two in particular conspicuously stand out: Louis-Ferdinand Céline and Marcel Proust.[28] From the early, parodic ramblings of le docteur Bardamu (pp.9–10), on through the 'guest appearances' of, say, Odette de Crécy (p.13) and the baron de Charlus (p.66), to the later pastiche of *A la recherche du temps perdu* (pp.91–4),[29] the influence of these two lions pervades the novel from start to finish, and it is not hard to see why: Modiano so respects this vaunted twosome that they become key poles of reference for him, a useful measuring stick as he tries to develop a 'style émotionnel' as individual as theirs.[30] Imitation, the adage tells us, is the sincerest form of flattery, and there is certainly a strong element of that here then. But there is clearly something much more important besides, for in talented hands parody and pastiche are not just a means of *emulating* revered novelists' techniques, they are also a way of *wiping the slate clean*, a way of getting the tendency simply to copy out of the system. 'Vous n'allez tout de même pas gaspiller votre jeunesse en recopiant *A la recherche du temps perdu*', the Marquise chides Schlemilovitch (p.94), and this is a warning which could be addressed with equal force to the author himself. For in order to plough his own furrow and create something original, he too must distance himself from the great stylists of the past.[31]

Underlying this use of pastiche and literary allusion (or intertextuality, as it is now often called)[32] there is, of course, ultimately, a much more fundamental obsession being expressed: the obsession with language, the vital importance of which manifests itself elsewhere in the novel in a variety of ways. First, through the fact that Raphaël's (multiple) identity is simply a linguistic construct. 'C'est surtout, à vrai dire, les auteurs antisémites qui m'ont aidé à prendre conscience de ce que je suis juif', Modiano has confided,[33] and Schlemilovitch could have said more or less the same thing, for as has been seen, he willingly lets anti-Semites, *by their utterances*, create both his character and his behaviour for him. Indeed, if this line is pursued further, the host of contradictions in the text no longer seem as puzzling as they did at first sight: the external, phenomenal world is not being used as a raw material, to be realistically (or Realistically) depicted; on the contrary, the language of the fiction is forming reality in front our very eyes, through a succession of signs on the page.[34] This first linguistic aspect of *La Place de l'Étoile*, which owes a considerable debt – conscious or otherwise – to Structuralism, is not totally unrelated to the second: the use of words as a weapon. 'J'aurais voulu répondre aux antisémites d'autrefois avec leurs propres armes: le langage', Modiano has said,[35] and he is palpably true to his word here, inverting anti-Semitic jibes and turning them back on their perpetrators almost incessantly, as when Raphaël explicitly notes: 'Maurras écrivait qu'on ne peut pas comprendre Mme de La Fayette [. . .] si on n'a pas labouré pendant mille ans la terre de France! A mon tour de vous dire ceci [. . .]: il faut mille ans de pogroms [. . .] pour comprendre le moindre paragraphe de Marx' (p.61). This quotation of Maurras (which further illustrates Raphaël's dependence on literary tradition) conveniently suggests a final reason why language has a vital role to play in the novel: linguistic expression automatically links the speaker to a nation and to a history, so it too represents a reassuring source of stability. As Modiano has himself admitted: 'J'ai l'impression d'être issu du néant. La langue française pour moi c'est un peu une amarre aussi',[36] which would in turn explain perhaps, looking back to Chapter 1, why he took up the pen rather than go into the cinema – being a *written*, non-visual medium, fiction offers the sort of *ancrage* that films and their like quite simply do not.

This tendency to associate Modiano with Schlemilovitch – a tendency which has built up over the last few paragraphs – is, in the circumstances, an eminently natural one to display, for the novel itself regularly, if somewhat allusively, shows that Raphaël owes a considerable debt to the man who invented him. For example, in at least one of his numerous lives, he too, like his creator, was born in Boulogne-Billancourt and was virtually two metres tall, he too could trace his family origins back to Thessalonika in Greece and he too lived on the quai Conti in Paris with his mother. There is a further, more resonant area of contact as well. 'Comment se fait-il que vous vous rappeliez tout cela', he is asked in the final pages, apropos of the Second World War, 'vous n'étiez pas né' (p.150). It is a remark which could just as pointedly be applied to Modiano himself, for as Chapter 1 has already indicated, he was not born until after VE Day either (not until 30 July 1945, it may be recalled). Because of this, then, *La Place de l'Étoile* can perhaps best be interpreted as an imaginary autobiography, a humorous, therapeutic exercise in which the memories evoked are almost entirely apocryphal – in short, a work designed to quell the anguish of narrator and novelist alike.[37]

Modiano's second novel, *La Ronde de nuit*, derives from exactly the same obsession which gave rise to – and permeated – every single line of his first: the problem of being both French and Jewish, torturer and victim, traitor and betrayed. For as the novelist himself noted in 1968:

> Partout . . . je suis le traître . . . Je suis avec des garçons de mon âge, ils ne savent pas que je suis juif . . . enfin à moitié . . . alors ils racontent des histoires antisémites . . . et j'ai envie soudain de les tuer . . . et quand je suis avec des juifs . . . ils se plaignent . . . ils sont trop juifs . . . [. . .] alors j'ai envie de les injurier . . . [. . .] je suis un traître . . . Parfois la nuit . . . je me pose cette terrible question . . . si j'avais vécu en quarante . . . moi Modiano? . . . Qu'est-ce que j'aurais fait? . . . Je crois bien [. . .] que j'aurais été un salaud . . . Enfin, j'aurais d'abord été un salaud . . . et puis j'aurais changé [. . .] j'aurais fini . . . non pas en héros . . . mais en martyr . . . Franchement, je le crois! Ça m'obsède.[38]

It is precisely this authorial obsession – *salaud* or martyr during the war? – which lies at the heart of *La Ronde de nuit*, and if, as was suggested above, the link with *La Place de l'Étoile* is already transparent here, then it becomes even more striking when the ultimate concerns of the two texts are in turn made explicit, as Modiano obligingly demonstrated during one of his interviews. 'Dans les deux livres', he insisted, 'c'est toujours la recherche d'une identité: l'identité juive, pour le premier et dans le second plutôt une fuite instinctive devant toute identification.'[39]

This informed assessment of *La Ronde de nuit* is tremendously helpful, because the central character of the work certainly does defy all attempts to pin him down. First, and perhaps most frustratingly, he has no fixed, administratively certified name to personalize him. 'Je n'ai jamais eu de carte d'identité', he admits at one stage (p.132), and shortly afterwards, when he elaborates the point, he manages to create even more uncertainty by referring to the only 'papiers' that he does possess: 'un faux passeport Nansen' (p.156).[40] Little wonder, then, that, at various times, he can claim to be Judas's younger brother, Maxime de Bel-Respiro, Marcel Petiot, Philippe Pétain, Landru, or even King Lear![41]

His professional activities further complicate this already perplexing picture, for here too it is impossible to decide precisely what his situation is. Initially – if the chronology of events is reconstructed – his status seems to be evident enough: he is Swing Troubadour, a *gestapiste* working at 3*bis* square Cimarosa for le Khédive and M. Philibert. Things become somewhat less straightforward, however, after he has been asked by his employers to infiltrate a Resistance group, the Réseau des Chevaliers de l'Ombre (R.C.O.). He successfully completes his task, receiving the *nom de guerre* Princesse de Lamballe in the process, but is then sent back by his new associates to join the Gestapo as a 'mole'. From this point onwards confusion cascades down around him, for his connection to both sides means, in effect, that he belongs to neither. Whenever he dons the mantle of *résistant*, his persona of Swing Troubadour is instantly erased and vice versa: 'Agent double? ou triple? Je ne savais plus qui j'étais. [...] JE N'EXISTE PAS' (p.132). Similarly, when he (falsely) denounces Lamballe as the commander of the R.C.O., he is both consolidating his own identity (usurping the stature of an awesome leader) and in the same breath palpably demolishing it (marking himself out for rapid execution).[42]

These two, mutually exclusive drives, one towards self-affirmation and the other towards self-destruction (or as Freudians might say, the Life instinct and the Death instinct), are present on almost every page of *La Ronde de nuit*, and manifest themselves in a variety of other guises as well. One of the most striking of these, arguably, is the narrator's willingness to dress up as a woman and affect a certain femininity (echoes of which are to be found in his *nom de résistance*, Princesse de Lamballe),[43] for this assertive act plainly has implications that are simultaneously destructive, if not in respect of his sexuality – he claims to have no taste for transvestism – then at least in terms of his gender: 'Is he masculine or is he feminine?' we are inevitably led to ask; but as with the question of whether he is a *gestapiste* or a *résistant*, the answer seems to be that he is both and neither. He is just not an easy man to classify; he is puzzlingly ambiguous.

The same ambivalence pervades his relationship with Coco Lacour and Esmeralda, his two imaginary friends. Being to all intents and purposes an orphan (his mother has fled Paris for Switzerland and his father, Alexandre Stavisky, is long since dead)[44] he finds in these fictitious companions a compensatory presence, an effective palliative to his inadequate family background: 'Nous menions, square Cimarosa, une vie de famille', he readily informs us, '[. . .] Mon amour ressemblait à celui que j'éprouvais pour maman' (p.163). Furthermore, before his mother left, he could use his ill-gotten gains to buy her presents, and thereby avoid worrying too much about the crimes he had committed: 'Maître chanteur, gouape, donneuse, indic, assassin peut-être, mais fils exemplaire. C'était ma seule consolation' (p.100). Now that she has departed, it is clearly Coco and Esmeralda who have taken over this role, providing him with an alternative means of boosting his self-image:

> De ma solitude quelque chose allait éclore [. . .]. Coco Lacour et Esmeralda. Misérables. Infirmes. [. . .] Que seraient-ils devenus sans moi? Je trouvais enfin une excellente raison de vivre. Je les aimais, mes pauvres monstres. Je veillerais sur eux . . . Personne ne pourrait leur faire de mal. Grâce à l'argent que je gagnais square Cimarosa, en qualité d'indic et de pillard, je leur assurerais tout le confort possible. (p.160)

Yet in spite of this overtly protective approach (and the increased self-esteem which goes with it!), he often feels like deserting his two vulnerable comrades, or, more perversely, actually killing them.[45] Given that the couple provide him, as we have just seen, with 'une excellente raison de vivre', their symbolic murder becomes tantamount to self-destruction, and the equivocal nature of his character is accordingly reinforced (all the more so in that, at the very moment when he mentally kills them – and, by extension, figuratively commits suicide – he gives himself power over others and hence, ironically, positively imposes himself).

Such blatantly paradoxical, Janus-like behaviour obviously raises questions about the narrator's moral status, but in this sphere too uncertainty reigns supreme, for not even his criminality is as clear-cut as we might normally tend to assume. First of all, his recruitment by le Khédive and Philibert in no way reflects a personal commitment on his part. Possessing, by his own admission, 'pas assez de force d'âme pour me ranger du côté des héros. Trop de nonchalance et de distraction pour faire un vrai salaud' (p.40), he teams up with the two men not through deliberate choice, but rather entirely by accident:

> Quelle drôle d'idée de m'être assis à la terrasse du *Royal-Villiers*, place Pereire, moi [. . .] qui voulais à tout prix me faire oublier. Mais on doit débuter dans la vie. On n'y coupe pas. Elle finit par vous envoyer ses sergents recruteurs: en l'occurrence le Khédive et M. Philibert. Un autre soir, sans doute, je serais tombé sur des personnages plus honorables [. . .]. Ne me sentant aucune vocation particulière, j'attendais de mes aînés qu'ils me choisissent un emploi. [. . .] Le plus curieux avec les garçons de mon espèce: [. . .] On en fait des héros. Ou des salauds. On ignorera qu'ils ont été entraînés dans une sale histoire à leur corps défendant. (pp.101–2)[46]

Once he has taken the plunge in this bizarre, inadvertent fashion, he finds it impossible not to hurtle on down the road to perdition, for his weakness of character means that he will do literally anything his new employers demand of him: 'Mouchard. Je deviendrai même assassin, s'ils le veulent' (p.21). Yet no matter how many offences he lets himself commit, he cynically absolves himself from all sense of responsibility and blame: 'Je n'étais pas plus méchant qu'un autre. J'ai suivi le mouvement, voilà tout. Je n'éprouve pour le mal aucune attirance particulière' (p.141). Such provocative shamelessness can have but one corollary, as Modiano himself most appositely points out: 'L'action se situe dans un contexte moral, mais elle est vécue par un être dépourvu de tout sens moral.'[47] In other words, Swing Troubadour/ Lamballe is multiply equivocal. Not only does he have no fixed nominal or physical identity; he has no ethical identity either.

This incertitude explains why the *ronde* emerges as a major leitmotif within the novel, its importance being immediately underlined in the very title of the work, a title which, fittingly, permits of a whole variety of interpretations itself. On the most prosaic level, *La Ronde de nuit* could refer to the narrator's night-time duties at the square Cimarosa, because (typically!) he has more than just one job to do there: 'Outre mon travail annexe de "récupérateur" en objets précieux, j'exerçais au 3bis la fonction de veilleur de nuit' (pp.156–7). Less mundanely, it might be his incessant journeys around Paris, from Gestapo to Resistance and back again, which are being conjured up in the reader's mind here. Alternatively still, and given that snippets of songs from the early 1940s punctuate the text,[48] the round mentioned could be of a distinctly musical nature, suggesting the novel be compared to a self-repeating dance or canon.[49] Perhaps the best interpretation of all, however, is to view the title metaphorically, that is to say as an allusion to the painful *vertige* that afflicts Swing Troubadour/Lamballe as he sinks down ever deeper into his dark and deadly nightmare. Certainly, when he realizes that Philibert and le Khédive will soon be insistently questioning him, the form that his anguish is given is most visibly that of the circle, the *gestapistes* – like his head – being expected to go into a disorienting spin: 'Une ronde autour de moi, de plus en plus rapide, de plus en plus bruyante, et je finirai par céder pour qu'ils me laissent tranquille' (p.90).

It is a mark of Modiano's precocious talent (already ably demonstrated in the pastiches of *La Place de l'Étoile*) that the narrator's turmoil is not simply conveyed explicitly, as is the case here, but is, above all, masterfully evoked by purely formal means. For once again realism has been abandoned in favour of a much less reductive, far more modernistic approach. Verb tenses are used so interchangeably that temporal uncertainty, rather than rigid chronology, is now the overriding order of the day, and more or less the same thing can be said about the narrative, since the work contains so many echoes of what has gone before that, as the title of the novel instantly suggests, the plot with which we are faced proceeds in a circular and not a linear fashion. For example, the opening section of the book turns back in on itself, beginning and ending with laughter in the darkness, and a whole host of sentences and phrases (not to mention incidents!) are leitmotivally reprised, with no – or little – variation: 'un beau coup de filet en perspective' (pp.15, 49, 68, 118, and 123); 'Aucune importance' (pp.133, 155, 156, 163, and 168); 'J'ai des billets de banque plein les poches' (pp.22, 73, 98, and 174); 'une place calme comme il en existe dans le XVIᵉ arrondissement' (pp.29, 77, and 83). Moreover – and more importantly – there is frequent reference to the Princesse de Lamballe's downfall, whether it be the last moments of the real-life aristocrat (p.61), the fairground attraction based on her demise (p.92) or the painting of her execution by Francisco de Goya (p.140). Princesse de Lamballe is, of course, the cover the narrator uses when he plays the role of *résistant*, so his death is implicitly forecast once more.

This sense of approaching doom is one of the most salient features of *La Ronde de nuit*, and is further generated by numerous other aspects of the text, not least among which are such dogmatic statements as 'Je n'avais aucune chance de salut' (p.124) and 'après des rondes et des rondes, mille et mille allées et venues, je finirais par me perdre dans les ténèbres' (p.125). It is in the final pages of the novel, however, that the impression of impending disaster is at its most acute. Having failed in an attempt to kill le Khédive (a self-assertive act which, predictably, is simultaneously self-destructive, most of the other gang members being present at the time), Swing Troubadour/ Lamballe is doing his utmost to speed away and effect an escape, but without success. The *gestapistes* are hot on his tail, pursuing him and tantalizing him, briefly allowing him to forge on ahead, and then quickly bearing back down on him again. 'Le Khédive, Philibert, tous les autres forment une ronde autour de moi', he had previously announced, '[. . .] Il faut que je trouve une oasis, sous peine de crever: mon amour pour Coco Lacour et Esmeralda' (p.73). No such oasis beckons for him now: as he drives round Paris and the *banlieue* in ever increasing circles, with his pursuers – and erstwhile colleagues – always threateningly in tow, he resigns himself to the fact that 'Coco Lacour et Esmeralda n'existaient pas' (p.175), and thereby acknowledges, indirectly, that all hope of salvation for him has gone. His days, quite clearly, are well and truly numbered.

Or are they? Elsewhere in the text the picture does not seem quite so distinct, for there are countless indications that, against all the apparent odds, Swing Troubadour/Lamballe actually emerged unscathed from his predicament.[50] Probably the best illustration of this is the incident which occurs, significantly, at more or less the halfway point of the novel. On a day when, again significantly, the sun is shining brightly, he walks into the square Cimarosa, looks at the façade of number 3*bis* and declares: 'Les volets sont fermés depuis longtemps. [. . .] Il se passait des choses bien curieuses [. . .] du temps où j'y habitais' (p.84). This revelation, fascinatingly, sets up another possible time-scale within the work: the events described, initially assumed to be part of a present located at some stage during the Occupation, could just as well be *memories* recalled years later, after the war, in the course of a stroll around Paris. For as Modiano himself has intimated: 'Le principal personnage de ce livre: Paris. Paris dont les avenues, les carrefours, les maisons évoquent des souvenirs pour le promeneur solitaire.'[51] This being the case, it seems highly appropriate that, at one stage on his travels, the narrator should chance upon '*La Ronde de nuit*, une opérette bien oubliée' (p.105); the operetta comes to symbolize his own *ronde de nuit, forgotten* in the sense that it belongs to a bygone era, yet still playing, still haunting him with immediacy.[52]

This is not to imply that memory is cast solely in an unfavourable light in the novel, though; reflecting the other positive/negative contrasts that underpin the work, it has a second, more appealing function to perform as well – that of an effective counter to the ravages of time. Throughout the book, Swing Troubadour/Lamballe is constantly aware of the fragile nature of everyday life, the way in which people and things disappear leaving no vestige at all of their former presence behind them. 'De tant de frénésie, tumulte, violences, que reste-t-il?', he muses, thinking back to the funfair at Luna-Park. 'Une esplanade vide en bordure du boulevard Gouvion-Saint-Cyr', is his melancholy reply (p.92).[53] But he does not simply sit back and resign himself to this ever beckoning obscurity; instead, he resolves to keep a faithful record of all his experiences, firm in the knowledge that, by conserving his precious memories in print, he can at least save something from the menacing jaws of oblivion: 'Le temps a passé. Si je n'écrivais pas leur nom: Coco Lacour, Esmeralda, il n'y aurait aucune trace de leur séjour en ce monde' (p.91). That these two characters are, in truth, entirely imaginary does not affect him in the slightest, since their appearance in his text accentuates – reassuringly – the ability of the written word to give permanent, concrete existence to even the most fanciful of recollections. But it *does* affect the reader, who must consequently recognize that, like *La Place de l'Étoile* before it, Modiano's second work takes on a specific, well-determined form – the form of an untrustworthy, frequently concocted memoir.

With this point now firmly established, it is but a small step to take to suggest that *all*, and not just some of the memories evoked in the novel could be fictitious, as Modiano himself seems to concede when he states: '*La Ronde de nuit* pourrait être, par exemple, la rêverie d'un promeneur solitaire, au mois d'août, dans le XVIe arrondissement. Le bruit de ses pas réveille les fantômes et il écoute, dans le silence de ce quartier, les secrets terribles que les pierres conservent depuis vingt ans.'[54] This readiness to admit that the past is preserved in the bricks and mortar of Paris, rather than in the recollective faculty of the narrator (the act of remembrance having been replaced by that of 'rêverie') is of undoubted importance, and leads on, opportunely, to two final ways in which the title of the book can be interpreted.

The first of these involves drawing a comparison with Rembrandt's famous masterpiece *The Night Watch*, which is also entitled *La Ronde de nuit* in French.[55] Like its literary counterpart, the old master's painting depicts an assembly of military men and has an atmosphere of dreamy unreality, but more notably, to the left of the picture, bathed in bright light, there stands a young girl. Many critics see in this figure a personal intrusion by the artist, the reflection of somebody close to him,[56] and this suggests that in the novel, too, the illuminated (or sunlit) character can be linked back directly to his creator.[57]

The second – and last – interpretation of the title gives rise to more or less the same conclusion, although the key to this assessment lies not now in the realm of fine art, but rather in the genesis of the text itself. 'Je me promenais dans [le XVIe] arrondissement abandonné. La nuit surtout', the novelist recollects, looking back to the time when he found his inspiration. '[. . .] Je voulus écrire un roman sur Paris en été. [. . .] Pensant à mes promenades nocturnes, je décidai du titre: *La Ronde de nuit*.'[58] So, once again, the link between author and text is manifest, and the ultimate corollary of this is equally clear: behind the walker of the streets of Paris (whether by day or whether by night), it is, seemingly, Modiano himself who is writing the imaginary autobiography.[59]

Fictitious though this life story may be, however, it has not been invented entirely from scratch, for as in *La Place de l'Étoile*, we find ourselves faced with a whole plethora of intertextual references. A good many of these, relating to fine art and popular song, have already been amply demonstrated above, but there is also another, previously unnoted source of cultural borrowing in *La Ronde de nuit*: the domain of literature, a domain which, if anything, is even more important than any of the others. To give only the more obvious allusions in this area, Esmeralda evokes – right down to her name – the heroine of Victor Hugo's *Notre-Dame de Paris*; Coco, her outsize companion, is a sort of Quasimodo as filtered through Vidocq;[60] the phrase, 'Décidément, le monde était plein de bruit et de fureur. Aucune importance' (p.155) is a close reworking of Shakespeare;[61] Scott Fitzgerald, first seen in the epigraph,[62] remains a constant presence throughout;[63] 'Dis, qu'as-tu fait de ta jeunesse?' (p.66) recalls the poet Paul Verlaine;[64] and last but not least, there is Swing Troubadour/Lamballe, who is a string of literary *clins d'œil* incarnate. '*Anthologie des traîtres, d'Alcibiade au capitaine Dreyfus, Joanovici tel qu'il fut, Les Mystères du chevalier d'Eon, Frégoli, l'homme de nulle part*' – all of these books, he admits (p.122), have helped shed light on his identity,[65] and although the titles quoted are no doubt imaginary, they none the less hint at the (written) sources absorbed by the author prior to the creation of his narrator. Furthermore, to this already impressive list can clearly be added Pierre Drieu La Rochelle's 'L'Agent double', Jean Genet's *Pompes funèbres* and Roger Nimier's *Les Epées*, for each of these texts likewise has a central character who is caught between two stools, a central character who, consequently, seems to have fed into Raphaël Schlemilovitch – the archetypal torturer/victim – as well.

This link back to *La Place de l'Étoile* could, at the present juncture, hardly be more timely, for as may now be apparent, the use of intertextuality in *La Ronde de nuit* is virtually the same (albeit not as blatant) as in the novel which precedes it. In both works, as has been seen, Modiano constructs a new, imaginary life for himself out of a broad network of cultural influences – but only out of those which have had the greatest impact upon him. And this is by no means fortuitous, for by homing in solely on the things which mean most to him, he can create the background that is best suited to meet his emotional needs. What is more, he can do something of no lesser import besides – he can purge himself, to re-evoke Proust,[66] of any temptation simply to *plagiarize* when henceforth putting pen to paper, free himself of each and every debt to his artistic forebears. In a word, he can, from this moment on, begin to forge his own, unique, individual style.

With his first two novels firmly behind him, Modiano, speaking in 1969, was quite open about the plans he had for his future works. 'Persistera toujours un climat policier, d'incertitude et de blackout', he opined,[67] and when his third major text, *Les Boulevards de ceinture*, duly appeared three years later,[68] the promised sense of continuity was delivered. Indeed, the more we read this book today, the more ties we find to link it back to its predecessors. The main temporal setting is still, we assume, the Occupation; the broad focus of the narrative – collaborationist journalism – recalls Schlemilovitch's stint at *Je suis partout*; incidents recounted earlier are reprised and elaborated upon; familiar characters return to act out their old roles again; and countless well-established phrases and images hauntingly resurface.[69] Moreover, the key theme of the work remains the thorny problem of identity, although the matter is now broached in a slightly different fashion – via a worried son's determined pursuit of his father.

It is the narrator, Serge Alexandre, who decides to embark on this quest, and not without considerable justification, it would seem: having lost touch with the man who begot him, and admitting that 'j'ai perdu mes papiers d'identité' (p.118), he appears, like his two precursors, to be somewhat of an orphan, a *déraciné* desperate to put down roots. But his task is far from being an easy one, for even when he enjoyed a paternal presence, his parent was not all that welcoming, as the 'épisode douloureux du métro Georges-V' demonstrates (p.105). Situated – significantly – at the mid-point of the novel (pp.105–13), this incident sees father endeavouring to push son under the wheels of an Underground train,[70] an action which, as things turn out, eventually comes to nought. Nevertheless, the symbolism of the deed is quite clear – the attempted murder translates the distance which exists between the two parties, a distance which is exclusively parental in origin. This being the case, if a subsequent reunion is to be brought about, it must be on the sole instigation of Alexandre, and this is where his problems begin to arise, for given that his father was, as it were, no less absent before his disappearance than after it, the 'orphan' has nothing on which to mount his quest but a void, nothing to prime his *retrouvailles* but speculation. As he himself remarks: 'Je me penche [. . .] pour retrouver [. . .] l'image fuyante de mon père. Je ne sais presque rien de lui. Mais j'inventerai' (p.82).

By using his creative faculties in this manner, Serge does eventually regain contact with his missing parent, who has appropriated for himself both the name of 'baron' Chalva Deyckecaire and an abandoned villa called Le Prieuré,[71] but all does not augur well for him as a result. The man he discovers is, and remains, very much a man of mystery. 'Apatride, sans raison sociale ni domicile fixe' (p.161), involved in unspecified 'combinaisons financières' (p.53), and having a marked affinity for extensive silences (pp.64–5), the 'baron' is, if anything, even harder to define than his son. And his acquaintances – Jean Murraille, Guy de Marcheret, Maud Gallas and Sylviane Quimphe – cannot be used to help pin him down either, for they too have been formed in exactly the same mould and are just as 'déclassés' and 'marginaux' as he is. Indeed, his very presence amongst such individuals – collaborators of varying degrees – is of itself extremely perplexing, for they are not so much his natural friends as his ostensible enemies, as Murraille's determination to kill him shortly demonstrates.[72]

This inability to 'flesh out' Deyckecaire as his search progresses is, on the face of it, bad enough as far as Serge is concerned, but at the end of the novel his trouble actually gets far worse. His *rêverie* proves to be as short-lived as any other dream, reality reimposes itself, and his father rapidly ages by thirty years as a consequence (p.197). In a word, Alexandre's lack of knowledge has become irrevocable, and this is all the more definitive an outcome in that, quite manifestly, his failure is absolutely total. For despite his lengthy contact with the 'baron', he has not cured his ignorance of his parent in the slightest. 'Qui êtes-vous?' he still wonders. 'J'ai beau vous avoir suivi pendant des jours et des jours, je ne sais rien de vous' (p.198). In fact, all he has managed to do, at the end of the day, is to arrive at the same dead end as Guy de Marcheret, of whom it is revealingly noted: 'Orphelin, Marcheret l'avait toujours été. Et s'il s'engagea à la Légion, ce fut peut-être pour retrouver la trace de son père. Mais il n'y avait au rendez-vous que la solitude, le sable et les mirages du désert' (p.75).[73]

This closing remark is well worth lingering upon, for one of the key qualities of *Les Boulevards de ceinture* is that the text itself shows Serge's quest to be doomed from the start, and this inbuilt sense of failure has its paradigm, precisely, in the evocative image of the mirage. There are two compelling reasons for this. The less obvious is that, just as they come and go in real life, mirages are mentioned time and time again throughout the novel (pp.65, 122, 137), and hence they help give the text, as its very title suggests, a form which is fundamentally circular in nature.[74] Admittedly, the countdown to the marriage of Guy and Annie and the chronological references to June (p.30), July (p.68) and August (p.172) create an appearance of linearity, but it is no more than that – a simple appearance. Overall, the text – like its narrator – just goes round and round in circles, to such an extent that, at the end of the book, we find ourselves back at the point at which we started: the description of the village on page 199 is a near reproduction of that on page 26, and the photo encountered in the final paragraphs harks back to the one seen at the outset of the work.

Mirages are also, of course, things which seem real, but which most definitely are not, and this is the other reason why they are paradigmatic in *Les Boulevards de ceinture*: the narrative has this selfsame ambivalence, deploying a whole host of devices to give the lie to its 'reality'. Most evident amongst these, perhaps, is a technique which Modiano has no doubt borrowed from the *nouveaux romanciers*: suggestions that entire sections of the book are little more than old photographs infused with life. The opening pages of the work would appear to provide the clearest demonstration of this procedure, but other scenes too betray their pictorial origins to the attentive reader, as when the text subtly reveals that Murraille 'laissait pendre sa cigarette au coin des lèvres comme elle y pend pour l'éternité' (p.38).[75] Less subtle are the numerous other ploys which help generate this element of *distanciation*: sounds and voices are overtly distorted; characters and settings slide in and out of focus; the light incessantly fades and intensifies; and 'dampening' verbs such as *étouffer* proliferate. Yet subtle or not, these ploys are certainly effective, especially when used in tandem or fused together by Modiano's masterful style, as the following extract ably demonstrates:

> Au-dessus de la silhouette rigide de Grève, une tête de chevreuil se détache du mur comme une figure de proue et l'animal considère Marcheret, Murraille et mon père avec toute l'indifférence de ses

yeux de verre. L'ombre des cornes dessine au plafond un entrelacs gigantesque. La lumière s'affaiblit. Baisse de courant? Ils demeurent prostrés et silencieux dans la pénombre qui les ronge. De nouveau cette impression de regarder une vieille photographie, jusqu'au moment où Marcheret se lève, mais de façon si brutale qu'il bute parfois contre la table. Alors, tout recommence. Le lustre et les appliques retrouvent leur éclat. Plus une ombre. Plus de flou. Le moindre objet se découpe avec une précision presque insoutenable. Les gestes qui s'alanguissaient deviennent secs et impérieux. Mon père lui-même se dresse comme à l'appel d'un 'garde-à-vous'. (pp.17–18)

Note how the sentences in this passage, although never long or complicated, nevertheless lengthen and shorten to create a rhythm, a rhythm which is perfectly in tune with the narrative it supports, undynamic and 'indifferent' at first, but then gaining both in certainty and momentum. Note too how the verbless phrases add to this contrastive movement, interspersing moments of activity with grammatical inertia. Note further how there is a poetic arrangement of long and short, soft and harsh sounds, from the lulling 'L'ombre des cornes [. . .] la pénombre qui les ronge' to the jarringly abrasive 'si brutale [. . .] contre la table'. And above all note how, when combined, these devices make the text oscillate between realism on the one hand and out-and-out *rêverie* on the other. It is this suggestive, cinematic half-light that will henceforth be Modiano's trademark.[76]

So, from start to finish, *Les Boulevards de ceinture* shows itself to be a 'mirage', undermining the narrator's quest before it really begins and imbuing the putative contact between father and son with vagueness, unreality and, ultimately, transience.[77] However, to deduce from this that the search has been a complete waste of time would be to make a most serious mistake, for two things have, unarguably, been achieved. First, although Serge may not have been able to discover what his parent was *actually* like, he has at least managed to fabricate a certain *type* of father for himself, one who fulfils all his emotional requirements: 'Pourquoi avais-je voulu, si tôt, être votre fils?' he revealingly observes (pp.142–3). And it matters not in the slightest to him that the details he dreams up cannot be corroborated, because he feels that they are undeniably valid, and that is the vital thing: 'Je n'invente rien. Non, ça n'est pas cela, inventer . . . Il existe certainement des preuves, une personne qui vous a connu, jadis, et qui pourrait témoigner de toutes ces choses. Peu importe. Je suis avec vous et je le resterai jusqu'à la fin du livre' (pp.161–2).[78]

This closing remark, felicitously, leads on directly to the second point, which is not totally unrelated to the first: Alexandre has also *assimilated* himself to the baron, following in his footsteps and moulding his conduct on the paternal model. Did his father once seek him out, and thereby set up family ties? He will repay the compliment. Does his father mingle with a group of collaborators? He will do the same. Is his father eventually arrested? He will join him in the police van (pp.197–8). Might his father look like a clown? He will be a clown with him (p.198).[79] Does his father do action X? He will follow suit – time and again this pattern is repeated, and it is not really hard to see why. As Norbert Czarny has intimated: 'La plongée onirique dans l'Occupation est une manière d'abolir l'écart des générations, en faisant "comme si". Retrouver ces temps troublés, c'est dire la solidarité.'[80] 'Dire la solidarité' it certainly does, and when this aim is added to that of *creating* a parent to order, the main, underlying benefit that Serge gains from his quest becomes clear: he is able to secure, albeit temporarily, the inherited identity that he currently lacks. For as he forthrightly admits: 'On est toujours curieux de connaître ses origines' (p.137).

Given this readiness, on Serge's part, to conjure up, and then associate with, an imaginary parent, our thoughts quite naturally turn to Sigmund Freud, whose theory of the *Familienroman* seems to find a discernible resonance here. Concocted in childhood, and essentially literary in character, 'le *roman familial*', as one summarizer has said, 'peut être défini comme un expédient à quoi recourt l'imagination', that is to say 'une fable biographique conçue tout exprès pour expliquer l'inexplicable honte d'être mal né, mal loti, mal aimé'.[81] This latter comment seems to fit Alexandre down to the ground, for quite apart from his forging of a custom-built father, he will – momentarily – dream up an idealized mother (and a sister?) for himself as well (pp.158–9).[82] However, in spite of all this, there are clearly times when Serge is not at one with Freudian theory. He does not, for example, imagine himself to be an *enfant trouvé* or a *bâtard*, as is normally the case, nor is his basic problem that of the well-known Œdipus Complex.[83] Quite the opposite, in fact, as he is the first to acknowledge after 'l'épisode douloureux du métro Georges-V':

> Qu'un père cherche à tuer son fils ou à s'en débarrasser me semble
> tout à fait symptomatique du grand bouleversement des valeurs que
> nous vivons. Naguère, on observait le phénomène inverse: les fils
> tuaient leur père pour se prouver qu'ils avaient des muscles. Mais
> maintenant, contre qui porter nos coups? Nous voilà condamnés,
> orphelins que nous sommes, à poursuivre un fantôme en
> reconnaissance de paternité. (p.168)

Perversely, then, it is Serge who fulfils the (traditionally paternal)
role of family-maker-cum-victim, and the father who adopts that
(classically reserved for the son) of family-breaker-cum-
murderer.

This inversion (which also provides an excellent example of
Modiano's irony) brings us back round to the 'climat policier'
with which this section began, for as Jules Bedner has rightly
observed, there is plainly an

> affinité entre la thématique de Modiano et celle du roman policier.
> C'est que le genre policier véhicule un mythe moderne de la
> persécution, où le persécuteur – porteur de la loi et justicier
> infaillible – joue en principe le rôle du père et le persécuté celui du
> fils. Rien d'étonnant à ce que ces rôles soient interchangeables, les
> pulsions étant susceptibles de se transformer dans leur contraire par
> le passage de l'activité à la passivité, comme la psychanalyse nous
> l'a appris. Le père peut donc être criminel, le fils policier.[84]

It is, exactly, this latter state which pertains in *Les Boulevards de
ceinture*, with Serge setting himself up as detective twice over.
Initially, in an 'intermède' which contrasts with most of the other
activities he admits to (writing false dedications in books,
trafficking, etc.), he is an active member of the police force,
working alongside Inspector Sieffer of the Vice Squad (pp.165–6).
And then, when this experiment turns sour, he continues to act
as an investigator – albeit in an amateur capacity – by deciding
to track down his own father. The photo with which the narrative
opens, the (implicit) witness statements of section two,[85] the
magazine mentioned in section three (p.33), the CVs of the
various characters (pp.69–82) – all of these 'clues' and
'testimonies' are the fruit of Serge's informal 'enquiries'.

Yet Alexandre is not uniquely a detective. Thanks to his status
as first-person narrator, and to his claim that – fittingly, given the
comments above about his *Familienroman* – his profession is
really that of 'romancier' (pp.40, 51), he is, more accurately, a

policier-novelist, the first in what will prove to be, as we shall see, a long line of such protagonists.[86] Furthermore, that we should actually encounter this double *métier* is entirely appropriate, for like so much else in *Les Boulevards de ceinture*, it serves to heighten the intrinsic tension of the work, the concerns of Serge-the-writer (invention, possibility, fiction) being the very antithesis of those of Serge-the-sleuth (fact, certainty, history). Not for nothing, then, will our narrator set off in search of his identity – the little he knows of himself already is fraught with contradictions.

It is more than the question of who he is that engrosses Alexandre, though, since he sees that this *particular* problem is tied up with a no less thorny, *universal* one, namely the ease with which time annihilates everything and everyone standing in its path. Were it not for this merciless destruction wrought over the years, he accepts, he would have no difficulty at all in discovering his missing origins, and so would not now be in the awful predicament that he is. As he himself says:

> On s'intéresse à un homme, disparu depuis longtemps. On voudrait interroger les personnes qui l'ont connu mais leurs traces se sont effacées avec les siennes. Sur ce qu'a été sa vie, on ne possède que de très vagues indications souvent contradictoires, deux ou trois points de repère. (p.148)

'Deux ou trois points de repère' – this is hardly a lot to go on;[87] and yet, like Swing Troubadour/Lamballe before him, Serge stoutly refuses to submit to the march of time. On the contrary, he determines to fight it to the best of his ability, doing all he can to preserve those vestiges of the past which still remain and immediately bequeath them to posterity, as his obsession with curricula vitae demonstrates:

> Je sais bien que le curriculum vitae de ces ombres ne présente pas un grand intérêt, mais si je ne le dressais pas aujourd'hui, personne d'autre ne s'y emploierait. C'est mon devoir, à moi qui les ai connus, de les sortir – ne fût-ce qu'un instant – de la nuit. C'est mon devoir et c'est aussi, pour moi, un véritable besoin. (pp.68–9)

Hence, whatever else Serge's quest may represent, it is, above all, an endeavour on his part to offset oblivion.

Now, this imperative to transfer knowledge from perishable memory into durable print seems, on the face of it, harmless enough. But as already suggested, there is something decidedly odd about the content of Serge's so-called 'memoirs' – despite such reassuring interjections as, 'Bien des années ont passé, mais les visages, les gestes, les inflexions de voix restent gravés dans ma mémoire' (p.172), the experience recalled is largely invented and far from unquestionable. For this reason, *Les Boulevards de ceinture* must be read with circumspection. The work is not the autobiography it often declares itself to be; it is, on the contrary, an imaginative fiction – the recollections presented are not those of its narrator.[88]

More significantly perhaps, they are not those of Modiano either, for there can be little doubt that, behind his lead character, it is the author himself who is embarking on the filial quest. Witness the paternal object of the venture, 'baron' Chalva Deyckecaire. A Jewish *apatride* linked to Alexandria, 'de type sud-américain' (p.111), a great frequenter of hotel lobbies, absent for the last ten years – all of these traits could apply to the novelist's own father as he writes. What is more, it is no coincidence that Serge Alexandre has the name that he does – this was an alias used by the swindler Stavisky,[89] of whom Modiano has quite openly opined: 'Il ne serait pas exagéré de dire que je voyais en lui une sorte d'image paternelle.'[90] Thus, there can be no mistaking the import of *Les Boulevards de ceinture*: through Serge and his assimilation to Deyckecaire, who in turn owes a sizeable debt to Stavisky,[91] it is the author himself who is walking in his father's footsteps, the author himself who, as in *La Place de l'Étoile* and *La Ronde de nuit*, is, in effect, ghostwriting the 'memoirs' being presented.

Ghostwriting is certainly the word, for just as Alexandre is divorced from his 'memories', so too, despite their similarities, are Modiano and his narrators far from identical. There is always a certain distance between them, a distance enshrined by irony. And it is here, as much as anywhere, that *Les Boulevards de ceinture* innovates, for the tone is now far more subdued, and the humour much more gentle, than in either of the preceding texts. *Gone* is the provocation of Raphaël Schlemilovitch;[92] *gone*, too, are the disturbing quips of Swing Troubadour/Lamballe,[93] while *in* has come a novel, tranquil self-mockery.[94] This new development – fully in tune with the ironic tensions in the work – is absolutely laden with significance, for it shows both that, as ever, Modiano's private life is affecting the substance of his writing (the part-dedication, 'Pour Dominique', revealing that he has found a soul mate,[95] and that, consequently, his own solitude and anguish – as reflected in his style – are gradually diminishing) and that, as will soon be confirmed, his mature technique as a novelist is starting to emerge. Or, put another way, Modiano has, at long last, begun to give himself a distinct *identity* – an identity both literary and personal.

Looking back over *La Place de l'Étoile*, *La Ronde de nuit* and *Les Boulevards de ceinture*, it becomes clear that a considerable amount of overlap exists between the three works, and so systematic does this linkage prove to be that a new, alternative line of attack instantly suggests itself. For although each novel can be read and appreciated quite independently of the others, there is a lot to be gained from considering them as part of something much bigger, as a sort of informal, loose-knit 'trilogy', as no less an authority than Modiano himself agrees:

> On pourrait dire qu'il s'agit d'un seul livre. On retrouve à travers les trois romans les mêmes thèmes, tantôt esquissés, tantôt amplifiés (ainsi le thème du père est esquissé dans le premier roman puis développé dans le troisième). Ces trois romans ne constituent pas une suite chronologique mais un enchevêtrement, une sorte de miroir dont les trois faces se renvoient les mêmes images.[96]

Some of these reflected images are plainly the themes of identity, time, memory and the past, all of which have already been highlighted in the course of this chapter. Less well documented, however, though hardly any less worthy of consideration, is another of Modiano's major leitmotifs, a leitmotif which it will therefore now be useful to analyse at much greater length: the focus on the dark and dreadful years of the German Occupation.

Without the slightest shadow of a doubt, it was the striking portrayal of the *années noires* in his fiction (and in *Lacombe Lucien* too, for that matter)[97] that helped propel Modiano into the public spotlight, all the more so in that, in so doing, he was unwittingly paving the way for the influential, all-embracing *mode rétro*, which was shortly to follow.[98] Yet it was not his use of the Occupation as a backdrop that so fascinated general readers and full-time critics alike, but rather the fact that, although he himself had no direct experience of the war, his knowledge of the period was so intimate as to be almost incredible.

Take, for example, *La Ronde de nuit*. Behind the *gestapistes* of 'la bande du square Cimarosa' it is not difficult to discern the real-life *bande de la rue Lauriston*.[99] Henri Normand, alias 'Le Khédive', has the same background and the same extravagant tastes as Henri Chamberlin-Laffont;[100] Monsieur Philibert – once 'le premier flic de France' (p.35) – bears a striking resemblance to Pierre Bonny;[101] Mickey de Voisins seems to evoke Guy de Voisin; le mage Ivanoff, Simone Bouquereau, Lionel de Zieff, Pols du Helder, Gouari l'Américain and Magda d'Andurian are no doubt inspired by le mage Popov, Sonia Boukassi, Lionel de Wiett, Paulo du Helder, Riri l'Américain and Marza d'Andurian; and this is not to mention characters such as Violette Morris, Armand le Fou and Danos (alias 'le mammouth'), who appear with no masking of their identities at all.[102]

Les Boulevards de ceinture further demonstrates Modiano's familiarity with the Occupation, for once again historical references can be seen to cover the length and breadth of the text. Celebrities such as Jean Drault, Darquier de Pellepoix, Professor Montandon, Mag Fontanges and Lionel de Wiet are all introduced under their real names;[103] Sézille, Suarez, Alain Laubreaux and Bouly de Lesdain can easily be spotted in the cryptic guises of Seyzille, Suaraize, Alin-Laubreaux and Mouly de Melun;[104] Jean and Corinne Luchaire, Guy de Voisin, and the brothers-in-law Robert Brasillach and Maurice Bardèche have, in turn, provided the inspiration for Jean Murraille, Annie Murraille, Guy de Marcheret, Lestandi and Gerbère;[105] Sylviane Quimphe owes a sizeable debt to the marquise d'Alès;[106] and there are allusions, too, to an infamous article published in *Je suis partout* on 27 June 1942 (P. A. Cousteau's 'Savez-vous jouer au tennis juif?'), and to the conference which the same newspaper held in the Salle Wagram on 15 January 1944 ('Nous ne sommes pas des dégonflés').

In spite of all this, however, *La Ronde de nuit* and *Les Boulevards de ceinture* cannot be said to be simply *des romans à clé*. They do, indisputably, have a certain historical tinge to them, as has just been demonstrated,[107] but this does not serve to supply the reader with a pre-established, easy-to-use interpretative grid, for as Modiano himself avers:

> J'ai employé un processus de mythomanie qui permet de mélanger réalité et fiction. En même temps j'ai l'impression que cette interférence crée un certain malaise qui n'aurait pas lieu si le lecteur

était sûr de se trouver soit dans l'imaginaire pur, soit dans la réalité historique. J'ajoute que beaucoup des personnages historiques cités relèvent presque pour moi de la légende. Je les ressens comme une espèce de mythe.[108]

Modiano's Occupation, therefore, is not realistic in the generally accepted sense of the word, but belongs rather to the less factual, more atmospheric domain of mythopoeia.[109]

So, from the solid basis offered by an acute grasp of historical fact, Modiano sets his imagination to work on the *années noires* and ends up engaging in a process of 'mythomanie'. But why? Why should he elect to home in on the 'dark years' in the first place? There are, it would appear, a number of possible reasons for this. The first of these relates to the fact that, as a novelist, he is well aware of the period's great literary – and essentially symbolic – potential. 'L'époque ne m'intéresse pas pour elle-même. J'y ai greffé mes angoisses', he has insisted.[110] And that is not all. He has also stressed the connection between the early 1940s and the present, and hence argued that, while superficially seeming to resurrect the past, he is, in reality, depicting 'l'image démesurément grossie de ce qui se passe aujourd'hui'.[111] This claim, quite obviously, is one with which it is almost impossible to take issue, for although the principal concerns of his first two texts – *la question juive* and treachery – were most visibly and poignantly highlighted during the war, few would deny that they remain matters of moment in the world of today.[112] And the same can be said of *Les Boulevards de ceinture*, because as the author himself points out:

> Ce père minable et fantomatique que recherche le narrateur peut être le symbole de beaucoup de choses. Symbole de l'effritement des Valeurs (avec un grand V), de la disparition de tout principe d'autorité et de toute assise morale, etc. . . . toutes choses qui étaient liées à l'image traditionnelle du Père. Le père des *Boulevards de ceinture* est une sorte de dérision désespérée du Père dans l'absolu.[113]

One reason for Modiano's interest in the Occupation is thus a purely professional one – it provides him with a suggestive, metaphorical setting in which a variety of timeless problems can be examined at one remove. But this is not the only motive he has for looking back to the 1940s; there is an acutely personal, exorcistic side to his retrospection as well.

This need for self-purging stems in large part from the conduct of his father during the Occupation. As a Jew, Modiano senior (false identity notwithstanding) was clearly in a vulnerable position after the Germans invaded France, and yet in spite of this, in spite of the risk of denunciation which constantly threatened, he still mingled with people whom he knew to be his sworn enemies.[114] Now, for him, such excursions into the lion's den were extremely rewarding, since he was not deported and so lived to fight another day.[115] But for his son the outcome was nothing like as positive – the future novelist became so fixated by what his parent had done that he had to seek therapy in fiction-writing. 'Ma mère est absente de mon œuvre', he would subsequently note,

> car je cherche à la préserver de l'impureté. L'affaire se situe entre mon père et moi. Mon père a pu préserver sa vie grâce à une attitude trouble, grâce à de multiples concessions. Ce qui alimente mon obsession, ce n'est pas Auschwitz, mais le fait que dans ce climat, pour sauver leur peau, certaines personnes ont pactisé avec leurs bourreaux. Je ne réprouve pas pour autant la conduite paternelle. Je la constate.[116]

In the light of this confession, it comes as no surprise to find Modiano adding that, in both the novels he had written up to that point, 'le fils se charge des faiblesses et de la lâcheté du père. Il y a une culpabilisation du fils qui endosse la veulerie du père, son comportement pendant l'occupation.'[117]

Be that as it may, Modiano's role here is far from being a totally passive and negative one. He may very well suffer from 'un certain remords par personne interposée', as he himself acknowledges,[118] but he does not achieve exorcism simply by taking 'la veulerie du père' to be his own. On the contrary, he considers it vital to improve on the paternal performance and actually fight back against the persecutors: 'Je me mets à la place de mon père. Il était muet devant [les antisémites]. [. . .] J'endosse sa propre peau pour répondre [. . .] il ne pouvait pas répliquer, il n'avait pas les armes.'[119] Modiano, of course, does have the means with which to riposte, and in particular he has language, which is a very flexible weapon indeed.[120] For example, in his first three novels, each of his central characters at some stage turns the tables on the unsavoury collaborators who surround him: Schlemilovitch kills Gérard le Gestapiste, Swing Troubadour/Lamballe shoots at le Khédive, and Serge Alexandre strangles Lestandi. Now as it is unlikely that such a pattern has emerged through mere coincidence, there must be some sort of ulterior motive at work here, and it is not all that hard to see what it is: the novelist is extracting, as only he can (through the new, linguistic reality he creates), a measure of revenge for the final solution.[121]

This is not to say, however, that exorcism is the principal driving force behind Modiano's focus on the Occupation. Nothing could be further from the truth. The novelist does see the 'dark years' as a source of anguish which needs to be purged from his system, as has just been demonstrated, but even more intensely he feels that this period, being the time when his parents first met, is the one in which he ultimately has his roots, the one which helped to form him. As he himself puts it: 'J'ai toujours l'impression que je suis le produit de l'Occupation. Pendant l'Occupation [. . .] des gens se rencontraient qui n'auraient jamais dû se rencontrer en temps normal [. . .] c'est un peu comme mon terroir.'[122] The *années noires*, then, represent the key to his identity, and as such they must inevitably feature strongly whenever he embarks on a quest for his origins.

Yet although this fact would, in itself, suffice to explain his fascination with the war years, there is patently much more to the matter than this, for as he discloses elsewhere, the behaviour of his father (once again!) severely exacerbated the issue: 'C'est juste au moment où je ne l'ai plus vu que j'ai appris ce qu'était cette époque, et que je n'ai pas pu lui poser les questions.'[123] One solution, of course, would have been for him to talk to friends and acquaintances instead, but here too the door had unfortunately been slammed in his face. 'Je connais leurs noms', he avows, 'mais [ces personnes] ont toutes disparu. Pas seulement les collaborateurs.'[124] With these admissions, the full extent of Modiano's predicament becomes clear – he is not just a child and heir of the early 1940s, he is, rather, their *orphan*. Accordingly, when he depicts the Occupation in his novels, linking it, as has been seen, with torment, a need for exorcism and the theme of the father-figure, what he is really doing is expressing one single, all-embracing obsession – he is evoking, to use his own words, 'la lumière incertaine de mes origines'.[125]

Notes

1. Savigneau, 'Les Chemins de leur carrière', p.13.
2. See Montalbetti, 'Patrick Modiano ou l'esprit de fuite', p.42.
3. This controversial approach to the *question juive* explains why publication of the novel was delayed: submission of the manuscript coincided with the Six Day War, and as most people in France were on the side of the Israelis, it was deemed better to bring the book out once passions had cooled. Note also that the success of the work had nothing to do with the 'events' of May 68, for as he has since acknowledged, Modiano shared none of the obsessions of those involved in the *événements*: 'Comment aurais-je pu "en être"? On se révoltait contre la famille, je n'en ai pas; contre l'Université, je ne l'ai guère fréquentée; contre la société et le système, j'en fais si peu partie' (Rolin, 'Patrick Modiano: le dernier enfant du siècle', p.64). Indeed, not only did he not share his contemporaries' concerns, he held the very opposite views to them. 'Cette décennie', he would recall, 'avait un côté futuriste [. . .]. On croyait encore au progrès' (Rondeau, 'Des sixties au Goncourt', p.23), whereas for him, as we shall see, it was the past that was all-important.
4. Jamet, 'Modiano s'explique', p.35.
5. Duranteau, 'Un début exceptionnel: *La Place de l'Étoile*, de Patrick Modiano', p.II.
6. Cf. André Gide: 'Je sens mille possibles en moi; mais je ne puis me résigner à n'en vouloir être qu'un seul' (*Journal 1889–1939* (Paris, Gallimard, Bibliothèque de la Pléiade, 1951), p.28).
7. Edmond Fleg (1874–1963) was a poet, playwright and essayist. Léon Blum (1872–1950) was a Socialist politician and Prime Minister of France (in 1936–37, 1938 and 1946–47). Henri Franck (1888–1912) was a poet.
8. *La Place de l'Étoile*, p.106. Henceforth, all page references will be incorporated into the text parenthetically (where possible).
   Guillaume Apollinaire (1880–1918) was a poet, novelist and dramatist. The reference here is to 'Marizibill', the lines to which Modiano alludes being: 'Elle se mettait sur la paille | Pour un maquereau roux et rose | C'était un juif il sentait l'ail' (Apollinaire, *Œuvres poétiques*, edited by Marcel Adéma and Michel Décaudin (Paris, Gallimard, Bibliothèque de la Pléiade, 1956), p.77).

9. Franz Kafka (1883–1924) was a Czech novelist who wrote in German. He did indeed die of tuberculosis.

10. During the Second World War, Philippe Pétain (1856–1951) was head of the right-wing Vichy regime which targeted Jews, trade unions and freemasons, while at the same time promoting a return to 'traditional values' (such as 'la terre'). The famous saying which Modiano exploits was uttered in a speech made on 25 June 1940, the full draft of which can be found in Jacques Isorni, *Philippe Pétain*, 2 vols (Paris, Table Ronde, 1972–3), II, pp.141–3, n.1. For Berl's role in its authorship, see Berl, '*Interrogatoire*', p.88. Finally, that Raphaël is again following Jewish precedent here can perhaps be confirmed by page 10 above, where Modiano admits that Berl is a great source of inspiration for him (for more on the relationship between the two men, see Assouline, 'Lieux de mémoire', p.46).

11. For fuller details of these characters, see Pierre-Marie Dioudonnat, '*Je suis partout*', *1930–1944: les maurrassiens devant la tentation fasciste* (Paris, Table Ronde, 1973) and, especially, Eugen Weber, *Action Française: Royalism and Reaction in Twentieth-Century France* (Stanford, Stanford University Press, 1962). The order in which Modiano lists his *Juifs maurrassiens* corresponds exactly (slight changes of name notwithstanding) to that found in Weber's seminal study (pp.195–6). Given that this work was translated into French well before *La Place de l'Étoile* appeared (Weber, *L'Action française*, translated by Michel Chrestien (Paris, Stock, 1964)), such correlation seems to give evidence of yet another 'borrowing' on Modiano's part.

12. Joseph Joanovici was one of the key *trafiquants* in the French black market during the Occupation. Perfectly at home in the company of Germans and members of the *Gestapo française*, he nevertheless used some of his profits to finance a Resistance network. Arrested after the Liberation, he was tried and sentenced (in 1949) to five years' imprisonment.

Maurice Sachs (1906–45) was another pillar of the *marché noir* in occupied France – until he left for Hamburg in 1942. Once there, he became a police informer, was eventually arrested, and died a violent death at the end of the war. In the France of today, he is perhaps best known for the first two volumes of his memoirs: *Le Sabbat* (Paris, Corrêa, 1946) and

La chasse à courre (Paris, Gallimard, 1948).

13. Reinhard Heydrich (1904–42) was a leading member of the Nazi security services and the man who, until his assassination, oversaw the infamous 'final solution'. Adolf Hitler (1889–1945) was, of course, the leader of Nazi Germany; along with his established partner, Eva Braun (1910–45), he committed suicide as the Allies moved into Berlin.

14. Texier, 'Rencontre', p.8. Cf. Chasseguet-Smirgel, *Pour une psychanalyse de l'art et de la créativité*: 'L'identification au persécuteur peut [...] avoir [...] pour fonction de le désarmer, de le rendre inopérant (c'est-à-dire, dans l'inconscient, de le châtrer), voire de l'anéantir' (p.235).

15. Cf. Chasseguet-Smirgel, *Pour une psychanalyse*, p.231n.: 'Le nom du héros est à lui seul révélateur de l'acceptation de l'identité juive et de ses racines: il est plus juif que nature.' Note also David Lodge's broader point: 'In a novel names are never neutral. They always signify' (*The Art of Fiction* (London, Penguin, 1992), p.37). As we shall see, Modiano will consistently exemplify this general 'law', favouring above all 'les noms à consonances cosmopolites et interlopes' ('Patrick Modiano répond au questionnaire Marcel Proust', p.26).

16. To confirm that (at least some of) these anti-Semitic jibes have actually been uttered, see Pascal Ory, *La France allemande* (Paris, Gallimard/Julliard, 1977), pp.71, 179–80.

17. Cf. Louis Malle's film, *Lacombe Lucien* (1974), the screenplay of which Modiano helped write, and whose main female character, France, can similarly be seen in symbolic terms. (Alternatively, consult the actual script of the film, published under the joint names of Malle and Modiano in 1974.)

18. Although not directly identified here, Sartre will soon crop up again in the (no less playfully dismissive) form of Jean-Paul Schweitzer de la Sarthe (a name which exploits the fact that Sartre was a relative of the famous Doctor Albert Schweitzer).

19. See *Réflexions sur la question juive* (Paris, Gallimard, 1954), pp. 156, 115 and 145 respectively. Of the other traits highlighted by Sartre, a good number have already been shown (albeit often implicitly) to be readily assumed by Raphaël, most notably 'l'ironie juive, qui s'exerce le plus souvent aux dépens du Juif lui-même et qui est une tentative perpétuelle

pour se voir du dehors' (p.119), 'le fameux "manque de tact" israélite' (p.153), 'l'*inquiétude* juive' (p.164), 'le "manque de pudeur"' (p.150), and, finally, the fact that 'il n'y a pas plus antisémite que le Juif' (p.127).

20. Of this list of people Joanovici, Sachs and Pétain have already been encountered above, and so need no further introduction here. Maurice Barrès (1862–1923) was a French novelist, essayist and nationalist politician, whose espousal of traditional values led him, like Pétain, to conduct a celebration of 'la terre'. Alfred Dreyfus (1859–1935) was the Jewish captain in the French army who, when falsely accused of treachery, became the focus of the (in)famous 'Dreyfus Affair' that rocked *fin-de-siècle* France. Erich von Stroheim (1885–1957) was a Hollywood celebrity renowned as 'The Man You Love To Hate', in which acting role he was often to be found in military attire. Simone Weil (1909–43) was a French author and philosopher of wealthy Jewish stock, but abandoned her *milieu* to throw herself into working-class life. Marcel Proust (1871–1922) was another French author from an affluent Jewish background, and is best remembered today for his classic masterpiece, *A la recherche du temps perdu*. Daniel Halévy (1872–1962) was the son of the famous librettist Ludovic Halévy, and a renowned historian and essayist in his own right. André Maurois (1885–1967) was a French writer best known for his (fictionalized) biographies. Louis-Ferdinand Céline (1894–1961) is still generally acknowledged as a rabid anti-Semite, and so appears to be blatantly miscast as a 'juif honteux' *à la* Simone Weil. However, there is at least one good reason why he should have been given this unlikely role, since Modiano once said of him: 'En lisant son œuvre romanesque, j'ai été frappé par le caractère assez juif de son esprit et de son style [. . .]. D'ailleurs, Céline avoue lui-même [. . .]: "Dans le fond mon œuvre est assez juive"' (Montalbetti, 'La Haine des professeurs', p.2). What Modiano actually means by this 'Jewish' strand in Céline's work can perhaps be ascertained from two of his later comments: 'Etre juif, c'est posséder la faculté de rendre les choses inquiétantes' (Jaudel, 'Quête d'identité', p.61). Or, more recently: 'je voyais le côté juif comme une sorte de génie en marge des choses, qui pouvait par exemple féconder la culture d'un pays' (Geille, 'Modiano

m'intimide', p.127). For further elucidation of this topic, see p.11 of *La Place de l'Étoile* itself.

21. There might also be yet another passing nod to Sartre, who observed in his *Réflexions sur la question juive*: 'Le sioniste s'irrite contre le Juif français qu'il accuse *a priori* d'inauthenticité' (p.174). (Note also Raphaël's comment on seeing Tel Aviv before him – 'Je ne suis pas tout à fait français [. . .], je suis JUIF français' (p.123) – and cf. Sartre, *Réflexions*, p.173: 'La meilleure façon pour [le Juif] d'être Français, c'est de s'affirmer *Juif français*.')

22. Cf. the relationship between France and Lucien in *Lacombe Lucien*. The general ambivalence of Modiano's depiction of Israel perhaps reflects his own views on the matter: 'Je ne fais partie d'aucune communauté juive. Je ne suis pas sioniste. Mais je me sens absolument solidaire des juifs dans l'adversité' (Jaudel, 'Quête', p.61).

23. More specifically, the allusion is to Sachs's *Le Sabbat*, which carries the subtitle *Souvenirs d'une jeunesse orageuse*.

24. Gustave Flaubert (1821–80) was a renowned son of Normandy and author of *L'Education sentimentale*.

25. For the original context of this phrase, see Gide, *Les Nourritures terrestres*, in Gide, *Romans*, edited by Yvonne Davet and Jean-Jacques Thierry (Paris, Gallimard, Bibliothèque de la Pléiade, 1958), p.186.

26. Lucien Rebatet (1903–72) was an anti-Semitic writer and journalist. Condemned to death on 23 November 1946, he was reprieved on 10 April 1947 and eventually freed on 16 July 1952.

27. The original text here is *Saint Genet, comédien et martyr* (Paris, Gallimard, 1952), Sartre's study of the playwright Jean Genet. Proof that Modiano has more than a passing acquaintance with this book is given, perhaps, by the fact that one of its chapter headings, 'Le Couple éternel du criminel et de la sainte', appears to have influenced Schlemilovitch's choice of title for part of his own monograph on a literary figure: 'Pierre Drieu la Rochelle ou le couple éternel du SS et de la juive' (p.22). More generally, the extent of Raphaël's allusions further suggest a debt to the author of the *Réflexions sur la question juive*, for in this latter text we discover that the Jew 'absorbe toutes les connaissances avec [. . .] avidité' (p.120), and often likes to 'assimiler les valeurs nationales (tableaux,

livres, etc.)' (p.122).

28. Two others, hitherto unmentioned, are not far behind: Scott Fitzgerald and Valery Larbaud. (There are also implicit signs of the influence of Arthur Rimbaud, for more on which see Jutrin, 'A propos de *La Place de l'Étoile* de Patrick Modiano'.)

29. Raphaël's title for part one of his work (*Du côté de Fougeire-Jusquiames*) obviously derives from Proust's *Du côté de chez Swann*, but the first words he writes are lifted more or less *tels quels* from *Le côté de Guermantes* – see *La Place de l'Étoile*, p.93 and cf. *A la recherche du temps perdu*, edited by Jean-Yves Tadié, 4 vols (Paris, Gallimard, Bibliothèque de la Pléiade), II, p.314.

30. For confirmation that this is his aim, see Montalbetti, 'La Haine des professeurs', p.2, and Duranteau, 'L'Obsession de l'anti-héros', p.13.

31. Fittingly (in the light of what was said above about imitation), Proust also 'cleansed' himself through pastiche at the start of his career: 'The whole thing for me', he wrote, 'was above all a matter of hygiene; one must purge oneself of the natural vice of idolatry and imitation. And instead of slyly doing Michelet or doing Goncourt while signing [one's own name], doing it openly in the form of pastiche, in order to go back to being no more than Marcel Proust when I write my novels' (cit. in Ronald Hayman, *Proust* (London, Minerva, 1991), pp.275–6).

32. In the plain language of David Lodge, intertextuality is a 'kind of gesturing from one text to another', and 'there are many ways by which one text can refer to another: parody, pastiche, echo, allusion, direct quotation, structural parallelism. Some theorists believe that intertextuality is the very condition of literature, that all texts are woven from the tissues of other texts, whether the authors know it or not' (*The Art of Fiction*, pp.96, 98–9).

33. Libermann, 'Patrick Modiano: *Lacombe Lucien* n'est pas le portrait du fascisme mais celui de sa piétaille', p.3.

34. Cf. Patricia Waugh: 'language *constructs* rather than merely *reflects* everyday life: [. . .] meaning resides in the relations between signs *within* a literary fictional text, rather than in their reference to objects *outside* that text' (*Metafiction* (London, Routledge, 1988), p.53). As we shall see (directly or indirectly) in the pages which follow, this modern view of

language, fiction and reality is one which characterizes the whole of *l'œuvre modianesque*.

35. Jaudel, 'Quête', p.61.

36. Brunn, 'Patrick Modiano', p.10.

37. This overlap between author and character allows yet another literary link-up to be made, this time with Joris-Karl Huysmans' *A rebours*. Like *La Place de l'Étoile*, *A rebours* mixes constant literary and cultural reference with overtly autobiographical elements, and thereby successfully cobbles together a personality for its central character. The name of this central character, des Esseintes, appears to be distinctly echoed by Modiano's Des Essarts.

38. Pivot, 'Demi-juif Patrick Modiano affirme: "Céline était un véritable écrivain juif"', p.16.

39. Montalbetti, 'Patrick Modiano ou l'esprit de fuite', p.42. Might there be yet another echo of Jean-Paul Sartre here? Sartre did, after all, say of The Jew that 'sa vie n'est qu'une longue fuite devant les autres et devant lui-même' (*Réflexions sur la question juive*, p.167).

40. Nansen passports were issued to *apatrides* after the First World War by the League of Nations, and owe their name to Fridtjof Nansen (1861–1930), a pioneering Norwegian explorer who became the League's High Commissioner for Refugees at this time. The fact that the narrator holds such a document automatically brings his *état civil* into question, our doubts being additionally fuelled by the use of the adjective *faux*.

41. Judas (the biblical traitor), Maxime de Bel-Respiro (Modiano's creation), Philippe Pétain (see Note 10 above) and the tragic King Lear (Shakespearian hero) really require no introduction, unlike (perhaps) Landru (1869–1922) and Marcel 'le Docteur' Petiot (1897–1944), both of whom were notorious mass murderers in France.

42. This being the case, we can see how appropriate his Gestapo alias is, for although the title Swing Troubadour relates, on the one hand, to Charles Trenet's 1941 song of the same name (extracts of which punctuate the text), it also has added significance, as Joseph Golsan points out: 'Swing [. . .] suggests a hopeless oscillation between labels which are [. . .] ultimately inadequate to self definition', while 'Troubadour [. . .] is suggestive of the character's rootlessness, because the

troubadours were wandering poets and minstrels' ('Author, Identity and the Voice of History in Patrick Modiano's *La Ronde de nuit* and *Les Boulevards de ceinture*', pp.188 and 188 n.2 respectively).

43. This name is all the more noteworthy in that there is not just an allusion here to the historical *woman*, called the Princesse de Lamballe (1749–92), who refused to shout 'Vive la Nation!' when faced with the guillotine. According to Pierre Daprini, 'une "princesse de Lamballe", dans un certain argot parisien, c'est un inverti qui se prostitue' ('Patrick Modiano: le temps de l'Occupation', p.198). Taking this point along with that made in Note 42 above, we can appreciate just how lacking in definition the narrator of *La Ronde de nuit* is – he has not one, but two aliases, both of which permit of at least two interpretations themselves!

44. Alexandre Stavisky (1886–1934) was the swindler at the heart of the infamous Stavisky Affair in France. His death, which some said was murder, others suicide, was one of the great *causes célèbres* of the Third Republic.

45. Cf. the closing scenes of *Lacombe Lucien*, where France and her grandmother seem to owe their continued survival to Lucien, a Lucien who, on one occasion, hides in a tree and apparently abandons them. Cf. also *La Place de l'Étoile*, in which Raphaël wants to kill his father, Tania and Des Essarts because: 'Moi, les gens que j'aime, je les tue. Alors je les choisis bien faibles, sans défense' (p.104). (Typically, there may be an allusion here to Oscar Wilde's famous saying (from his 'Ballad of Reading Gaol'): 'Yet each man kills the thing he loves' (Wilde, *Complete Works* (London/Glasgow, Collins, 1966), p.844)).

46. Again cf. *Lacombe Lucien*, the (anti-)hero of which ends up in the Gestapo simply because his bike has an unexpected puncture. Cf. also Modiano's own comment on the *années noires*: 'Tel garçon un peu léger [. . .] en 1938 devenait en clair un délateur. Paris sous l'occupation, c'est en effet mon univers, à cause de cette façon dont les êtres, autrement éclairés, se divisent en héros et en salauds' (Duranteau, 'L'Obsession de l'anti-héros', p.13).

47. Montalbetti, 'Patrick Modiano ou l'esprit de fuite', p.42.

48. In addition to 'Swing Troubadour' (see Note 42 above), there is clear reference (though often with some adaptations) to:

Léo Marjane's 'Seule ce soir' (1941), Charles Trenet's 'Fleur bleue' (1937), 'Bonsoir, jolie madame' (1939) and 'Que reste-t-il de nos amours?' (1943), and Johnny [Hess] and Charles [Trenet]'s 'Quand les beaux jours seront là' and 'Maman, ne vends pas la maison'. Note also the connotations of the square Cimarosa, Domenico Cimarosa (1749–1801) being an Italian composer of operas. (For details of the German songs used in *La Ronde de nuit*, and more on Modiano's use of music in general, see Coenen-Mennemeier, 'Le philtre magique', in Bedner (ed.), *Patrick Modiano*, pp.55–71.)

49. Cf. Bruno Doucey, who likens the work to a fugue (*'La Ronde de nuit': Modiano*, pp.42–3).

50. Unless, of course, he is simply anticipating escaping! Cf. *La Place de l'Étoile*, in which there is similar uncertainty: 'Ma tête éclate, mais j'ignore si c'est à cause des balles ou de ma jubilation' (p.149).

51. Modiano, 'Un roman sur Paris en été', p.5. There is certainly good cause for considering Paris as the key character in the work, for in essence, it is no different to Swing Troubadour/Lamballe – just as our protagonist is a huge collection of contrasts (*résistant/collabo*, masculine/feminine, protector/enemy, etc.), so too is the French capital portrayed in terms of binary oppositions: it is split into two by the Seine, with the *rive gauche* (and the Resistance) on one side, and the *rive droite* (and the Gestapo) on the other; it is known as the *Ville lumière*, yet is now entirely blacked out; and so we could go on. Not for nothing, then, will the narrator say: 'Cette ville déserte correspondait à mon état d'esprit' (p.109) – the city is no more at one with itself than he is!

52. The symbolism here appears all the more blatant in that, as has been seen, the novel too has a strong musical element to it.

53. Cf. pp.87, 159–60.

54. Modiano, 'Un roman sur Paris en été', p.5.

55. Although Modiano's text does not itself make this comparison, its repeated mention of artists (such as Goya and Franz Hals) encourages the link to be established. For a fuller discussion of this debt to Rembrandt, see Doucey, *'La Ronde de nuit'*, pp.71–7.

56. The association is normally with Saskia, Rembrandt's wife. See e.g. *Rembrandt* (Paris, Hachette, 1965), p.181 or *Rembrandt:*

La Terre et le Ciel (Paris, Tallandier, 1976), p.35.

57. This interpretation, of course, is no more definitive than anything else connected with the novel. Doucey will argue, for instance, that it is Esmeralda who evokes Rembrandt's little girl figure (*'La Ronde de nuit'*, p.77).

58. Modiano, 'Un roman sur Paris en été', p.3.

59. Cf. Kanters, 'La Nuit de Patrick Modiano', p.24. For further validation of this contention, recall Modiano's reference to the 'promeneur solitaire' above, and cf. his comments about his own relationship with the Occupation: 'Je n'ai pas connu cette époque mais il suffit de laisser parler les pierres. La nuit surtout. Les façades des immeubles et des hôtels particuliers dégagent encore, vingt ans après, une sorte d'éclat ténébreux' ('Un roman sur Paris en été', p.4).

60. Quasimodo is, of course, the hunchback of *Notre-Dame de Paris*. The connection to Vidocq is articulated by Bruno Doucey: 'Coco Lacour peut faire songer à Coco-Latour, chef de bande et bagnard évoqué en 1828 dans les *Mémoires* de François Vidocq (1775–1857), ancien forçat devenu chef de la Sûreté sous l'Empire' (*'La Ronde de nuit'*, p.52 n.1).

61. Cf. Golsan, 'Author, Identity and the Voice of History', p.195. The lines in question (from *Macbeth*) are: '[Life] is a Tale | Told by an Ideot, full of sound and fury, | Signifying nothing' (*William Shakespeare: The Complete Works*, edited by Stanley Wells and Gary Taylor (Oxford, Clarendon Press, 1986), p.1127 (ll.2006–8)).

62. The quotation, 'Pourquoi étais-je identifié aux objets même de mon horreur et de ma compassion?' is taken from Fitzgerald's 'The Crack-up', the original form of words being: 'I only wanted absolute quiet to think out [. . .] *why I had become identified with the objects of my horror or compassion*' (author's italics; *The Bodley Head Scott Fitzgerald*, [edited by J. B. Priestley and Malcolm Cowey], 6 vols (London, Bodley Head, 1958–63], III, p.400).

63. Apart from the links implied by the epigraph, see e.g. Modiano's comment on Luna-Park above and cf. Fitzgerald's 'The Last of the Belles': 'This place that had once been so full of life and effort was gone, as if it had never existed' (*The Bodley Head Scott Fitzgerald* (cf. Note 62), V, p.488). Other possible debts to Fitzgerald, both here and (as we shall see) throughout the *œuvre*, include: the use of historical figures,

fashions and popular songs to situate the narrative in time; the focus on dreaming and dreamers; the liking for evocative names; the transience of all things on Earth, and the preserving quality of memory.

64. Cf. Verlaine, *Œuvres poétiques complètes*, edited by Y.-G. Le Dantec, revised by Jacques Borel (Paris, Gallimard, Bibliothèque de la Pléiade, 1962), p.280: 'Qu'as-tu fait, ô toi que voilà | Pleurant sans cesse | Dis, qu'as-tu fait, toi que voilà, | De ta jeunesse?'

65. Alcibiades (450–404 BC) was the Athenian statesman and general who, having first called for an expeditionary force to be sent to Sicily, then turned traitor and ensured the venture ended in failure. The chevalier d'Éon (1728–1810) was a French embassy official renowned for dressing as a woman and claiming to be a lady. Leopoldo Fregoli (1867–1936) was an Italian actor, singer, dancer, mime artist and illusionist who was famous the world over; he is still remembered in France today as a *comédien à transformations*. For details of Dreyfus and Joanovici, see Notes 12 and 20 above. (Note also that the Joanovici book title, promising an account of the man 'tel qu'il *fut*', suggests that the subject is now dead and that the narrator could not, therefore, have read it until well after the war had ended – a further clue that the Occupation is being remembered/imagined, and not directly experienced.)

66. See Note 31 above.

67. Texier, 'Rencontre', p.8.

68. While working on this *récit*, Modiano also tried his hand as a journalist, publishing 'L'Anti-Frank' (a riposte to Bernard Frank's attack on *La Place de l'Étoile*) and three brief studies of well-known writers: 'Je me sens proche de lui' (on Albert Camus), 'Hervé Bazin vu par Patrick Modiano', and 'Un martyr des lettres' (on Marcel Proust).

69. See e.g. p.58, where the theme of the *ronde* crops up again.

70. Cf. *La Ronde de nuit*, in which Swing Troubadour/Lamballe considers killing Esmeralda and Coco in the very same manner. For the import of the simultaneous contrast between the two incidents (Serge is the intended *victim*, not, as his predecessor was, the would-be *murderer*), see p.36 below.

71. Considering that the 'baron' seems to be Jewish (see e.g. pp.144, 185), there might be a (typical) allusion here to *A la recherche du temps perdu*, in which Proust has M. de Charlus,

'le "baron" de Charlus, comme il se fait appeler' (IV, p.254), say: 'Dès qu'un juif a assez d'argent pour acheter un château, il en choisit toujours un qui s'appelle le Prieuré, l'Abbaye, le Monastère, la Maison-Dieu' (III, p.490). Additionally, it might be that Modiano has been struck by this specific feature of the place which inspired him: Barbizon. For as Ferny Besson has observed, when *récit* is compared to village, 'On reconnaît la Grand'rue, les pistes cavalières, l'auberge avec sa façade anglo-normande, et jusqu'à la longue villa **La Barraka**, ici rebaptisé **Mektoub**, **Le Monastère** devenu **Le Prieuré**, bâti sur le chemin du Bornage' ('*Les Boulevards de ceinture*, par Patrick Modiano', p.17).

72. This readiness of the father-figure to court danger is a constant in Modiano's early work. See e.g. *La Place de l'Étoile*, p.41. Note also Horn's suicidal visit to the Gestapo HQ in *Lacombe Lucien*.

73. Cf. Modiano's own assessment of *Les Boulevards de ceinture*: 'C'est l'histoire d'une quête qui ne peut déboucher sur rien de stable [. . .], mais sur du sable mouvant, un climat de désarroi et d'inquiétude' (Malka, 'Patrick Modiano', p.2).

74. Further contributors to this circularity are recurrent phrases such as: 'L'épisode douloureux du métro Georges-V' (pp.105, 116, 137, 167), or 'Aucune importance' (pp.29, 48, 146, 153). As has been seen, leitmotifs were also a feature of *La Place de l'Étoile* and *La Ronde de nuit* (both of whose titles likewise allude to the concept of the circle), and this constant use of repetition is worthy of note on two counts. First, because it generates a certain rhythm, the 'petite musique' which the author so values (see Rambures, 'Comment travaillent les écrivains', p.24, and cf. Montaudon, 'Patrick Modiano: le plus agréable c'est la rêverie', p.15). Second, because it highlights the role of *fantasy* in the three texts, imagination being, as the poet Coleridge once suggested, rather like 'undulating folds, for ever varying and for ever flowing into itself – circular, and without beginning or end' (cit. in A. S. Byatt, *The Game* (London, Vintage, 1992) p.6).

75. Photographs, as we shall see, will be a constant feature of *l'œuvre modianesque*, and understandably so – quite apart from their regular exposure of the fiction, they are in themselves (like most of the other old *documents* that Modiano exploits) largely ambivalent, and so add to the

overall sense of uncertainty. As Susan Sontag has helpfully noted: 'A photograph is both a pseudo-presence and a token of absence' (*On photography* (London, Penguin, 1979), p.16 – see ibid., *passim*, for more on the ambivalence of photography).

76. 'A cinematic novelist', David Lodge has said, '[. . .] is one who [. . .] imagines and presents his materials in primarily visual terms, and whose visualisations correspond in some significant respect to the visual effects characteristic of film' (*Working with Structuralism* (London, Routledge, 1991), p.96). As may now readily be conceded, Lodge could be referring directly to Modiano here, especially as the latter has openly avowed: 'Je suis d'une génération qui a été intoxiquée par le cinéma. Il est normal qu'elle soit beaucoup moins rhétorique que la précédente' (Rambures, 'Comment travaillent les écrivains', p.24). We will have cause to return to the novelist's cinematic style in the pages which follow, but as an appetizer, we can instantly savour two other regular features of this filmic approach: the rarity of (causal) conjunctions, which leads to sentences' being juxtaposed rather like the different shots of a movie (a technique well illustrated in the passage above), and the abandonment of normal chronology, whether through the exploitation of flashback (already discussed sufficiently), or through the unconventional use of verb tenses (a subject addressed, with examples from *Les Boulevards de ceinture*, in Brouwer, 'L'Emploi des temps verbaux chez Patrick Modiano').

77. Cf. Czarny, 'La Trace douloureuse': 'Le récit baigne dans un climat onirique, entre cauchemar et réalité, et rien ne permet de conclure, comme si l'auteur, en jouant sur le trouble, cherchait à prolonger chez le lecteur l'impression de malaise qui caractérise la relation entre le père et le fils' (p.172).

78. As is so often the case in Modiano's work, this reliance on imagination and what is felt to be right has distinct precedents in French literary tradition. See e.g. Jean-Jacques Rousseau, speaking about his memoirs (*Les Confessions*):

> Je les écrivois de mémoire; cette mémoire me manquoit souvent ou ne me fournissoit que des souvenirs imparfaits [. . .]. Je disois les choses que j'avois oubliées comme il me sembloit qu'elles avoient dû être, comme elles avoient été peut être en effet, jamais au contraire de ce que je me rappellois qu'elles avoient

été. (Rousseau, *Œuvres complètes*, volume I, edited by Bernard Gagnebin and Marcel Raymond (Paris, Gallimard, Bibliothèque de la Pléiade, 1959), p.1035).

This tendency towards imaginary autobiography (not to mention the implicit search for an identity which accompanies it) would perhaps explain, at least in part, why Rousseau's influence is so visible in *La Place de l'Étoile* as well.

79. Cf. *La Place de l'Étoile*, where no sooner has Schlemilovitch *père* been described as a 'gentil clown' (p.49) than Raphaël partners him (imaginatively?) in a *clownesque* double act (pp.52–3).

80. 'La Trace douloureuse', p.176. For an earlier example of this drive towards solidarity, see *La Place de l'Étoile*, pp.49–50, 121–2.

81. Marthe Robert, *Roman des origines et origines du roman* (Paris, Grasset, 1972), pp.43n and 46 respectively.

82. As ever, cf. *La Place de l'Étoile* and *La Ronde de nuit*, whose child-like narrators have likewise been seen to 'adopt' a surrogate family.

83. For a concise summary of the classic symptoms, see Bruno Vercier and Jacques Lecarme, *La Littérature en France depuis 1968* (Paris, Bordas, 1982): 'Tout enfant, selon Freud, est à certains âges un petit romancier qui rêve sur ses origines, s'imagine enfant trouvé ou bâtard, et par ces fantasmes, essaie de résoudre la crise œdipienne' (p.130).

84. 'Modiano ou l'identité introuvable', p.60.

85. Note the repeated use of the telltale *on* on pp.26–32: 'On a fort bien compris que', 'On s'explique mal que', etc.

86. There were, of course, elements of this detective strand in Schlemilovitch and Swing Troubadour/Lamballe, but it is only with Serge that we effectively start to see signs of a protracted, police-style *enquête*, complete with various *indices* and apparent *documentation*.

87. This problem has certain echoes of Scott Fitzgerald's *The Great Gatsby* – there too the narrator tries to record a mysterious man's life, but is plagued by information which is fragmentary, partial and often contradictory (see *The Bodley Head Scott Fitzgerald* (cf. Note 62), volume I).

88. If we assume that they are his own recollections, the chronology of the text falls apart – see e.g. Jacques Brenner,

Histoire de la littérature française de 1940 à nos jours (Paris, Fayard, 1978), p.540.

89. See Eugen Weber, *Action Française: Royalism and Reaction in Twentieth-Century France* (Stanford, Stanford University Press, 1962), p.320. This nominal 'borrowing' on Serge's part (and of a pseudonym at that) should not surprise us in the slightest: it simply confirms the pattern set in *La Ronde de nuit*, where the lack of a true patronymic (or, for that matter, metronymic) became the symptom of a much more general loss of identity.

90. Duranteau, 'L'Obsession de l'anti-héros', p.13. Retrospectively, these words can be applied to *La Place de l'Étoile* and *La Ronde de nuit*, for in these works too, the same 'image paternelle' is in evidence: 'En France, il devint le secrétaire de Stavisky', Raphaël says of Schlemilovitch *père* in the former (p.41), while in the latter, the 'adoption' of the crook is far more explicit (see p.24 above).

91. See e.g. *Les Boulevards de ceinture*, pp.91–7, and cf. William Shirer, *The Collapse of the Third Republic: An Inquiry into the Fall of France in 1940* (London, Heinemann/Secker and Warburg, 1970), pp.188–90. Alternatively, see the direct comparison in Nettelbeck and Hueston, *Patrick Modiano*, p.49.

92. Recall, for example, the gallows humour of his claim to be a Jewish Nazi, or a 'juif collabo', etc.

93. See e.g. *La Ronde de nuit*, p.129: 'Obligado écrivait un "journal politique". "Nous devons témoigner, m'expliquait-il. C'est un devoir. Je ne peux pas me taire." Pourtant le mutisme s'apprend très vite: il suffit de recevoir deux coups de talon dans les gencives.'

94. Self-deprecation had marked both of Modiano's earlier narrators as well, but it had always been somewhat abrupt, as with this put-down from *La Ronde de nuit*: 'Toutes les fées se sont penchées sur mon berceau. Elles avaient bu sans doute' (p.74). Such abruptness no longer applies.

95. He married Dominique Zehrfuss on 12 September 1970. (The two witnesses were Raymond Queneau and André Malraux.)

96. Malka, 'Patrick Modiano', p.2.

97. For more on this link between Modiano's novels and *Lacombe Lucien*, see Golsan, 'Collaboration, Alienation, and the Crisis of Identity in the Film and Fiction of Patrick Modiano'.

98. The *mode rétro* embodied a nationwide renewal of interest in

the Occupation, and was one of the most dominant trends in France in the 1970s and early 1980s. For fuller details of the movement and Modiano's part in it, see my book *Collaboration and Resistance Reviewed: Writers and the 'Mode Rétro' in Post-Gaullist France* (New York/Oxford, Berg, 1992).

99. Modiano himself acknowledges this debt to history – see Modiano, 'Un roman sur Paris en été . . .', p.5. For a good idea of the extent of Modiano's familiarity with the gang (also demonstrated in *La Place de l'Étoile*), see Philippe Aziz, *Tu trahiras sans vergogne* (Paris, Fayard, 1970), or Marcel Hasquenoph, *La Gestapo en France* (Paris, de Vecchi, 1975). (Revealingly, neither of these books had been published when Modiano was putting pen to paper.)

100. When war was declared Laffont was actually calling himself Henri Normand – see Hasquenoph, op. cit. Note 99, p.133.

101. Aziz reveals where Modiano probably found the name for his character, referring to 'Georges Garance, dit "Monsieur Philibert", [. . .] organisateur attitré des soirées mondaines et des orgies de la rue Lauriston' (op. cit. Note 99, p.69). Interestingly, one of the *gestapistes* in *Lacombe Lucien*, Pierre Tonin, was also an inspector and 'un policier exceptionnel' (p.37) before being dismissed from the force. Anyone wishing to pursue this matter further could usefully consult the biography written by Bonny's son, Jacques: *Mon père, l'inspecteur Bonny* (Paris, Laffont, 1975).

102. The use of 3*bis* square Cimarosa as the gang's address is no coincidence either. 3*bis* place des États-Unis was another of Laffont's haunts (cf. *La Place de l'Étoile*, p.127) and one of the streets leading towards it from the rue Lauriston is the rue Cimarosa. In the light of what was said earlier about the importance of closed shutters at Swing Troubadour/ Lamballe's former abode (see pp.27–8 above), it might be useful to recall here the following statement by Pascal Jardin: 'Au 3*bis*, place des États-Unis [. . . Laffont] commet de telles atrocités qu'en 1973, l'hôtel n'est toujours pas réhabité' (*Guerre après guerre* (Paris, Grasset, 1973), p.195). It should also be noted, to avoid the lure of reductionism, that much of the ambience *chez* Philibert and le Khédive derives from another group of infamous French *gestapistes* – the *bande à Berger* from the rue de la Pompe (see Nettelbeck and Hueston, *Patrick Modiano*, p.27).

103. Jean Drault (as activist in the *Ligue antijuive universelle*), Darquier de Pellepoix (as head of the Commissariat aux questions juives) and Georges Montandon (as academic pseudo-scientist) were all renowned anti-Semites. Mag Fontanges was a lesser member of the *bande de la rue Lauriston*, as of course was the aforementioned Lionel de Wiet.

104. Captain Paul Sézille (*Les Cahiers jaunes*), Georges Suarez (*Aujourd'hui*), Alain Laubreaux (*Je suis partout*) and Jacques Bouly de Lesdain (*L'Illustration*) were all journalists on collaborationist publications.

105. Jean Luchaire (*Les Nouveaux Temps*, *Toute la Vie*), Robert Brasillach and Maurice Bardèche (both *Je suis partout*) were all active in collaborationist journalism; Corinne Luchaire was Jean's daughter and an established actress in her own right, while Guy de Voisin was an ex-legionnaire, Corinne's husband and a frequenter of 93, rue Lauriston. For authorial confirmation that these are his models, see Jaudel, 'Quête', p.61. Cf. *Lacombe Lucien*, which sees the Corinne Luchaire–Guy de Voisin couple reincarnated as Betty Beaulieu and Jean-Bernard de Voisins (in addition to the clue of Jean-Bernard's surname, Annie and Betty have both appeared in the film *Nuit de rafle(s)*). Note also that, when naming his actress character, Modiano may have been thinking of Annie Mouraille, the *comédienne* who was involved in the killing of Marx Dormoy (see Philippe Bourdrel, *La Cagoule* (Paris, Albin Michel, 1970), pp.251–4).

106. For more about the marquise d'Alès and her likeness to Sylviane Quimphe, see Chapter 7, Note 48 below.

107. Note also their Fitzgeraldian use of period detail, such as the reproduction of song lyrics, or the mention of popular nightclubs.

108. Montalbetti, 'Patrick Modiano ou l'esprit de fuite', p.43. For illustration of this latter point, see *Les Boulevards de ceinture*: 'Eddy Pagnon ... Encore un nom qui court dans ma mémoire. Personnage? Je ne sais pas' (p.54). Pagnon is in fact a historical character – a member of the Bonny–Laffont gang, he was executed on 26 December 1944. (Fuller details of this *gestapiste*, and of Modiano's interest in him, can be found in Chapters 6 and 7 below.)

109. Cf. *Lacombe Lucien*, apropos of which Modiano has stated:

'C'est d'une occupation un peu rêvée qu'il s'agit, comme déformée à travers une glace, revue par l'imaginaire' (Libermann, 'Patrick Modiano', p.3). Such avowed recourse to myth further underlines the point that has already been stressed throughout this chapter – namely that Modiano's work is immensely unreliable as regards the information it imparts.

110. Jamet, 'Modiano s'explique', p.36.
111. Rambures, 'Comment travaillent les écrivains', p.24. Note also Modiano's alternative line of argument: 'Finalement, on ne peut pas faire autrement que décrire son époque même si superficiellement on a l'air de décrire le passé. Ce sont tout au plus les nostalgies de l'époque' (Jamet, 'Modiano s'explique', p.36).
112. Note also the rather ambiguous comment by the narrator of *La Ronde de nuit*: 'Délations, passages à tabac, vols, assassinats, trafics de toute espèce – choses qui sont, à l'heure où j'écris ces lignes, monnaie courante' (p.72).
113. Malka, 'Patrick Modiano', p.2.
114. Cf. one of his famous acquaintances, Maurice Sachs, who not only mixed with the same collaborators as he did, but also leased the flat at 15, quai Conti before he moved in (see Sachs, *La Chasse à courre* (Paris, Gallimard, 1948), pp.67–8). Thanks to these, and other similarities between the two men (their Jewishness, their dubious deals, etc.) Modiano comes to see Sachs as a substitute father *par excellence*.
115. He did have at least one very close call, though – see Chapters 6 and 7 below. For more on Albert Modiano during the war, see Jamet, 'Modiano s'explique', pp.31–2, or Assouline, 'Lieux de mémoire', p.38.
116. Texier, 'Rencontre', p.8. As has been seen, this bizarre linking of victim and torturer is a theme of Modiano's work.
117. Ibid.
118. Libermann, 'Patrick Modiano', p.3.
119. Brunn, 'Patrick Modiano', p.10.
120. In addition to the points which follow, recall p.21 above.
121. That it is principally *anti-Semitism*, and not so much collaboration in the abstract, that is the novelist's main target would appear to be confirmed by the following authorial comment: '[Les gens de la rue Lauriston] étaient d'abord des truands. [. . .] Je ne dirai pas qu'ils étaient plus

sympathiques . . . mais à côté des gens comme Rebatet . . .' (Josselin, 'Mondo Modiano', p.60). Note also that the cathartic intent may help to explain the use of humour in the 'trilogy', for as Bruno Doucey has observed: 'l'humour, fût-ce le plus noir, est un moyen d'exorciser la peur, une façon de conjurer le mal' ('*La Ronde de nuit*', p.68).

122. Geille, 'Modiano m'intimide', p.65.

123. Jamet, 'Modiano s'explique', p.32. This is not to say, though, that Albert never mentioned the period at all. 'J'en ai toujours entendu parler dans mon enfance', his son will elsewhere admit, before adding, significantly, '[. . .] mais en termes assez vagues' (Libermann, 'Patrick Modiano', p.3).

124. Jamet, 'Modiano s'explique', p.32. This lack of surviving witnesses meant that he had to rely heavily on books for his information. Some of these, no doubt, were those that Maurice Sachs had left behind when he moved out of 15, quai Conti (see *Un cirque passe*, p.144). Most, however, were uniquely parental in origin: 'Mon père avait [. . .] acheté des livres pendant l'occupation, Rebatet, Céline, toute la clique. C'était toute la production d'une époque dont je me suis imprégné' (Jamet, 'Modiano s'explique', p.35).

125. Ezine, 'Sur la sellette', p.5.

3

'Plus ça change. . .': 'Villa Triste', 'Livret de famille' and 'Rue des Boutiques Obscures'

J'ai vraiment le sentiment d'écrire le même livre, depuis le début.

Patrick Modiano

On vit plus dans la vie qu'on n'a pas que dans la vie qu'on a.

Jules Barbey d'Aurevilly

Le grand, l'inévitable sujet romanesque, c'est toujours [. . .] le temps.

Patrick Modiano

One of the hardest hurdles to climb for any novelist, it is often said, is that of the second novel, since buoyed by the success of the first, expectations have rocketed and are lodged at their most intense. As Chapter 2 has endeavoured to demonstrate, this pitfall, clearly, was not one to which Modiano fell prey. *La Ronde de nuit* is, if anything, even better than *La Place de l'Étoile*. But the problem of the next work never really goes away, and by the time Modiano had concluded his third foray into the Occupation, thereby terminating his informal trilogy as well, the question of how best to expand his *œuvre* was evidently a pertinent one. Should he produce more of the same? Should he change direction entirely? True to his goal of always keeping one step ahead of himself, he had the answer well before *Les Boulevards de ceinture* was completed. 'Ce livre', he tells us through the mouth of Serge Alexandre, is intended to be 'le dernier concernant mon autre vie' (p.162). So, a break with established practice would appear to be on the cards. Yet as this chapter will attempt to show, the following three texts, *Villa Triste* (1975), *Livret de famille* (1977) and *Rue des Boutiques Obscures* (1978),[1] by no means mark a radical departure from their predecessors. Important differences are in evidence, it is true, but so too are numerous continued similarities, and to such an extent that there is only one possible conclusion to be drawn: all in all, as the adage says, 'plus ça change et plus c'est la même chose'.

'Il fait si noir', the narrator says towards the end of *Les Boulevards de ceinture*, 'que je ne peux pas me rendre compte du chemin que nous prenons. Rue des Saussaies? Drancy? La villa Triste?' (p.198).[2] Typically, we never do find out, in literal terms, what the final stop will actually be – as in so many other aspects, the narrative here leaves us guessing. Yet on a more allusive, self-referential level, the last destination cited is without doubt the most convincing of the three, for the next work of fiction on Modiano's own (literary) journey is, precisely, *Villa Triste*.

Fresh from completing two other (for him) pioneering missions, one into the cinema, through a collaboration with Louis Malle on the script of his successful film *Lacombe Lucien*, and the other into the theatre, by means of a disastrous play called *La Polka*,[3] Modiano came to *Villa Triste* with novelty very much to the forefront of his mind. Little wonder, then, that, at first glance, novelty is exactly what he seems to deliver.

The most telling sign of this, arguably, is the subject-matter he chooses to exploit in the work. Having focused up until this point on what, loosely speaking, can be called the war novel format, he now switches genres entirely and turns his hand to the love story, in the form of the idyllic relationship which binds his narrator, Victor Chmara, to an aspiring young actress called Yvonne Jacquet. And idyllic is certainly the word here, because the closest we ever get to real passion is Victor's rather deflatingly subdued: 'Quelque chose se dilatait du côté gauche de ma poitrine, et j'ai décidé que ce jour était le plus beau de ma vie' (p.25).[4] Nevertheless, understated or not, this *histoire d'amour* still represents something of a new departure for the author.

Newness can likewise be found in certain structural and technical aspects of the book, and in particular in the way that repetition and circularity, previously the very bedrock of *l'œuvre modianesque*, have now been replaced at the heart of the text by their exact opposites. Not that the circle and echoes have been *totally* abandoned – as we shall see, they still have a role to play; it is just that, relatively speaking, their importance has visibly diminished. For example, the narrative has become much more linear in nature, proceeding in almost chronological fashion along two distinct levels in time: the first, the early 1960s (probably 1962), when Chmara and Yvonne fell in love in the company of their close friend, Dr René Meinthe, and the second, twelve years later, when, in the same lakeside spa town, the narrator apparently sees the doctor again and thinks back to their earlier activities together.[5] Significantly, and further to distinguish the two epochs, the 1960s romance takes place amidst the summertime atmosphere of happiness, brightness, hustle and bustle, whereas the later *retrouvailles* are set in winter, and are associated with sadness, darkness, death and inertia.

Implicit in all of this, of course, is another tremendous innovation for Modiano: the leap forward in time from the 1940s to the 1960s, which clearly demonstrates that, as he suggested in *Les Boulevards de ceinture*, he has indeed abandoned the 'autre vie' that he 'lived' during the Occupation.

Yet despite this undoubted progress, such a change of temporal setting is perhaps somewhat misleading, for the underlying atmosphere of the new period is, in many ways, in perfect harmony with that of the old one. We may well have moved on twenty years, but we have not left all trouble and strife behind us; we have simply gone from one conflict to another, from the *années noires* to the war in Algeria. Consequently, when the background situation is described in *Villa Triste*, it is in terms which would not be out of place in any of Modiano's previous novels. Paris, we are informed (p.14), is characterized by 'une ambiance policière déplaisante', 'beaucoup trop de rafles' and by exploding bombs, and things are hardly any better in Geneva, peopled, as it is, by 'agents de toutes sortes. Polices parallèles. Réseaux clandestins' (p.161). Indeed, even the colonial allusions which are such a feature of this latest work had already been linked to war in *Les Boulevards de ceinture*.[6]

There are other respects, too, in which established practice is obviously repeated, most notably in the continued focus on identity, as exemplified, once again, by the uncertain character of the narrator. Apparently parentless, an *apatride*, living under the assumed name of Count Victor and having to admit, 'Je n'ai jamais éprouvé une très grande confiance en mon identité' (p.87),

Chmara, like each of his three predecessors, is totally adrift in the world and hence marked by 'le désir de ne plus marcher sur du sable mouvant, de [se] fixer quelque part' (p.152). One way in which he tries to resolve this problem is through our old friend, the *Familienroman*, which allows him to lay down roots in, of all places, Tsarist Russia (p.112).[7] Another way, no less familiar to us, is by forging ties with the people around him, people such as Pulli ('Je pourrais être votre père, Chmara' – p.182), or Yvonne, a possible wife. Now admittedly, the former, being an exile, is more a reflection of him than the ideal answer to his prayers, and the latter would appear to be no panacea either, for her father is a barely mentioned man of mystery, and almost all her other *attaches* were severed when she set off on her acting career: 'Il semblait qu'Yvonne n'eût rien laissé derrière elle, dans cette ville, et je m'étonnais qu'on pût couper aussi vite ses racines quand, par chance, on en avait quelque part' (p.149).[8] But she does still have an uncle – Roland Jacquet, the *garagiste* – and this is the important thing, since it means she does have at least one form of *ancrage*. And Chmara quickly recognizes this. No sooner has he met Roland than he is irrevocably attracted to him, because of what he represents. 'Il était paternel', he confesses (p.125), and immediately feels at home with him. So much so that, in next to no time he is referring to himself and the two Jacquets as 'trois personnes de la même famille' (p.131). Given that he has already made such revealing statements as 'je ressentais une grande volupté à dire "ma famille"' (p.56), the procedure he is employing here is clear: through Yvonne and her uncle, he is locking himself into the family structure that he himself lacks.

In much the same way as this cult of the family has its source in Modiano's previous novels, so too is the destruction of time carried over into *Villa Triste*. 'J'essaie simplement de montrer comment le temps passe et recouvre tout, choses et gens', the novelist readily admits,[9] and he has certainly succeeded in implementing this plan. The whole of Chapter I is a melancholy catalogue of how the town has changed (for the worse) in the course of just twelve years, and over and over again, subsequently, things which seemed so enduring are said to have totally vanished, which is perhaps why we get the endless allusions to the colonies: they too are rapidly being lost, and so they too conjure up visions of impermanence and decay.[10] People are scarcely any more imperishable either. Errol Flynn, Henri

Garat, Ali Khan, Queen Astrid, Belinda Lee, Marilyn Monroe, Daniel Hendrickx, the Belgian baron, Lana Turner's lover – all of these individuals are now dead, we are informed,[11] and to this already impressive list we must add Dr René Meinthe, who tragically commits suicide by gassing himself and who, as Nettelbeck and Hueston rightly say, 'représente le passé qui sera balayé par une vie et une énergie nouvelles'.[12]

More than in any of the previous novels, this destructive march of time is essential in *Villa Triste*, for the nostalgia it generates underpins one of the other principal themes of the work: the unavoidable loss of youth. When Chmara falls in love with Yvonne, for example, he is interested not only in what his girlfriend is like at present, but also in her early childhood, as demonstrated by his visit to her old bedroom at her uncle's garage. He examines everything closely there, 'espérant découvrir un vestige de l'enfance d'Yvonne' (p.132), and eventually comes upon her old school satchel, which is certainly a link to her younger days, but not an entry into the sought-after *paradis perdu*. 'Un premier soir de vacances', he realizes, 'Yvonne l'avait fermé définitivement' (p.133), and its musty smell confirms that time has unhaltingly and irrevocably moved on. (Shortly afterwards, he will see Yvonne from a distance and think that she is a 'petite fille' (p.140), but only until she walks forward and takes on her true proportions again.)[13] The man 'à tête d'épagneul' similarly underlines this vital point.[14] When the narrator recognizes him as a familiar face from his childhood – the owner of the model *Kon Tiki* boat[15] – he momentarily thinks of talking to him about their previous encounters, but then decides that the boat has probably been lost, and so says nothing more than a simple 'goodbye', which would once more seem to suggest (albeit figuratively) that the work really is the 'sorte d'adieu à la "jeunesse"' that the author intended.[16]

There is, of course, one obvious way in which this sense of loss can be to some extent countered: the power of recollection. And as ever in Modiano's work, this is apparently what happens here. The text flexibly expands into a whole range of registers as *documents*-cum-fossilized-memories (newspaper articles, Meinthe's letters, cinema programmes, etc.) are preserved in print *tels quels*, while a string of explicit phrases such as 'je me souviens' constantly remind us that the now lost summer of 1962(?) lives on into the present, in the recollective faculty of the narrator. Indeed, this resurrectional quality of memory is conveyed quite superbly when Victor looks in at a dinner dance and sees some old acquaintances there: 'Ils se mêlent aux autres danseurs, là, sous les averses de confettis. Et tout cela vire et volte, tourbillonne et s'éparpille dans mon souvenir. Poussières' (p.178). The immediacy of the *là* and the decay implicit in the final word say it all – what is actually dead is being made to live again.

This use of remembrance to recapture things past smacks, most manifestly, of the influence of Marcel Proust. As has already been seen, Modiano readily acknowledges how much he owes to his celebrated predecessor, and in *Villa Triste* the debt is palpably at its most acute to date. Apart from the more specific allusions, such as the comment: 'Après douze ans, je me rendais compte que je ne savais pas grand-chose sur René Meinthe et je me reprochais mon manque de curiosité à l'époque où je le voyais chaque jour' (p.162),[17] there would initially appear to be three broad areas of intertextual exchange. First, the character of Victor Chmara. Budding writer, monocle-wearer, occasional snob and, in one interpretation of his background, an invalid member of the Jewish bourgeoisie, Chmara unarguably has a good many Proustian traits to his person (often caricaturally so!). Second, the evocative nature of names, whether they be the names of places, like that of the Villa Triste (p.150), or the names of people, like those of the narrator's vague acquaintances (p.36). Third, and finally, the thematic focus. Love, jealousy, homosexuality (in the figure of Meinthe), these are all the stuff of *A la recherche* too (even if Modiano treats them in nothing like the same depth as his famous mentor).[18] And this is not to mention the shared themes of identity, time, memory and the past which have already been dealt with amply above.

Another major concern for Proust is, of course, the power of the imagination, and here again the link with *Villa Triste* seems to be quite manifest, for Modiano's text is literally packed with examples of escapism and *rêverie*. Pulli, for one, is demonstrably prone to this tendency. Pining for his much-loved but distant Egypt, he has built a restaurant called Le Khédival,[19] which, being an exact replica of a restaurant in Cairo, allows him to realize his dream and return to his native land in spirit, if not exactly in person. Chmara similarly shows a marked propensity to day-dream, and to such a degree that, if he is not forging the aforementioned *Familienroman* for himself, he is letting his mind wander with only the slightest of alternative stimulations. 'La lecture de tous ces magazines m'avait fortement impressionné', he observes at one stage. 'Et je rêvais. Alors j'évitais les gestes trop brusques et les questions trop précises, pour ne pas me réveiller' (pp.52–3).

Of all the various clues that establish escapism as a key feature of the work, however, one of the most telling is surely the constant reference to America. In the phrase 'c'est l'Amérique' or its converse, the French language itself enshrines the USA as a symbol of the ideal, and Modiano exploits this association to the full in his novel. Yvonne's uncle, who is seen in an extremely positive light, earns his living by selling spare parts for American cars (although, living on the poor side of town, he can hardly be called *un oncle d'Amérique!*); Chmara admits that his great wish is to live with Yvonne in Wyoming; and when models are chosen for the two young lovers they just happen to be Marilyn Monroe and Arthur Miller, and Paulette Goddard and Erich Maria Remarque (Hollywood is, after all, sometimes known as 'the dream factory').[20]

But there is much more to the role of imagination in *Villa Triste* than this. The thematic function it fulfils only accounts for part of its overall importance; it has a more fundamental task to perform as well, a task which relates to the (at least partial) abandonment of realism in the work. And that Modiano has indeed, once again, eschewed the realistic approach, there can be little doubt. 'Ni [Yvonne] ni Meinthe ne m'ont jamais raconté leur vie en détails, mais par indications vagues et contradictoires', the narrator is forced to concede (p.146), and the text itself reflects this uncertain reality, constantly self-destructing in purely logical terms.

Take the geographical setting for instance, as Jacques Bersani has.[21] The rue Royale, the avenue d'Albigny, the rue Sommeiller, the rue Vaugelas – these and numerous other references establish the lakeside *ville d'eau* as Annecy. Yet the Boulevard Carabacel, which is also mentioned, is one of the main thoroughfares in Nice, and if Switzerland is on the other side of the lake, the French spa town in question must inevitably be Évian.

More worryingly perhaps, the chronology of the narrative does not hang together either. On page 12, Meinthe sees off the Paris train which, we have already been informed, 'passe à minuit six' (p.11). We then follow him as he walks to the Cintra bar (Chapter

IV), where he has a drink (Chapter VIII), and where he is still sitting when we discover that it is now 'bientôt minuit' (p.157)! Furthermore, despite the numerous allusions to his exact age 'il y a douze ans', none of the varying (and in themselves contradictory) possibilities turns out to be consistent with the later revelation that he was 37 when he died (p.159). Now it would, admittedly, be quite possible to explain these temporal discrepancies by a lack of care and attention on Modiano's part, but such an explanation appears to be unlikely. The fact that the clock at the garage strikes twelve every hour suggests, immediately, that traditional chronology has *intentionally* been discarded,[22] and Chapter XII gives a good indication of why this should be. In yet another puzzling development, the narrator learns from the newspapers (pp.159–60) that Meinthe has died the previous evening, and this causes him to think back to their common adventures at the start of the 1960s. Yet he does not reflect on their apparent meeting of only a few hours earlier (the doctor's last movements are those observed in Chapters I, IV, VIII and XII). What is more, the references to the arcades of the rue de Castiglione (p.159) or, say, the Louvre (p.160) unquestionably show that he is no longer in a lakeside town in Haute Savoie, but, rather, in central Paris. So what has happened? Does he not remember being with his old friend only a day or so earlier? Did he dash away from the *ville d'eau* before the news of the suicide broke locally? One way of overcoming these problems is to conclude that he never was with Meinthe leading up to his death, but has simply *imagined* his friend's last moments on the basis of the sparse details given in the articles he has discovered. Or, even more radical, perhaps he never knew the dead man at all. Perhaps even the events from the 1960s which he 'remembers' are entirely imaginary. Certainly, Modiano himself has implied that this is the case, opining of his work in 1975: 'C'est la nostalgie de quelqu'un qui se fabrique des souvenirs imaginaires, parce qu'il en a le temps; c'est la nostalgie de quelqu'un qui puise dans cette vie rêvée les ressources qui manquent à la sienne.'[23]

Such recourse to fictitious memories has, it may be recalled, been a feature of Modiano's whole *œuvre* up to this point,[24] and should any doubts persist as to whether or not *Villa Triste* is yet another work of *rêverie*, these can quickly be dispelled by highlighting three other similarities with the preceding novels.

First, the continued use of blatant (and often cinematic) distancing devices.[25] As ever, or so it seems, events are said to take place in slow motion, voices are muffled, characters slide in and out of focus, scenes are compared to nightmares and sounds are distorted, all of which serves to erode the 'reality' of the text at the very moment that it is created. This 'double mouvement de création et de gommage', as a famous New Novelist might call it,[26] leads on conveniently to the second link to the 'trilogy' – the use of humour. Whether through the basic irony of the 'double movement', the ludic, often pastiching nods to literary predecessors,[27] or the clearly parodic treatment of love (see above), the narrative never allows us to take what it says too seriously. Nor – and this is the third and final point – does it allow us to proceed in a straight line, for in spite of the aforementioned move towards increased linearity, Modiano has, once again, peppered his work with images which are decidedly circular in nature, as the closing pages of the novel ably demonstrate. Having set out his luggage 'en demi-cercle' (p.176) and soon, like Yvonne's uncle before him (p.135), to indulge in the act of blowing smoke rings (p.181),[28] Chmara is waiting at the train station, becoming more and more aware that his dream of a settled life with Yvonne has disintegrated, and so preparing to return to the instability which was his before he fell in love, a rootlessness which his impending journey in itself effectively represents. Yet this is not the only clue that he is going back to square one, as it were. The train he is planning to catch is the 00.06 to Paris, the same one he apparently watched Meinthe see off in Chapter I,[29] while his comment: 'J'ai pénétré dans le café en rotonde, à côté de l'hôtel de Verdun. S'appelait-il des Cadrans ou de l'Avenir?' (p.177) deliberately harks back to the paragraph with which the novel actually opened (note the use of 'en rotonde' as well). Now obviously, such consistent exploitation of circular forms cannot be the product of mere coincidence. It must be pursued with some aim in mind, and it is not difficult to suggest what this might be: the circle, which has no precise beginning or end, and from which it is impossible to break out, is the ideal image to convey Chmara's tendency towards *rêverie*. For as he himself remarks at one stage: 'Par un phénomène d'alternance ou de cyclothymie, un rêve succédait à un autre' (p.177).[30]

Yet not all of his dreams quickly collapse, to be instantly

Patrick Modiano

replaced by others. One, at least, proves to be much more enduring in character – the one which, seemingly, transports him out of Paris and into the *ville d'eau* in the first place, the one where, it would appear, he begins by dreaming up a past for himself (in the Haute Savoie of the 1960s), only, therein, to dream up yet another past for himself (the *Familienroman* set in Russia). This Chinese-box effect, or, as it is often called, this *mise en abyme*, serves, most evidently, to emphasize the subtle circularity of the work, and to underline (as does the aforementioned inter-textuality) just how *fuyante* its 'reality' is. But it also does something more besides – it confirms the narrator's status as a *novelist*, for as Francine de Martinoir has rightly said: 'Le mouvement du personnage mythomane est au fond le même que celui du romancier.'[31]

This *jeu de miroirs* tends to suggest, of course, that, ultimately, it is Modiano himself who is playing the 'mythomane'/ 'romancier', and there is much in the text to encourage this inference. The mentions of 'mon père' might have come from the author's own mouth;[32] the love element reflects his own recent romance, and whole chunks of the work are modelled on his own time spent in and around Annecy.[33] Thus, at the end of the day, *Villa Triste* is essentially no different to the three novels which precede it. Depicting memories which, as has been seen, cannot logically be ascribed to its protagonist, it marks a further venture by Modiano into the realms of imaginary autobiography. And that it is indeed the novelist who, yet again, is the prime actor in this endeavour, there can really be no question at all, since in a revealing summary of the book he has removed even the slightest possibility of confusion. 'C'est encore le rêve', he insists. 'C'est moi, mais à travers une autobiographie [. . .] rêvée.'[34]

One of the most striking features of Modiano's practice thus far has been his tendency to use suggestive titles for his texts, and thereby give his readers immediate insights into the nature and structure of the works in question. *Livret de famille*, his fifth novel, is even more informative in this respect, since by taking its name from the document which is presented to all newly married couples in France, and in which various family details (births, deaths, and so on) are intended to be recorded, it visibly reveals the real-life source which served to inspire it.

It is no doubt because of these roots in concrete reality, at least in part, that the work maintains the quest for innovation which was first pursued in *Villa Triste*. For example, as Nettelbeck and Hueston have pointed out, 'aux quinze pages du livret correspondront les quinze chapitres de *Livret*, lui aussi une anthologie d'*extraits* de diverses vies qui constituent progressivement un registre familial',[35] and the end result of this is that, on the face of it, we seem to be dealing not now with one basic narrative, but rather with a collection of fifteen self-standing short stories. The focus on matters of *état civil* similarly gives rise to a certain novelty, for although there is much of Modiano's own life history in all of his texts, the personal allusions here are so precise that we often seem to be moving in the realms of pure autobiography.[36] Pages are devoted to the author's grandmother, his mother, his wife and his daughter, and there is mention, too, of his father, his grandfather and the ill-fated Rudy. Furthermore, the narrator is overtly identified as Patrick or Modiano at certain moments.[37]

This pronounced movement away from 'une autobiographie [. . .] rêvée', and towards a more (traditionally) autobiographical form of writing may seem somewhat surprising at first glance, but on reflection there would appear to be at least two very convincing explanations of this development.

First, it could well be that courtship and marriage have made their mark on Modiano's life, and that he has now become more optimistic – and therefore more loquacious – about the composition of his *état civil*. Certainly, when he recalls his time in Tunisia with his young fiancée, he does tend to suggest that, at long last, he has managed to procure the roots he yearns for: 'Le vent m'apportait les derniers échos d'Alexandrie [. . .] de Salonique et de bien d'autres villes avant qu'elles n'aient été incendiées. J'allais me marier avec la femme que j'aimais et j'étais enfin de retour dans cet Orient que nous n'aurions jamais dû quitter' (p.162). This novel sense of stability and contentment is further seen in his reference to his new-born daughter Zénaïde. Sound asleep in her cot as the text commences, with a plane tree gently 'caressing' her window and her face bearing nothing less than 'une expression de béatitude' (p.9), Zénaïde is, from the outset, the symbol of all that is positive in life, the very model of hope incarnate. For as the narrator remarks after registering the birth (having earlier eaten in a restaurant called L'Esperia!): 'Cette petite fille serait un peu notre déléguée dans l'avenir. Et elle avait obtenu du premier coup le bien mystérieux qui s'était toujours dérobé devant nous: un état civil' (p.22). In other words, the family heritage is guaranteed for the future, no matter how uncertain it may have been in the past.[38]

The second reason for the more autobiographical slant of *Livret de famille* relates to Modiano's wish, already demonstrated in his previous texts, to use his writing as a means of acquiring a new, more appealing identity for himself – by filling his work with a mass of incontestable facts, he can ensure that it will never be dismissed as pure invention, and hence establish it as a convincing version of the full, real-life *livret de famille* after which he so desperately hankers.

But of course, if facts can, as it were, be used to 'upgrade' the traditionally lower status of fiction, than the reverse must also be true, with the writer's imagination 'compromising' the historical predominance of the world around us. And this is precisely what happens, for although the work, like its predecessors (but more fully) contains a wealth of personal truths, we, as readers, are not always sure exactly where to draw the line. More importantly, neither, or so it would appear, is Modiano himself, for as he has stated in typically tantalizing fashion: 'Je crois que tout est vrai [. . .] peut-être tout est faux [. . .] C'est très difficile. Qu'est-ce qui est vrai? A part [. . .] ma petite fille, ma femme, ma mère, ça j'en suis sûr. C'est vrai. Le reste?'[39] Thus, appearances certainly can be deceptive. Despite our initial temptation to do so, we should not jump to the conclusion that *Livret de famille* is in large part an autobiography. On the contrary, we must, at the end of the day, situate it in that category of writing which bears the heading 'imaginative'.

And should any lingering doubts about this remain, they can quickly be dispelled by referring not now to the *content* of the work, but rather to its *form*.[40] Take, say, the structure of the narrative. Not for us a linear, basically chronological progression, but rather one which, quite visibly, is much more indirect in nature. Over and over again we travel backwards and forwards in time (both as we move from one chapter to the next, and within individual chapters themselves), and then, having been introduced to a succession of different characters, we actually end up back where we started, with Zénaïde (albeit a year further on). Now, this return to the *point de départ* is intended, no doubt, to highlight the significance of the baby girl for the novelist-parent, in much the same way as Chapter VIII, the strategically-placed middle chapter, recounts how he managed to firm up his identity in not too dissimilar a manner: by obtaining his certificate of baptism. Yet such structural emphasis has little part to play in conventional biography.

There is another aspect of *Livret de famille* which would not be appropriate here either: the use of linking devices to fuse the various parts of the work together into one unified whole. Hardest to spot amongst these are the simple, brief reiterations of detail. The evocation of Bourlagoff as a baby, secure in his 'nursery bleu ciel' (p.77), is a reflection of Zénaïde in Chapter I; the two ladies in the registry office 'qui se ressemblaient comme des jumelles' (p.16) are echoed later by the twin sisters from Indonesia (p.107); the leopard skin on Denise's bed (p.144) harks back to the one in the Moulin Yang Tsé (p.139); mention of pyramid follows mention of pyramid (pp.74, 82, 145); and so on and so forth, from the first page through to the last.

Far easier to discern than these subtle links are the more extensive repetitions, which result in the creation of leitmotifs, such as the loss of youth, the cinema, 'le hasard', the Orient, or the destruction of dreams.[41] And if just one chapter has to be chosen to show how skilled Modiano is in drawing the different threads of his narrative together, it must surely be Chapter XIV, where almost everything that has gone before is masterfully and unifyingly recapitulated. The mention here of Koromindé, Toddie Werner, Bülow and Flo Nardus brings Chapters I, VI, XII and XIII respectively back to mind; the reappearance of the narrator's mother, father, brother and daughter provides outward connections to Chapters I, IV, V, VIII and XV; the reference to the Second World War mirrors the allusion to two other wars, in Chapters III and VI; the June setting is the same as those in Chapters VIII and XI; the cinematographic strand is carried over from Chapters I, IV, VII, IX, X, XI, XII, XIII; and there are numerous other intertwining elements too. Thus, just before Chapter XV takes us back to Zénaïde and the point at which we (more or less) started, we are given what amounts to the thematic climax of the work.[42] And once again, indisputably, this procedure is that of a novelist, not a biographer.[43]

Exactly the same can be said about the question of humour, which must be kept to an absolute minimum in formal life stories. Not so here. As ever, we are treated to Modiano's full repertoire of comic effects, from the farce of the journey to, and arrival at, the registry office (pp.13–16), on through the ludic parody of Switzerland (Chapter IX),[44] to the blatant irony of the Moulin Yang-Tsé (pp.130–41) – never, for one moment, are we deprived of at least the prospect of some light relief, and never, as a consequence, are we allowed to get too carried away with what we are actually being told.

All things considered, then, Modiano has scarcely changed his approach to writing at all. 'Il y a toujours une part autobiographique dans un roman', he asserted in 1972,

> mais il faut la transposer, l'amplifier, essayer de retrouver l'essence des êtres et des choses à travers leur apparence quotidienne, structurer ce qui, dans la vie, est désordre... Si on ne se livre pas à ce travail de 'filtrage' et de stylisation, on risque de donner une impression de 'débraillé', de 'document vécu', de 'déballage' qui est le contraire de la littérature.[45]

These words, most manifestly, could still be applied to *Livret de famille*. For as may by now be apparent, intrinsically, this text is no different to its four predecessors – it, too, on the whole, is an imaginary autobiography.

This, in turn, explains why Modiano's key themes are also repeated in the work. Themes such as the onward march of time, which afflicts most of the characters portrayed and creates in the narrator, to use his own words, 'une impression de vide qui m'était familière depuis mon enfance, depuis que j'avais compris que les gens et les choses vous quittent ou disparaissent un jour' (p.158).[46] Or memory, which, ambivalent as ever, both rescues the past from oblivion and thwarts our attempts to forget.[47] Or, more fittingly perhaps, considering that we are dealing with an imaginative *Livret de famille*, the 'adoption' of a surrogate family to make up for a flawed identity, for as we learn early on in the narrative: 'J'ignore [. . .] où je suis né et quels noms, au juste, portaient mes parents lors de ma naissance' (p.10).

Yet in spite of this uncertain status of both parents alike, it is only on the figure of the father that, as usual, the pursuit of replacement relatives tends to concentrate. The man in the registry office, with his 'regard très doux, presque paternel' (p.20), is one evident example of this. Le Gros, who announces 'J'ai envie de vous adopter' (p.125), and Marignan, 'l'une des multiples incarnations de mon père' (p.23), are quite palpably two more.[48] Uncle Alex ('Ton père et moi, nous sommes des hommes de nulle part' – p.130) cannot possibly be omitted from a list of this sort. Nor can a plethora of others, for as Georges Rollner unwittingly implies, almost every man in the film world would fit the bill as well: 'Il me souriait et me tapotait le crâne, d'une main paternelle. "[. . .] Nous sommes tous parents entre nous . . . Le cinéma est une grande famille . . ."' (p.90).

Harry Dressel once appeared in a film, we are told (pp.157–8), so it comes as no surprise that he, too, should quickly emerge as another stand-in father. Or so we are led to believe, for nowhere is he overtly given this role; it is just that, once the narrator sets out to write his biography, a surrogate parent–son relationship appears to come into play. For example, the biographer soon falls in love (and moves in) with his subject's daughter, Denise, with the result that the man he is working on becomes a kind of emotional 'in-law' for him. Yet there is a good deal more to the Dressel episode than this implicit 'adoption'. Much of Modiano's own writing is, of course, itself a sort of search for an absent parent, so a link between character and author is immediately created in the reader's mind. And as the chapter progresses, this parallelism becomes even more prominent and discernible. Comments such as 'Entre Le Caire et Alexandrie, j'étais chez moi' (p.156) seem to have authorial authority, and when Denise's helper is eventually identified, it is as none other than one P. Modiano!

One aspect of this association of novelist and fictional counterpart (or *mise en abyme*) has already been elaborated upon above, but there is another which it will be well worth mentioning here: from the way the life of Dressel is reconstructed, we can learn much about the techniques which Modiano himself employs to produce his novels. First of all, we can see how he prepares himself for his creative writing. 'Il fallait d'abord réunir les preuves matérielles du passage d'Harry Dressel sur la terre', we are informed. '[. . .] Je dressais [. . .] de longues listes de gens susceptibles, s'ils vivaient encore, de me parler de lui. Et cela nécessitait l'acquisition de vieux annuaires de toutes espèces' (p.153). Then, once this proof (which is bound to be fragmentary) has been assembled, the time comes for *rêverie* to be given full rein: 'Mon dossier était bien mince, mais je comptais laisser aller mon imagination. [. . .] Il suffisait de rêver sur les deux ou trois éléments dont je disposais, et je parviendrais à restituer le reste, comme l'archéologue qui, en présence d'une statue aux trois quarts mutilée, la recompose intégralement dans sa tête' (p.155). The simile is a striking one, and the aesthetic comparison is certainly not misplaced, for as has already been seen, this is precisely the technique which governs each of Modiano's first four novels.[49]

Before moving on from Harry Dressel, there is one final point which can usefully be made about him, a point which further illustrates the self-referentiality of Modiano's work: the sense of *déjà vu* he evokes. 'Avais-je rencontré cet homme au cours d'une vie antérieure?' the narrator wonders at the start of Chapter XII (p.142), and the answer to this question might well be an emphatic 'yes', for the selfsame Dressel had earlier, if somewhat fleetingly, appeared in *Villa Triste* (pp.35, 38). And that is not all. So too had Géza Pellemont from Chapter XIV. Thus, Modiano is engaged in a twofold act of unification. Not only does he forge the various chapters of *Livret de famille* into one, coherent whole, he also links his latest work to its predecessors, and thereby unifies his *œuvre*.[50]

An additional example of this is the vital theme of the Occupation, the re-emergence of which (after its virtual neglect in *Villa Triste*) takes us back so familiarly to the world of *La Place de l'Étoile*, *La Ronde de nuit* and *Les Boulevards de ceinture* that it is as if we had never really been away. Once again we are apprised, though more explicitly than in any of the previous works, that 'sans cette époque, sans les rencontres hasardeuses et contradictoires qu'elle provoquait, je ne serais jamais né' (p.173). Once again we see that, accordingly, the period represents for the author 'ce terreau d'où je suis issu' (p.169). Once again we discover, in all its terror, the menace which hung over occupied Paris, and more particularly over Modiano senior who, it would now seem, was actually arrested by his persecutors, only to escape by a stroke of good fortune (p.106).[51] And once again we find, time after time, that all sense of security during the 'dark years' was ill-founded and ephemeral, if not downright impossible. Witness the leitmotif of the-haven-that-is-illusory, normally symbolized by Switzerland.[52] 'Géza Pellemont [. . .] était citoyen suisse', we are informed towards the end of the novel.

[. . .] Mon père m'a souvent dit que lorsqu'il s'asseyait sur la banquette de la Ford de Pellemont, il avait l'impression illusoire de se trouver hors d'atteinte de la Gestapo [. . .], parce que cette voiture était, en quelque sorte, un morceau du territoire helvétique. Mais les miliciens la réquisitionnèrent un peu plus tard et ce fut dans cette Ford qu'ils assassinèrent Georges Mandel. (p.168)[53]

As may perhaps readily be conceded, the symbolism here (as ever) is nothing if not blatant, and it becomes even more so when viewed alongside the foreshadowing events of Chapter IX, for there, plagued by his memories of the Occupation (the negative side of remembrance and, implicitly, the past again!), the narrator likewise sees the answer to his problem as lying in the soothing effect of Switzerland. And no sooner has he left France behind him than he begins to feel the benefit of his journey: 'J'étais heureux. Je n'avais plus de mémoire. [. . .] J'avais atteint cet état que j'appelais: "la Suisse du cœur"' (p.98). Unfortunately though, as is always the case in Modiano's work, such solace proves to be little more than a mirage. Into the dream walks a living nightmare, in the form of Gerbauld, alias D., 'le personnage le plus hideux du Paris de l'Occupation' (p.105),[54] and as a result, the longed-for feeling of tranquillity rapidly disappears: 'Il n'y avait plus qu'à se laisser submerger par cette léthargie que je m'obstinais à appeler: la Suisse du cœur' (p.120).[55] 'La Suisse du cœur' – Modiano could hardly have concocted a more revealing phrase to use in the present context, for this metaphor visibly confirms the contention made with such confidence above, namely that Switzerland is being employed symbolically, as a token of unattainable serenity and contentedness – in short, as a sort of ideal counterweight to the oppressive, anguish-laden Occupation.[56] And, of course, to the painful memories it evokes.

Now, that the young narrator, like the author himself, should actually be able to recall the 'dark years', let alone suffer from such recollections, may seem totally incongruous at first sight,[57] yet this bizarre power of remembrance is not without justification in *Livret de famille*. 'Ma mémoire précédait ma naissance', we are advised in no uncertain terms. 'J'étais sûr, par exemple, d'avoir vécu dans le Paris de l'Occupation puisque je me souvenais de certains personnages de cette époque et de détails infimes et troublants, de ceux qu'aucun livre d'histoire ne mentionne' (p.96). Admittedly, such an astounding statement barely even scratches the surface of credibility, but it does have an intrinsic significance nonetheless. If we assume that, here as elsewhere, Modiano has chosen to place his own words in the mouth of his narrator, then he has clearly come a long way since he declared in 1968:

> Il y a longtemps que je baignais dans cette atmosphère, elle a fini par s'intégrer à moi [. . .]. Ce n'est qu'*a posteriori*, en réfléchissant à cette époque, que j'ai vécu de manière hallucinatoire la période 35–45. J'en ai fait mon paysage naturel que j'ai nourri de lectures appropriées: Mémoires, pamphlets, romans, études historiques.[58]

Obviously, the fruits of this early research have been blended with family anecdotes, marinated by his imagination and then moulded into the prenatal remembrance to which he now most earnestly lays claim.[59] In other words, his stated objective has successfully been achieved – he has indeed forged a new memory for himself out of the 'borrowed' memories of his elders.

'J'aime les auteurs de Série noire qui expriment des problèmes d'identité', Modiano was to confess in 1981,[60] and from the very start, his liking for the *roman policier* had filtered through into every area of his creative activity. In *Les Boulevards de ceinture*, we may recall, he had made Serge engage in unpaid police work, trailing people for the paternal inspector Sieffer, and the upshot of this was that 'Tous ces inconnus, je m'identifiais à eux. C'était *moi* que je traquais sans relâche' (p.166). Two years later, in 1975, he had changed tack slightly and let Chmara claim to be writing a *polar* in *Villa Triste*.[61] However, despite this persistent interest in the detective novel, he had never really given himself over entirely to the genre in his fiction. His sixth novel, the Goncourt-prize-winning *Rue des Boutiques Obscures*, finally remedied this neglect.[62]

The work revolves around the central figure of *privé* Guy Roland, and if the choice of generic focus itself represents something of a novelty within the *œuvre modianesque* – we have clearly moved on from the earlier flirtations with the war novel (*La Place de l'Étoile*, *La Ronde de nuit* and *Les Boulevards de ceinture*), the love story (*Villa Triste*) and the autobiography (*Livret de famille*) – then so too (typically) does the way in which the author decides to treat his subject, for Guy's main characteristic is that he is an amnesiac, so his powers of detection have to be directed inwards and applied to his own extremely enigmatic case. And as he thus sets off in search of his past, more and more new ground is visibly broken by the author.

Perhaps the most prominent of these new developments is the fragmentary nature of the narrative, a form which is in perfect harmony with story-line of the work, in so far as one exists. 'Tout m'a semblé si chaotique, si morcelé . . .', Guy reflects towards the end of his investigation. 'Des lambeaux, des bribes de quelque chose, me revenaient brusquement au fil de mes recherches . . . Mais après tout, c'est peut-être ça, une vie . . .' (p.202). This could serve as a perfect summary of *Rue des Boutiques Obscures*, formally speaking, for all types of *document* are reproduced therein: telephone numbers, police *fiches*, Bottin entries, letters, notes, a birth certificate, a paper cutting, and so on and so forth, almost without end. Now admittedly, *Villa Triste*, say, had also employed different discursive genres, but only in relatively small doses, and even then in the midst of a unifying prose text. The point here is that the technique is greatly extended and so systematic that the merest name and address is sometimes transformed into a self-standing chapter.[63] Nowhere previously had Modiano resorted to this degree of fragmentation!

Nor had he chosen to set any of his earlier texts outside Western Europe, or at the very least (allowing for a few pages in *Livret de famille*) Mediterranean North Africa, so in this respect, too, *Rue des Boutiques Obscures* can be seen to innovate somewhat. For at the end of the book, after a glimpse of a woman living in Valparaiso, we follow Guy across the Equator and on to a lonely island in the South Pacific, which is almost as far from the Old Continent as it is actually possible to get.

This new (albeit brief) internationalization of the setting in turn reflects another step forward from Modiano's previous practice. The fact that the narrator is plagued not now by a memory he would prefer not to have, but rather by having no memory at all, allows the problem of recollection to be explored in greater depth and *universalized*. In particular, it allows us to see, more clearly than ever before, just how fundamental remembrance is to the concept of identity. Because Guy has forgotten everything he experienced prior to his amnesia, he has no individual, personal past to speak of, and it is this, as much as his more obvious lack of a name (his present *état civil* derives only from after his illness), that causes him to ask himself exactly who he is. For a name without a history is in no way a self.[64] And that is not all. It might also be argued, as Alain Poirson has, that 'Guy Roland [. . .] essaiera de savoir qui il est, et la meilleur manière n'est-elle pas d'interroger ceux qui vous ont connu? Nous sommes construits par les autres, et notre identité n'est que la somme des regards qu'autrui porte sur nous.'[65] Now without wishing, necessarily, to accept the theoretical subtext here, the basic contention is essentially sound: it is not simply our own memories which make us what we are; the memories of others have a role to play as well.[66]

In a whole variety of ways, then, *Rue des Boutiques Obscures* introduces a certain novelty to Modiano's work. Yet that said, the break with previous practice cannot be characterized convincingly as radical. As the preceding paragraph implicitly suggests (the claim of innovation notwithstanding), the thematic focus of the novelist has hardly altered in the slightest: once again we find ourselves dealing with time, memory, the past and identity, and once again, ultimately, these concerns are shown in an already established light.

Take the matter of temporality as an obvious case in point. As symbolized, most strikingly, by the *merles des Moluques* – 'ils rongeaient tout, le papier, le bois, les murs même des maisons' (p.213) – this phenomenon is shown, as ever, to be more or less synonymous with destruction, with neither people nor places, things nor hopes in any way able to resist its deadly impact.[67] Alternatively, take Guy and his long-lost *état civil*. Now so vital as to merit a search, but (probably) abandoned years earlier for an alias, Roland's true name, like identity elsewhere in the *œuvre*, is viewed with a certain ambivalence to say the least.[68] Finally, and to stick with ambiguity, take the treatment of memory in the work. After its initial presentation as an immensely positive faculty (something which, as fossilizer of days gone by, it is essential for everyone to have), the power of remembrance is finally seen in patently negative terms, with the past that Guy recalls being (again ambiguously) one that he would no doubt actually prefer to forget, a past which climaxes with an unsavoury incident from – where else? – the Occupation. This eventual return to the *années noires* completes the thematic circle, as it were, and illustrates, perhaps better than anything else, that Modiano has not really turned over a new leaf. On the contrary. He is, quite visibly, still writing the same book, but constantly changing the paragraphs around to achieve refreshingly new effects.

This basic consistency of approach is further demonstrated by the background features of the text, with almost everything – or so it seems – again conveying the narrator's desperate lack of an *ancrage*. The secondary characters, for instance, are anything but stepping stones to fixity, for they, too, are often cut off from their roots, whether these roots lie in Russia (Paul Sonachitzé, Stioppa de Djagoriew, Gay Orlow), Holland (Léon Van Allen), America (Waldo Blunt, Freddie Howard de Luz), Great Britain (André Wildmer), Egypt (Alexandre Scouffi), Greece (Pedro Stern), or the Baltic States (Constantin von Hutte).[69] The settings of the work are hardly omens of stability either, comprising, as Alain Bony has said, 'un archipel dans les nuages, une succession de lieux dispersés, isolés, appartements, chambres d'hôtel, cafés, salles de restaurant désertes, chalet dans les montagnes; lieux provisoires et menacés, refuges (planques) plutôt que demeures'.[70] Even the weather adheres to this overall pattern, with fog, rain, snow and *buées* distorting all around them. Never, for one moment, therefore, does Guy have anything solid to cling on to – his isolation is as much sensory as it is physical.

This sense of being adrift leads on to another area of contact with the preceding texts: the deceptive, subtly treacherous nature of the narrative, a narrative all the more perfidious in that, at first glance, everything appears to be so simple. We follow Guy from witness to witness, more or less day by day, as his *enquête* proceeds, in fittingly linear fashion, towards its surprising conclusion; we note how, at roughly the mid-point of the book, two 'déclics' mark the point at which his memory returns; and we appreciate, stylistically, the symbolic poles within which his search is placed: black/white, dark/light, fog/clarity, etc. Yet the more we examine the profusion of detail before us, the more we come to realize that, like the château where Freddie once lived (p.75), the façade and what lies behind it are two totally different things, for the novel is not linear at all in the final analysis. It is, rather, intrinsically circular, beginning with nothingness ('Je ne suis rien' – p.7) and ending with a question (p.214), and embodying a search which, on the whole, peters out at the two very points at which it commenced: the rue Anatole-de-la-Forge (pp.12, 206) and the photo of Gay Orlow (pp.37, 214). Furthermore, within this overall circle lie a great variety of smaller circles, like the one described by Hutte (pp.11, 148–9), or those formed by the succession of leitmotifs and echoes.[71] Little wonder, then, that, at the end of the day, the maze should prove to be a key symbol in the work.

Even more problematic, if anything, than this use of circularity is the cultivation of facts which, to say the least, do not always result in total consistency. Guy, for example, has been a private detective for eight years, and yet, when we see him actively searching for himself, his dominant character traits seem to be apprehension and fear – hardly the traditional qualities of a successful sleuth![72] Similarly, is it really credible that he should not have wanted to unearth his lost past before now? And when he does actually discover that, back in 1943, he collapsed in the snow, exhausted and lost, during an abortive attempt to escape into Switzerland (the so-called haven once again proving to be unreachable), how could he possibly not have perished on the spot there and then?

It is the blatant contradictions within the work, though, that present us with the greatest cause for concern, and setting aside those incongruities which could possibly be explained by lapses of memory, or the mere passage of time (Denise has hair which is sometimes blonde, sometimes brown, and she should be twenty-five when she disappears, not twenty-six), we are left with one fundamental problem: illogical chronology. And this is a problem which is in evidence from the very start of Guy's *enquête*, for the line of enquiry on which he embarks is initially flawed, as close attention to the detail of the text reveals. In Chapter II, Heurteur produces a newspaper cutting announcing that Marie de Rosen died on 25 October, and that she will be buried on 4 November, with a church service to follow the next day (p.20). Thanks to this information, Guy turns up on 5 November (p.24) and eventually makes contact with Stioppa (p.32), who invites him back to his flat and shows him photos of Gay Orlow (pp.36–7), which allows him to obtain her *fiche* (pp.43–4), which in turn leads him on to Waldo Blunt (Chapter VII), and so on and so forth, in the linear fashion already referred to above. But all is not as straightforward as it seems. The date on Gay's *fiche*, showing when it was drawn up, is 23 October 1965, that is to say before Guy had even discovered the existence of the woman![73] So, from the word 'go', the realism of the narrative is subtly subverted.

Taking their lead from this early inconsistency, the later

Chapters XXVI, XXXII and XLIII likewise seem geared to rule out any realistic interpretation of the work. Why? Because they contain information about missing elements in the narrative jigsaw (witnesses not tracked down), and hence make us wonder exactly where this information originates.[74] Guy, quite clearly, cannot be at the root of these facts, for as the novel ends the only lead he has left is Pedro's old address at 2, rue des Boutiques Obscures in Rome. This being the case, our search for a source must obviously be directed elsewhere. Yet of the two possibilities remaining to us, neither is consistent with the conventions of realism either. We could, for example, say that the so-called facts are not real, but totally fictitious, and that Guy has simply *imagined* them, perhaps during a bout of wishful thinking, to give himself hope.[75] But if we resort to imagination here, why not use it to resolve all the other contradictions we encounter? Why not conclude that everything in the novel, *documents* and memories included, might also be concocted? Why not suggest that, if the text strikes us as linear, it is not because one discovery automatically opens the door to the next, but because each stage in the story actively *generates* the next, in a permanent process of imaginative creation?[76] Guy does, after all, make no bones about his tendency to fantasize, as when he considers a photo of Scouffi: 'Il se détache peu à peu de la photo, s'anime et je le vois marcher le long du boulevard, sous les arbres, d'un pas claudicant' (p.130).[77] Ultimately, of course, what all this equates to is something resembling the way in which fiction is written, and this brings us on nicely to the second possible source of Chapters XXVI, XXXII and XLIII: some sort of implied author, standing at one remove from the narrative voice, and able to know things that the limited first-person narrator cannot – an implied author whose presence serves not to hide the artificiality of the text but openly to flaunt it.[78]

This aim of deliberate self-exposure further manifests itself through the playful nature of the narrative, for Modiano has chosen not so much to write a typical detective story as openly to create a pastiche of one.[79] Clichés from the genre are employed with gay abandon (Guy is seen in the position of a suspect being questioned, with a bright light shining in his eyes – pp.7, 15–16;[80] he leaps into a taxi and virtually says 'Follow that car' – p.30);[81] red herrings are thrown in to confuse and to mislead (Freddie is not, after all, the answer to the enigma); *pistes* are laid so that readers can outguess the nominal detective (the missing Oleg de Wrédé could well be Scouffi's killer, and therefore contactable as 'Cavalier bleu' on the unofficial chatline,[82] but this line of enquiry, teasingly, is never followed up); the idea of a witness with revealing information is pushed to its absurd – and humorous – extreme (Guy is bombarded with tins full of photos and mementoes until he meets Hélène, who produces a gilded box which simply contains cigarettes – pp.35–9, 80–1, 94, 98–9); and the pathetic fallacy is deployed in all its triteness (Hutte's departure is accompanied by rain, his joy in Nice presaged by a summer scene – pp.7, 42). Yet of all the stereotyped devices employed, arguably the most effective is the 'lucky break', which in Modiano's hands is so exponential that it comes to defy credulity. Time and again we see that 'il y a parfois de mystérieuses coïncidences' (p.160), and the reason for this insistent focus is clear. On the one hand, it demonstrates to us, in much the same way as Guy's discovery of some people from the past and not others, that naked contingency governs our lives, rendering everything we hope to achieve uncertain, and on the other, paradoxically, it shows that an all-powerful force is at work within the novel, a force able to produce any number of 'chance' encounters at will – that ultimate puller of strings, the author.[83]

Is this author the implied one already encountered above, or have we moved on in our discussion of authorship? To try and answer this question, it will be useful to return to another point made earlier, namely that Guy's search for an identity has much in common with the process of literary creation – it too, we may recall, begins with nothingness, and it too then progressively fills in the void. Or perhaps it would be more enlightening here to rephrase this and say that, by engaging in research, consulting archives, accumulating documents, interviewing key contacts, and finally using his imagination to paper over any gaps, Guy is able to use the pasts and the memories of other people to construct a past and a memory for himself. For when summarized in these terms, the procedure being followed can hardly be mistaken – it is Modiano's own technique that we are witnessing.[84]

Given that Guy eventually comes to identify with Pedro, the question now is whether the novelist can, in turn, be seen to slip into the character of Guy, and to a large extent, it would certainly appear to be that he does, as a comparison between *Rue des*

Boutiques Obscures and *Livret de famille* indicates. Consider, for the sake of argument, three of the people whom we encounter during Guy's investigation: Denise Coudreuse, wearer of a 'parfum poivré' reminiscent of the bride's, and possessing 'un visage d'Asiatique, bien qu'elle fût presque blonde. Des yeux très clairs et bridés. Des pommettes hautes' (p.114); Alec Scouffi, 'un Grec d'Alexandrie' (p.122), author of two books (pp.121, 131) and the victim of an unsolved murder (p.132);[85] and Waldo Blunt, who lives just off the Avenue de New-York, and who is forced to walk the streets of Paris when his young wife throws a party.[86] Without the slightest shadow of a doubt, each of these characters has manifestly been prefigured in the previous novel: Denise in the form of Denise Dressel, who, we are told, 'sentait un parfum qu'il m'arrive de reconnaître au passage de quelqu'un d'autre' (p.155), and who 'était de taille moyenne, blonde, les yeux clairs et bridés [. . .]. Ses pommettes [. . .] lui donnaient un air mongol' (pp.143–4); Scouffi, with no change to his identity at all (p.101); and Blunt in the guise of Henri Marignan, who lived at 62, Avenue de New-York, and who likewise fled the parties which his partner held there (p.25). Thus, quite visibly, the people who emerge to fill Guy's past are the same as those whom, already, Modiano has closely linked to his own.[87]

Now this is all very well, but why should the novelist associate himself with his narrator like this? Why not choose to maintain a guarded distance? Once again, *Livret de famille* would appear to hold a (if not the) clue, for what we learn about the author's father there is undoubtedly significant. For example, Modiano senior, we discover, initially called himself Guy during the Occupation (pp.10–11); he visited Megève shortly before the Liberation (p.10); and was friendly with a Japanese actor and a blonde who lived at 14, rue Chalgrin (p.169). In *Rue des Boutiques Obscures*, revealingly, more or less the same applies: the narrator similarly uses the alias 'Guy'; he too seems to have stayed at Megève during the war (Chapter XXXVII); and he too seems to have socialized with the couple from the rue Chalgrin (p.206). Putting two and two together, then, what is going on here is quite transparent: the memories of the *années noires* which, through Guy, Modiano recalls are those which belong to his father, or those which might well belong to him.[88] In other words, the author has returned to the same venture he embarked on before: he has again put himself in his parent's shoes to compose an imaginary autobiography. And the ultimate reason for this, as ever, is not hard to discover. Being the first, and only, text in the *œuvre* to bear the dedication 'Pour mon père', *Rue des Boutiques Obscures* can be interpreted as a sort of filial adieu, a final, valedictory attempt to exorcize the paternal past – and along with it, of course, the period it so largely comprises: the traumatic 'dark years' of the Occupation.[89]

Notes

1. During this period (late 1972–8) Modiano also produced a number of short stories – 'Courrier du cœur' (1974), 'Johnny' and 'Soir de Paris' (both 1978) – a variety of journalistic works – 'Vingt ans après' (1972), *'Les Écrivains de la nuit*, de Pierre de Boisdeffre' (1973), 'Au Temps de Lacombe Lucien' (1974) and the *Interrogatoire* of Emmanuel Berl (1976) – at least two screenplays for television – an episode of *Madame le juge* ('Un Innocent') and an adaptation of Kessel's *L'Équipage* – a play – *La Polka* – and (in tandem with Louis Malle) the film script of *Lacombe Lucien* (1974).
2. Number 11, rue des Saussaies was one of the addresses of the Gestapo in occupied Paris; Drancy was a holding camp in the *banlieue* and an infamous step on the road to deportation; la villa Triste seems to have no significance in the French context, although there does appear to have been a place of torture of this name in Milan (see Raleigh Trevelyan, *Rome '44* (London, Coronet, 1983), p.323).
3. First performed in May 1974 (at the Théâtre du Gymnase in Paris) and still unpublished today, this play seems to have been part of Modiano's work schedule since 1972, when he claimed to be writing for the theatre in order to 'me forcer à faire parler des personnages' (Dormann, 'Modiano apprivoisé', p.100). Needless to say, perhaps, this wish to perfect the art of dialogue (like the aforementioned ventures into the short story, literary criticism and, a year or two later, work for television) further illustrates the novelist's search for new avenues to pursue.
4. For more on this non-physical portrayal of love, see Martinoir, 'Patrick Modiano: *Villa Triste* (II)', p.6.
5. This increased linearity is further demonstrated by Modiano's

choice of title – the first which does not allude to some form of ring – and by the fact that, for the first time ever, he divides his novel into numbered chapters.

6. Note that the spa town backdrop has associations as well – see Chmara's mention of 'le charme factice d'une station thermale, tout ce décor d'opérette' (p.115) and cf. Jean-Pierre Azéma's comment on the appearance of wartime Vichy: 'une capitale d'opérette, avec son établissement thermal ceinturé d'hôtels blancs' (*De Munich à la Libération* (Paris, Seuil, 1979), p.148).

7. Cf. Bedner, 'Modiano ou l'identité introuvable', p.59.

8. Although this *deliberate* cutting of links seems to suggest that Yvonne is different to Chmara, in most other respects she is not – she, too, for example, 'donne peu de détails sur sa vie passée et s'invente sans doute une enfance différente de celle qu'elle a vécue' (Martinoir, 'Patrick Modiano: *Villa Triste* (II)', p.3). For more on this linking of characters, see ibid., pp.3–5.

9. Ezine, 'Sur la sellette', p.5.

10. This might also explain, at least in part, why they have already featured in *Les Boulevards de ceinture* – what better reference point could there be for collaborators described as 'des condamnés à mort en sursis' (p.127)? Incidentally, this phrase provides yet another example of the influence of Céline on Modiano, for in *Voyage au bout de la nuit* there is mention of 'condamnés à mort différés' and 'mon destin d'assassiné en sursis' (Céline, *Romans*, volume I, edited by Henri Godard (Paris, Gallimard, Bibliothèque de la Pléiade, 1981), pp.35 and 52 respectively). The *Amiral Bragueton*, the boat which transports Bardamu to colonial Africa (pp.112ff.) would also appear to have inspired the *Amiral Guisand* of *Villa Triste*.

11. Daniel Hendrickx and the Belgian baron are Modiano's own inventions. Errol Flynn (1909–59) was an Australian-born Hollywood movie star. Henri Garat (1902–58) was a French music-hall singer and actor. Aly Khan (1911–60) was the playboy son of the Aga Khan. Astrid (1905–35) was Queen of the Belgians. Belinda Lee (1935–61) and Marilyn Monroe (1928–62) were screen actresses and sex symbols. Lana Turner's lover was Johnny Stompanato (??–1958).

12. *Patrick Modiano*, p.70. *La Polka* also features a doctor who gasses himself.

13. This seems to confirm what Modiano said in an essay while still at school: 'Le monde de l'enfance [. . .] est [. . .] *le pays où l'on n'arrive jamais* [. . .] ce pays que nous portons chacun en notre cœur et dont nous garderons toujours la secrète nostalgie' (Morel, 'Une dissertation de Modiano', p.38). Significantly perhaps, when asked, a few years later, where he would like to live, the novelist replied, 'Au pays où l'on n'arrive jamais' (Modiano, 'Patrick Modiano répond au questionnaire Marcel Proust', p.24).

14. Just as this character is associated with a dog, so too is Yvonne's *dogue allemand* made almost human: belonging to a special breed that often commits suicide, it is clearly meant to make the reader think of Meinthe. (This is, of course, yet another example of the aforementioned contrasts in the novel, contrasts which, embodying 'a negative kind of similarity' (Lodge, *Working with Structuralism* (London, Routledge, 1991), p.11) will, eventually, link into a network of echoes.)

15. The real Kon-Tiki (a balsa-wood raft) hit the headlines in 1947, when it was sailed from Peru to the South Sea Islands. For more on this venture and its leader, Thor Heyerdahl, see Heyerdahl and Christopher Ralling, *The Kon-Tiki Man* (London, BBC Books, 1990).

16. Ezine, 'Sur la sellette', p.5.

17. Cf. *A la recherche du temps perdu*: 'Je me reprochais de ne pas avoir fait assez attention à [Swann . . .], de ne pas l'avoir bien écouté quand il me recevait' (III, p.708).

18. See the earlier reference to love (p.64 above) and cf. Modiano's summary treatment of jealousy (*Villa Triste*, pp.85-9). In no way does Modiano *analyse* these phenomena, as does Proust. For more on the links and differences between the two authors, see Martinoir, 'Patrick Modiano: *Villa Triste*' (parts I and II).

19. Note the (typical) backward glance here to Le Khédive in *La Ronde de nuit*.

20. Arthur Miller (1915–) is an American dramatist and film script writer. He was married to Marilyn Monroe (see Note 11 above) from 1956 to 1961. Erich Maria Remarque (1898–1970) was an American (though German-born) novelist. He married film star Paulette Goddard (1911?–90) in 1958.

21. 'Patrick Modiano, agent double', p.81.

22. Cf. Eugène Ionesco's play, *La Cantatrice chauve* (in Ionesco, *Théâtre*, volume I (Paris, Gallimard, 1954)), where the same device is used (but more absurdly).

23. Ezine, 'Sur la sellette', p.5. Note also how this statement demonstrates, once again, that Modiano's work has a contemporary relevance, the escapism stemming from an unfulfilling *present* (cf. Note 111 to Chapter 2 above).

24. Even in *La Polka* 'un homme meurt au milieu des souvenirs qu'il n'a pas eus' (Sénart, 'Revue théâtrale', p.181).

25. For more on Modiano's debt to the cinema in *Villa Triste*, see (in addition to the points which follow) Martinoir, 'Patrick Modiano: *Villa Triste* (II)', p.13.

26. See Alain Robbe-Grillet, *Pour un nouveau roman* (Paris, Minuit, 1963), p.127.

27. Apart from Marcel Proust (see above), another of the author's mentors here is our old friend Scott Fitzgerald – with its opening focus on the destruction of time, its manifest sense of dream and nostalgia, its use of expressive names, its citing of period songs, its theme of the cinema and its riotous parties at lakeside villas, this book smacks of Fitzgerald as insistently as – if not more so than – each of the previous works we have studied. Additional (and often related) debts are clearly owed to Valery Larbaud and Paul Morand, as Jacques Bersani indirectly notes: 'comment ne pas reconnaître, dans [. . .] *Villa Triste*, le charme discret du parfait récit à la française, modèle 1920, marque N.R.F.?' ('Patrick Modiano, agent double', p.78).

28. Cf. Le Khédive (*La Ronde de nuit*, p.15) and Deyckecaire (*Les Boulevards de ceinture*, p.54). This echoing of the 'trilogy' in matters of detail is another feature of *Villa Triste*, and further adds to the sense of circularity it creates. (Cf. Note 19 above.)

29. This imminent return to the capital further serves to signal the end of his *mental* journey, the journey which, as illustrated above, appears to take him from his Parisian base of the present to the Haute Savoie of the past. Note also that the broad-based theme of the voyage, already discernible in the 'trilogy', will prove to be a key feature of the *œuvre* as a whole, as we shall shortly see.

30. See also Note 74 to Chapter 2 above.

31. 'Patrick Modiano: *Villa Triste* (II)', p.10.

32. See e.g. the reference to the father's *Société africaine*

d'entreprise (p.151) – the company run by Albert Modiano in real life.

33. See Morel, 'Une dissertation de Modiano', p.37.
34. Jamet, 'Modiano s'explique', p.27.
35. *Patrick Modiano*, p.79.
36. This is where we discover, for instance, that Modiano was born on 30 July 1945. Up to this point, as noted in Chapter 1, he had led everyone to believe that the year of his birth was 1947 (no doubt in memory of his brother Rudy, whose death, as we have seen, had a profound and lasting effect on him).
37. This 'confessional' approach, added to the choice of title, establishes a definite link to Drieu la Rochelle's *État civil* (Paris, Gallimard, 1921). Drieu has, of course, already inspired previous works in the œuvre (see Chapter 2 above).
38. This notion that parents can, retrospectively, gain more satisfactory roots through their children is a constant feature of Modiano's work. Cf. e.g. *Les Boulevards de ceinture*, pp.87–90, 109. Cf. also *Lacombe Lucien*, in which, by Modiano's own admission, France is so named because her Jewish father 'se voulait "assimilé"' (Libermann, 'Patrick Modiano', p.3).
39. Cau, 'Patrick Modiano marié, un enfant et un livret de famille de 180 pages', p.13. For a more theoretical (and general) discussion of this merging of fiction and reality (including the use of the author as character) see, *passim*, Waugh, *Metafiction* (London, Routledge, 1988).
40. Note also that Modiano is not always in line with the leading theorist on autobiography in France, Philippe Lejeune. For the latter's (evolving) views on the genre (and hence an idea of where *Livret de famille* stands in relation to it) see his two seminal works, *L'Autobiographie en France* (Paris, Colin, 1971) and *Le Pacte autobiographique* (Paris, Seuil, 1975).
41. These leitmotifs are in turn intertwined for even greater coherence. The dreams which crumble, for instance, are often associated, as in *Villa Triste*, with the world of the cinema – see e.g. Claude Chevreuse (pp.121–2) or Le Gros (p.126). Note also the combination of the Orient and the loss of youth in, say, the cases of Marignan (p.34) and the narrator's parents (p.172).
42. This technique is well-established, and can already be seen in *La Place de l'Étoile* and *La Ronde de nuit*.
43. Or, perhaps, that of a composer, the use of theme and climax

in a *livret* (libretto) having musical connotations as well. For more on the musicality of the text, see Nettelbeck and Hueston, *Patrick Modiano*, pp.86–92. Note also that Elgar's *Enigma variations*, like Modiano's *Livret de famille*, is in fifteen parts of different lengths, each with autobiographical connections, and each echoing other variations/chapters.

44. Great play is made of the national stereotype: neutrality and slowness. There is even a character called Muzzli (= muesli/müsli)!

45. Malka, 'Patrick Modiano', p.2.

46. Cf. p.9 above. To gain an idea of just how great this erosion is in *Livret de famille*, see e.g. André Bourlagoff (p.74), James Levy (p.38), Sessue Hayakawa (p.172), the guests at Toddie Werner's (p.168), Fantasia music (p.108), and Marignan's China (p.30), all of whom and which are shown to have disappeared.

47. This ambiguity is summed up in the epigraph from René Char, 'Vivre, c'est s'obstiner à achever un souvenir', *achever* meaning both to complete and to kill off. Note also that, implicit in this, is a view of the past as similarly equivocal – it is either so good as to be worth recalling, or so bad as to be best forgotten.

48. Having 'died' in Germany in 1945 (pp.25, 26), Marignan can be seen to evoke the shadowy form of Maurice Sachs, who, as seen in Note 114 to Chapter 2 above, likewise has the role of substitute parent to fulfil. (Certain aspects of Chapter V, where there is reference to a book called *La Chasse à courre*, further encourage us to detect Sachs's ghostly presence in the work – to elucidate the allusion here, and to show Sachs's influence throughout the *œuvre*, see *Un cirque passe*, p.20 and cf. *La Ronde de nuit*, p.91.)

49. To recall only *Villa Triste*, we may remind ourselves that Chmara refers to his 'vieux bottins, et les numéros de *Match*, *Cinémonde*, *Music-hall*, *Détective*, *Noir et Blanc* des dernières années' (p.47), and later says of Yvonne's uncle: 'Je ne comprenais qu'un mot sur deux mais cela suffisait à rétablir le reste' (p.140). That Modiano is divulging his own approach here is confirmed by confessions such as: 'J'ai besoin d'un tas d'archives, vieux journaux, plans de ville, pour situer ce que j'invente' (Rolin, 'Patrick Modiano', p.63); or, more recently: 'Pour que je me mette à écrire un roman, il faut qu'il y ait des

détails précis [. . .]. Alors, je peux laisser libre cours à ma rêverie' (Maury, 'Patrick Modiano: travaux de déblaiement', p.100). See also Note 59 to Chapter 2 above and, for a more detailed discussion of Modiano's technique, Rambures, 'Comment travaillent les écrivains', p.24.

50. There are plainly touches of Proust and Balzac here and, like them, Modiano gains more from the technique than mere unity – by reintroducing characters at different moments of their lives and in different settings, he can describe them from different viewpoints, show the fragmentary nature of our perceptions, and (perhaps above all) highlight the corrosive impact of time.

51. Cf. *La Place de l'Étoile*, in which Schlemilovitch *père* is picked up by Gérard le Gestapiste, but somehow flees to safety (p.96), and *Les Boulevards de ceinture*, where Deyckecaire, as we may recall, is similarly taken into custody (pp.197–8).

52. The 'normally' is important here, for other countries sometimes fulfil this role as well. Belgium, for instance: Félix Openfeld (to stick with *Livret de famille*) flees Hitler's Germany to seek the shelter of 'la neutralité belge' (p.45), but then has his asylum ruined when the Führer's armies invade in 1940 (his predicament in many ways having been foreshadowed by *Les Boulevards de ceinture*, where baron Deyckecaire tries to 'filer en Belgique' (p.197), but is arrested before he gets anywhere near the border). Or Spain: *Lacombe Lucien* shows Horn making costly arrangements to decamp over the Pyrenees, only to realize that 'Ça n'existe pas l'Espagne . . .' (p.114), a conclusion strikingly confirmed by Lucien's later attempt at the same journey, which is aborted when his car breaks down *en route*.

53. Georges Mandel (1885–1944), a former minister and a strong opponent of the armistice proposed by Pétain in 1940, was indeed killed by members of the French Milice – on 7 July 1944.

54. The brief biography that Modiano gives of this character (p.111) suggests that he was inspired in large part by the infamous Louis Darquier de Pellepoix.

55. Cf. *La Ronde de nuit*, in which Swing Troubadour/Lamballe thinks he can escape from his predicament by running away to Lausanne, but eventually concedes: 'Lausanne ne me suffirait pas' (p.174).

56. Although the *années noires* scarcely feature as such in *Villa Triste*, we still get a wartime atmosphere of fear and insecurity, so the same technique is exploited – see *Villa Triste*, pp.14–15. Note also that, significantly in the light of Note 52 above, the USA also acts as refuge in this work, with a key part of Chmara's dream being to build an idyllic, yet impossible love-nest in America: 'c'était dans ce pays qui n'existe pas [. . .] que j'aurais voulu vivre avec Yvonne' (p.167). (Cf. Modiano's earlier comment in interview, when asked about his plans for his next novel: 'Cela s'appellera sans doute "La Californie". C'est la chose que l'on n'atteint jamais' – Leclère, 'Il a vingt-deux ans et il méritait le Goncourt', p.139).

57. Cf. Gerbauld's imagined reaction to identification as D.: 'Mais comment le saviez-vous? Vous n'étiez pas né' (p.119). The echo here of *La Place de l'Étoile* (p.150) and, implicitly, *Les Boulevards de ceinture* (p.199) further shows the unified nature of Modiano's work.

58. Montalbetti, 'La Haine des professeurs', p.2.

59. Cf. his comment on the Occupation in interview: 'J'en ai entendu parler, autrefois, par des proches, à mots couverts, en des termes qui ont frappé mon imagination enfant. [. . .] Je n'ai pas oublié' (Jaudel, 'Quête', p.61). Cf. Note 123 to Chapter 2 above.

60. Pudlowski, 'Modiano le magnifique', p.28.

61. Note also that all of Modiano's narrators have, hitherto, had something of the informal sleuth about them, thanks to their manic recording of incidents, statements and names in a desperate attempt to preserve/reconstruct the past.

62. For background information on the history and modern exploitation of the detective novel, see Jacques Dubois, *Le Roman policier ou la modernité* (Paris, Nathan, 1992), or Ronald Walker and June Frazer (eds), *The Cunning Craft: Original Essays on Detective Fiction and Contemporary Literary Theory* (Macomb, Western Illinois University, 1990). (Pages 166–73 of this latter text deal directly with *Rue des Boutiques Obscures*.)

63. As many critics have noted, the constant blank spaces which this results in *visually* convey the absence at the heart of the work.

64. Cf. *A la recherche du temps perdu*: 'Je ne savais même pas [. . .] qui j'étais; [. . .] mais alors le souvenir [. . .] venait à moi

comme un secours [. . .] pour me tirer du néant d'où je n'aurais pu sortir tout seul' (I, p.5). For another of the many (and now predictable) Proustian touches in *Rue des Boutiques Obscures*, see the mention of 'les noms, comme celui, pourpre et scintillant, de: "Rubirosa"' (p.176) and cf. 'ce nom inconnu et si doux de "Champi" qui mettait sur l'enfant [. . .] sa couleur vive, empourprée et charmante' (*A la recherche du temps perdu*, I, p.41).

65. 'Le Malaise du passé', p.41. As may be recalled, Modiano has already exploited this view of identity in *La Place de l'Étoile*.

66. Cf. Guy's confidence in Sonachitzé and Heurteur: 'Heurteur aussi avait de la mémoire. A eux deux, ils résoudraient certainement "l'énigme" que je posais' (p.14).

67. See e.g. the erosion wrought on the 'bande de Stioppa' (p.19), Waldo Blunt (pp.46, 56), 'l'homme des plages' (p.60), the metaphorical racehorses (p.162), Porfirio Rubirosa (p.163), or the symbolically-named Garage de la Comète (p.204).

68. Cf. Bedner, 'Modiano ou l'identité introuvable', p.60.

69. Note how (as ever) the names of the characters are evocative of their rootlessness, both in their general exoticism, and in their frequent cross-cultural origins.

70. 'Suite en blanc', p.661.

71. See e.g. (again) Hutte, who from the very start takes on the role of *Doppelgänger* to Guy – he, too, has initially 'perdu ses [. . .] traces' (p.11), and so similar to his young *protégé* does he feel that, quite visibly, he acts as surrogate father for him (it is, we recall, he who gives Roland his identity, 'naming' him in much the same way as a parent names a new-born baby). Note also that the negative side of memory, which Guy eventually discovers, finds a resonance in Jean-Michel Mansoure (pp.116–17, 120–6) and Mme Kahan (pp.149, 173). For leitmotival threads in the novel, see e.g. the mention of billiards (pp.78–9, 110, 125, 148, 189), or the recurrent phrase, 'Vous ne trouvez pas qu'il me ressemble?' (pp.37, 57, 66, 77).

72. For more on this topic, see Scherman, 'Translating from Memory: Patrick Modiano in Postmodern Context', p.297.

73. Gerald Prince (in *Narrative as Theme*, p.123) quite rightly suggests that, as the year is only specified on Gay Orlow's *fiche*, Guy could have met Stioppa in, say, 1964. But as Prince himself then recognizes, 'nothing else in the text points to this conclusion'. Furthermore, if we opt for this early meeting, we

are scarcely any better off, for why would Guy wait eleven months (or longer) to follow up his new-found *piste*?

74. Cf. Côté, 'Aux rives du Léthé: Mnémosyne et la quête des origines chez Patrick Modiano', p.326.

75. Note how these chapters are essentially positive – bathed in sunshine and sporting the theme of *l'enfance* (the symbol of the (assumed) happiness now forgotten), they hold the promise of success for Roland, a promise all the more powerful in that, as we have seen, his 'double', Hutte, shows him that a past and childhood 'lost' *can* actually be recaptured.

76. See e.g. Waldo Blunt. No sooner do we learn that he married Gay in the United States (p.43), than Guy meets up with him in Paris – working at the hotel Hilton (an American concern) and living near the Avenue de New-York (pp.45, 54–6).

77. This view of the text as *rêverie* is supported by one interpretation of the book's title – *Rue des Boutiques Obscures* might be an allusion to Georges Perec's *La Boutique Obscure* (Paris, Denoël, 1973), which, as its subtitle of *124 rêves* makes clear, has a narrative composed entirely of the author's dreams. (The themes of this latter work – the war years, Jewishness, fear of arrest, the cinema, etc. – further underline the links to Modiano.) Note also the circular elements in Guy's quest and cf. the final point of Note 74 to Chapter 2 above.

78. For more on the concept of the implied author, see the brief history of the term in Belsey, *Critical Practice* (London, Routledge, 1987), pp.30–1.

79. The parody has other targets too:

> Le héros anonyme qui marche [. . .], la figure du labyrinthe devenue cliché, [. . .] l'œuvre s'élaborant à mesure qu'avance l'enquête [. . .] invitent à penser que Modiano raille les techniques du Nouveau Roman ésotérique. De même les signes surréalistes, les symboles freudiens [. . .], les divans de toutes formes, les boîtes à tous usages ridiculisent la littérature des profondeurs et de la libido. (Wardi, 'Mémoire et écriture dans l'œuvre de Patrick Modiano', p.47)

80. This also illustrates another ludic aspect of the text – the way in which light, normally linked to clarity and clear vision, now often represents the very opposite. Cf. the names Pedro

Stern (star in German), Freddie Howard de *Luz* (light in Spanish) or the chalet called the Croix du Sud (Southern Cross) – none of these, ultimately, elucidates the problem posed by Guy.

81. The fact that these clichés may derive from the cinema does not invalidate the point, since Modiano has clearly aimed to introduce this medium (like so many others) into *Rue des Boutiques Obscures* – witness the aforementioned black-and-white imagery, which additionally serves to evoke the feel of the old *films noirs* and B movies. Note also that, as already shown, the cinema has been a constant intertext for the *œuvre* hitherto.

82. See pp.122–3 and cf. p.174.

83. Cf. David Lodge:

> There is always a trade-off in the writing of fiction between the achievement of structure, pattern and closure on the one hand, and the imitation of life's randomness, inconsequentiality and openness on the other. Coincidence, which surprises us in real life with symmetries we don't expect to find there, is all too obviously a structural device, and an excessive reliance on it can jeopardize the verisimilitude of a narrative. (*The Art of Fiction* (London, Penguin, 1992), p.150)

Chance being, as we have seen (and shall see), a theme of most of Modiano's texts, these points would apply equally well to the *œuvre* in its entirety.

84. It is also very much the technique of Georges Simenon, of whom Modiano himself observes: 'Il n'y a personne dont je me sente plus proche' (Rolin, 'Patrick Modiano', p.63). For full details of Simenon's approach to writing (and, indeed, his other, more general links to Modiano), see, *passim*, Simenon, *Quand j'étais vieux* (Paris, Presses de la Cité, 1970) or Fenton Bresler, *The Mystery of Georges Simenon* (London, Heinemann/Quixote Press, 1983).

85. Scouffi actually existed, and did indeed write the two books Modiano mentions (p.131) – a further example of the author's tendency to mix real and invented characters, and thereby increase the element of uncertainty in his works (cf. pp.40–1 above).

86. Blunt's isolation from the party builds on that of the bride in Chapter II, and looks forward to that of Pedro and Denise in

Chapter XXXVII. This provides yet another illustration of how one incident in the work feeds into another.

87. Note also that the narrator of *Livret de famille* had said: 'J'aurais donné tout au monde pour devenir amnésique' (p.96), a wish clearly implemented through Guy.

88. Cf. Magnan, 'Les Revenants de nulle part', pp.184–5. Note also that the man with whom Guy eventually identifies, Pedro, was born in 1912 (p.152) – just like Albert Modiano.

89. This figurative lowering of a curtain can no doubt be linked to the fact that Modiano's father had recently died.

4

Making a Break: 'Une jeunesse' and 'De si braves garçons'

Il faut changer à des choses contemporaines, se débarrasser du passé, de la vieille peau.

Patrick Modiano

Modiano semble [. . .] être passé du modernisme miroitant à un classicisme aux teintes passées.

Bruno Vercier and Jacques Lecarme

By the time *Rue des Boutiques Obscures* won the prix Goncourt in 1978,[1] Modiano had arrived at something of a crossroads in his career. Up until now, as has been seen, he had tended to live in the shadow of his past, repeatedly fashioning dream lives for himself out of the memories of other people. But as the 1980s approached, he had reached the stage where this procedure could readily be abandoned, for the rootlessness which gave rise to it had gradually disappeared, and no longer did he feel so stricken by pangs of instability. On the contrary. A successful novelist, happily married, and with two children to delight in,[2] he currently had all the security he could ever have possibly wished for, a security so strong that it could not fail to alter his literary outlook. 'Je ne peux ressasser éternellement les mêmes fantasmes', he was shortly to announce, underlining his intention to begin a new phase in his work, and later in the same interview he would add by way of explanation: 'Il vient un moment où on peut parler de soi-même, où l'on commence à posséder un passé à soi et où l'on n'a plus besoin de celui des autres.'[3] Nowhere is his change of direction more visible than in this remark,[4] yet the break with the past did not materialize immediately. For a year or two, he seemed to mark time, committing himself only to relatively minor projects: a succession of short stories ('Lettre d'amour',[5] '1, rue Lord-Byron', 'Docteur Weiszt', 'Memory Lane', and 'La Seine'), a preface for a French edition of a text by Rilke (*Les Cahiers de Malte Laurids Brigge*), and the scenario of a film on the criminal Jacques Mesrine.[6] But all the time his search for novelty was proceeding, and after the turn of the decade, fittingly, it was to come to fruition in his next two major prose works, *Une jeunesse* (1981) and *De si braves garçons* (1982), as the pages which follow will endeavour to demonstrate.

'A 33 ans je ne peux pas rechercher toute ma vie l'image de mon père', Modiano declared after the publication of *Rue des Boutiques Obscures*. 'Quand on a des enfants, on est père à son tour, et l'on peut oublier un peu le passé [. . .] je ne crois pas que je vais parler tout le temps de la guerre.'[7] Sure enough, in his next novel, *Une jeunesse*, he visibly translates these words into action: the time-scale takes in the 1980s and the 1960s, but the Occupation, previously omnipresent (except in *Villa Triste*), is now given hardly any significant mention at all.

And this is by no means the only way in which *Une jeunesse* marks a development in Modiano's *œuvre*; there are numerous other, much more obvious changes besides. The most immediately recognizable of these is the very title of the work, which breaks with the evocative, polysemic phrases of earlier texts, in favour of something far less equivocal if not downright bland. Indeed, once this unfamiliar note of simplicity has been struck, it is maintained throughout the narrative which follows, and it is here that the author's innovations are at their most blatant. Gone, for instance, is the anguished, isolated *je*, replaced by a more objective, third-person narration and a double focus on Odile and Louis Memling, both as individuals and as a contented couple.[8] Gone too is the problem of identity, at least as expressed through the use of aliases. Also gone is the litany of place-names and the 'cast of thousands', which had been such a feature of the *œuvre* up to this point. Gone as well, and most significantly of all perhaps, is the sense of temporal uncertainty, for never before has chronology had such an important role to perform. Admittedly, there are still a number of flashbacks and 'flashforwards', but overall, linearity is the order of the day, with past, present and future all falling into easily distinguishable blocks, and with no glaring contradictions to confuse matters.

In fact, this dividing of time into separate segments proves to be a key element in the structure of the text, since the narrative itself is composed of a succession of 'fresh starts'. The middle-aged Brossier stops working for Bejardy in order to spend more time with his student girlfriend, and adopts a more youthful lifestyle in the process. 'J'ai fait table rase de toute une période de ma vie', he confesses. 'Je suis un tout autre homme, maintenant' (p.162). Louis, on the other hand, moves in exactly the opposite direction, proceeding not backwards towards a lost youth, but forwards towards greater maturity, yet still putting the past very firmly behind him. When he completes his military service he throws his old shoes away, 'et ce geste solonnel marquait la fin d'une période de sa vie' (p.23). Later, like Brossier, he too abandons Bejardy, stealing the money he is supposed to smuggle into Switzerland, and running away with Odile, with the result that, at the end of the book, another transformation has taken place: 'Quelque chose, dont il se demanda plus tard si ce n'était pas tout simplement sa jeunesse, quelque chose qui lui avait pesé jusque-là se détachait de lui, comme un morceau de rocher tombe lentement vers la mer et disparaît dans une gerbe d'écume' (p.193). Fifteen years further on, the money, we assume, having been invested in a 'home d'enfants' in the mountains, the time has come again to move on. 'Le home d'enfants, c'est fini', we learn (p.8), and the main question now is: 'Est-ce qu'il peut vous arriver quelque chose de neuf à trente-cinq ans? [. . .] Est-ce que parfois la vie recommence à zéro à trente-cinq ans?' (p.10).

As the page references of these last two quotations indicate, Modiano has decided to place his conclusion (chronologically speaking) at the start of his narrative, and this is significant, for it illustrates yet another innovation on his part. In addition to establishing the contentment which Louis and Odile feel *in the present*, the displaced 'ending' infuses the text – given that most of the 'action' takes place in flashback – with a clear sense of *the future*, a definite reason for optimism. Or to use the words of the critic Norbert Czarny: 'Le temps passé ne renvoie pas à la souffrance de ce qui n'est plus, à un manque, mais à la plénitude d'un présent.'[9] As may by now be apparent, never before has a novel by Modiano seemed so positive in outlook.

This is no doubt because the author himself has never been happier in his personal life, for there can be no denying that he has put much of himself into the work he has created. Like Louis, he is (as he writes) about thirty-five, with a wife and two children to delight in; like Brossier, he was 'une sorte d'étudiant fantôme';[10] like Odile and Bellune, he has experience of the French music industry;[11] and like all his main characters, he knows exactly what the 1960s were like and just how problematic they could be:

> Je ne suis pas passé par les mêmes péripéties que les personnages, mais c'est tout à fait l'ambiance et la lumière dans lesquelles je vivais lorsque j'avais 19–20 ans, à Paris. Le climat dans lequel j'évoluais, les lieux que je fréquentais sont à peu près ceux que je décris dans ce livre. À l'époque, je ne savais pas ce que j'allais faire. J'avais l'impression d'être à la dérive dans une ville un peu grise.[12]

In the light of this looming authorial presence, we should not be too surprised by the aforementioned succession of 'fresh starts' which we encounter in the text – this is just one more way in which Modiano draws his own line under the past, one more way in which he shows that his state of 'dérive' is now over.[13]

Such personal involvement in the fiction is, of course (like the circularity which comes from placing the 'end' of the novel at its head), a permanent feature of *l'œuvre modianesque*, so *Une jeunesse* can hardly be said to provide a complete break with previous practice. Quite the opposite in fact. Despite the glaring innovations already outlined above, the text plainly has a good deal in common with its predecessors.

Take, for example, the thematic aspect of the work. 'Jamais [. . .] un livre de Modiano n'a été plus centré sur le Temps', Norbert Czarny has observed,[14] and it is true that time – and the destruction it wreaks – continues to be a key concern for the author, as seen most noticeably through the characters of Bellune and Bauer. Bellune is one of the kindest people encountered by Odile in the 1960s, yet he is most manifestly a relic from a bygone age. Celebrated in the field of operetta before the war, and having fled Vienna for France to escape the Nazis (adapting his old name of Blüene in the process – yet another new start), he has, when we first meet him, once again been overtaken by events, for although he is still working in the music business, the burgeoning 'pop scene', with its youthfulness and vigour, is far removed from his own fundamental tastes and values.[15] Not for him the exploitative, 'casting-couch' approach of the despicable Vietti. But not for him either the feeling of power and influence –

the phone in his office, revealingly, never ever rings. All his glories, then, are most patently in the past, and thus left behind by the calendar's advance, he acknowledges his state in the most striking – and symbolic – of manners: he chooses to commit suicide.

Suicide is also evoked by Bauer's appearance in the novel, though only in passing, for when he produces his photo album and remarks that some of the people featured there took their own lives, he is not so much highlighting the means by which they died as the fact that death descends upon everybody at one stage or another. 'C'est triste de penser que tous ces beaux gosses ont vieilli ou bien disparu', he says; '[. . .] quand je feuillette cet album et que je les regarde les uns après les autres, j'ai l'impression que ce sont des vagues qui sont venues se briser au fur et à mesure' (p.181). And not even the living and healthy can avoid this inexorable erosion, as Louis himself rapidly comes to realize: 'Sans doute Bauer collerait-il leur photo sur son album avec la date, et Odile, lui et le chien n'auraient été, après tant d'autres, qu'une vague' (p.183).[16] As may quite readily be agreed, the metaphor employed here is an effective one, and could, moreover, be applied to Modiano's *œuvre* as a whole. It too proceeds wave-like from book to book, with each component part coming to an end only to be evoked anew in the form of its successor, the resultant non-stop ebb and flow leaving behind it little but a profound sense of memory, the past and, above all, the destructive passage of time.

This being the case, it is perhaps fitting that the familiar theme of reverie should likewise be carried over into *Une jeunesse*, for although there is now, as we have seen, no central *je* to produce a *texte-rêve*, the characters of the work still manifest a marked propensity to dream – characters such as Mary (p.110), or Bellune (p.33), or Brossier (p.67), or Vietti (p.102), or Axter (p.150), or all the hopefuls auditioning for the talent-spotter (p.27); or, of course, the two main characters: Louis, who dreams of seeing his father ride his bike in the velodrome, and Odile, who longs to become a successful singer, and both of whom, tellingly, enjoy going to a café called *Le Rêve*, because 'cela les amusait [. . .] de dire: "Rendez-vous à cinq heures au *Rêve* . . ."' (p.108).[17]

If this tendency to fantasize already links Louis and Odile back to previous Modiano (anti-)heroes, then this connection is cemented by other familiar aspects of their make-up. They too, for example, are still children, all alone in an indifferent yet hostile world. They too are rootless, disoriented orphans, living, in the 1960s, 'un de ces moments où l'on éprouve le besoin de s'agripper à quelque chose de stable et de demander conseil à quelqu'un. Mais il n'y a personne' (pp.124–5).[18] They too home in on parental surrogates (Brossier, Bejardy, Bellune) like so many safe ports in a storm (pp.40–1, 67, 69). And they too are far from being elevating and exceptional individuals. In short, the novelty of their status as a couple notwithstanding, they have been formed in precisely the same mould as the first-person narrators whom they have replaced.

So, despite the significant innovations in *Une jeunesse*, there remains, overall, an undoubted element of consistency with the past. Indeed, the more one studies the text, the greater the sense of continuity becomes, extending even to the level of detail. To give only some of the endless possible illustrations of this: Louis's and Odile's excursion to Boscombe College in Bournemouth reminds us that, in *La Place de l'Étoile*, Raphaël had similarly visited 'un manoir proche de Bournemouth' (p.15); the opening of the novel, with the Memling family happily settled in the mountains, harks back to *Rue des Boutiques Obscures*;[19] Vertbois, the 'propriété familiale, en Sologne [. . .] berceau des comtes Bejardy' (pp.116–17) evokes *Livret de famille*;[20] there are the (by now) usual allusions to chance ('Avouez qu'il y a parfois des coïncidences' – p.178) and to Proust ('Louis lisait les aventures de Burgess et de ses amis, et ce nom, Guy Burgess, suffisait pour lui faire retrouver toute l'atmosphère de Bournemouth' – p.151); the leitmotif of the butterfly (pp.28, 51, 52, 53, 72–3, 152) is just as insistent as ever;[21] and once more we encounter the mysterious garage, the selfsame garage which, no doubt, had already been evoked in *Livret de famille* and *Rue des Boutiques Obscures*. And, of course, in *Villa Triste*.

This final comparison can usefully be expanded, for of all the previous texts which *Une jeunesse* evokes, the one with which it has the most in common would appear to be, precisely, *Villa Triste*. Modiano's fourth novel, it may be recalled, was basically a love story of circular structure, relying heavily upon contrasts and parallels for its development. As may already have been inferred, exactly the same can be said of his seventh major work. We follow (chronologically speaking) Louis and Odile first individually in alternation, and then, after their meeting,[22] together as a couple, finishing at a similar point to where we began – at a time of great transition in their lives – and discovering along the way that their position relates to those of numerous other characters in the book: Brossier, like them, is somewhat adrift in Paris, having long felt 'un besoin vital d'"organisation" et de "guides"' (p.167); almost everyone they meet shares their propensity to dream, as seen above (although whereas Odile's main wish, like Chmara's, is eventually dashed – 'Le rêve s'est cassé. Elle ne chantera plus' (p.104) – Mary's seems to be realized (p.176)); Louis commits a crime against his boss, Bejardy, just as Bejardy had against his (even if theft hardly compares to murder); and so the echoes and oppositions go on.

Yet it is not just on the structural level that links exist with *Villa Triste*. There are other areas of contact as well. Bellune, the relic of the past escaping a new age through suicide, has distinctive overtones of René Meinthe; the setting of the French Alps, near a lake, harks back to Victor Chmara's retreat (all the more so in that Louis went to school in Annecy); and finally, for good measure, there is a reference to a man nicknamed 'la Carlton' (p.191). 'La Carlton' has, albeit fleetingly, already appeared in Modiano's fourth novel. Once again, then, the reintroduction of characters brings a sense of continuity to the *œuvre*.

A further, and final, element of this continuity can be found in the atmosphere of *Une jeunesse*, the composition of which, as in previous works, is part menace and part uncertainty. The menace, as ever, derives from the streets of Paris, and seems to belong to the very fabric of the French capital.[23] In Odile's case, it takes an overtly sexual form. She is exploited by the police to catch a sex attacker, used by Vietti to satisfy his desires, and even prostituted by him when he agrees to give her money.[24] For Louis, on the other hand, the main threat comes from his employer, the murderer and 'escroc' Roland de Bejardy, and in particular from the (apparently) criminal activities in which he involves him. Or so we assume, for real though the impression of menace appears to be for us, for our two 'heroes' there is little obvious cause for concern – they just accept without demur the activities they are invited to engage in.

And this brings us round to the question of uncertainty, since one of the main sources of ambiguity in the work is, precisely, this (typical) avoidance on Modiano's part of any moral comment.[25] Odile may well (more or less) sell her body, Louis turn into a smuggler, and both of them abscond with Bejardy's money, but not once do they feel pangs of conscience, and not once are they authorially condemned. Consequently, at the end of the novel we are not entirely sure whether their theft and flight represent an escape from immorality (their decisive action showing their new-found independence and maturity) or the ultimate proof that they have strayed even further from the straight and narrow.[26] Their current contentment and respectability might suggest that the first of these two interpretations is the better, but then again, such a reference to the present might simply serve to confuse the issue further, as John Sturrock rightly realized:

> Louis and Odile's past does not explain their present [. . .]. Because Modiano says not a word of the intervening twelve years between [their] escape from Paris and the present moment, their ordinariness remains interrogatively at odds with the doubtful story of how it was achieved. [. . . They] have their past but one which verges all the while on the imaginary, as if it were indeed the future, the beginning again of which Odile has been thinking [. . .]. If their past is a projection from the present, then their present is similarly a projection from their past. We are caught between two mirrors. *Une jeunesse* is an exceedingly clever, well-made novel; and a deeper one than the casual realism of its manner suggests.[27]

This closing remark is undoubtedly true; there is certainly much more to *Une jeunesse* than meets the eye. But not in the sense that, say, *Rue des Boutiques Obscures* was deceptively simple. There, it may be recalled, the past had to be imaginary, since the narrative deliberately undermined its own verisimilitude. Now, however, things are noticeably different. The realism may be somewhat 'casual', to take up Sturrock's term, but a more traditional form there is none the less: no longer does the text *automatically* self-destruct. Perhaps this, then, more than anything else, should warn us that the familiar aspects of the work are in many ways misleading. At the end of the day, without a doubt, an important break with the past has been made. But it is a break which, all in all, is sadly not for the better.

With the (at least partly) innovatory *Une jeunesse* completed and behind him, Modiano seems, between 1981 and 1983, to have embarked on a period of consolidation, reworking old material for the most part, yet in such a way as to maintain his avowed quest for novelty. *Memory Lane* (1981), his next book, consists of his earlier *récit* of the same name embellished with (photo-like) drawings by Pierre Le-Tan, and this new venture into illustrated writing is followed up almost immediately by another (and with the same artist): *Poupée blonde* (1983), a light-hearted theatrical script-cum-programme which, quite clearly, has its roots in the abortive 1974 play, *La Polka*.[28] Modiano's eighth major work, *De si braves garçons*, similarly manifests a considerable debt to the past, incorporating adapted versions of 'La Seine' (pp.58–77), 'Docteur Weiszt' (pp.93–101) and 'Johnny' (pp.125–9), although only those familiar with all aspects of the *œuvre modianesque* are likely to be aware of this massive self-quotation – those who are acquainted uniquely with the novels will, on the contrary, tend to be struck simply by what is new in the work. For newness there most certainly is, and in a number of different areas at that.[29]

One radical change of approach in *De si braves garçons* is apparent to even the most casual of observers: building on the split narrative focus of *Une jeunesse*, Modiano has taken one step back to his favoured first-person narrator of pre-1980 days, and two steps forward to a *je* which is no longer merely singular, but rather the embodiment of two different characters (at least). The more minor of these is Edmond Claude, a bit-part actor who, fittingly, has little more than a walk-on role in the book either, addressing us in only two of the fourteen chapters it comprises. The main narrative voice on the other hand (assuming it to be a single entity) seems to be much more interesting and noteworthy. Eventually identified as a Patrick born in July 1945, characterized on more than one occasion as a 'rêveur', and now the father of two young daughters and a writer of detective stories, this second *je* has many obvious links with Modiano himself.

And this brings us on to another novel aspect of *De si braves garçons*, for although such autobiographical elements have, of course, been a feature of the author's whole *œuvre* up to this point (adding to the real/imaginary tension therein), the personal experience which generates the text is no longer the same as that exploited previously: out goes the evocation of the novelist aged twenty, and in comes a sketch of him five years earlier as a schoolboy. Or as Jacques Pécheur has so tellingly put it: 'La photo de classe succède au *Livret de famille* pour ces nouvelles variations sur la mémoire.'[30] But where, exactly, was this suggestive 'school photograph' taken?[31] Scrutiny of the details which Modiano divulges seems to provide the answer. Valvert, the fictional *collège* in question, is situated to the south-west of Paris on the Bièvre, near to the aerodrome at Villacoublay, within walking distance of the 'hameau des Metz' (p.107), and in a village once inhabited by the *teinturier* Oberkampf. From these details alone, and armed only with the relevant maps (or with our first-hand knowledge of the region), we can easily spot the town that Modiano is recalling: Jouy-en-Josas. And the school is no real mystery either, for two of the pupils at Valvert, Winegrain and Bourdon, had earlier appeared in *Memory Lane*, and there they were said to have studied at the (real-life Josassian) collège du Montcel. So, it would seem that Modiano, too, is an old boy of le Montcel.[32]

This is well worth establishing, for it throws an interesting new light on *Rue des Boutiques Obscures*. In this work, it may be recalled, Guy Roland sets off in search of his past, and two of the key staging posts on his journey turn out to be the Collège de Luiza et d'Albany and the Howard de Luz's château at Valbreuse. Now, at the time, these two places did not seem especially significant, but when reconsidered after a reading of *De si braves garçons*, they exhibit an overtly discernible resonance. The head of the collège de Luiza et d'Albany is a certain Monsieur Jeanschmidt, who just happens to be the same man who is in charge of Valvert, and when Guy arrives in Valbreuse, he could almost be visiting our small town on the Bièvre.[33] Putting two and two together, then, there would appear to be absolutely no room for doubt – in his prix-Goncourt work as well, if less directly, Modiano has felt the need to evoke his schooldays in his fiction.[34]

The reason for this is not hard to discover, although, predictably, it is at the very least twofold. First, Modiano is again engaging in nostalgia. Through his aforementioned links to Guy and use of the theme of childhood,[35] he is evoking his own pre-adult innocence, in much the same way as, in *De si braves garçons*, he depicts an *enfance* lost and apparently regretted – why else should 'Patrick' return to Valvert in memory and, moreover (in the final chapter), physically with Charrell? Second, and conversely, he is alluding to a more negative aspect of his past, an aspect which may, perhaps, actually be best *forgotten*. For as *De si braves garçons* further suggests, his adolescence was an unsettled time for him, a time which, as already noted, was to mark him for the rest of his life. Not, of course, that we are informed of this explicitly (nothing is ever explicit in the *œuvre modianesque*!); but we can, nevertheless, make certain inferences about 'Patrick' (and, through him, the author) on the basis of the classmates he mixes with. Christian Portier, for instance, is 'un enfant naturel' (p.133) who tries so hard to be grown up that he acquires a 'voix grave d'enfant trop vite mûri' (p.132); Michel Karvé is plagued by parents who 'ne lui adressaient pas la parole et même lui témoignaient une totale indifférence' (p.33); Daniel Desoto is expelled 'à cause de son attitude nonchalante et ses caprices d'enfant gâté' (p.94), while 'la seule famille de Bob [McFowles] était une grande-mère américaine' (p.46). Hence, as one of the old teachers at Valvert remarks: 'Il y avait de drôles de gens dans ce collège... Tous perturbés par leur situation familiale' (p.25). And the more we read, the more we assume that this applies to the main narrator as well, for never is there any mention of *his* parents, and never does he once dissociate himself from his colleagues – it is always to '*nous* qui étions des enfants du hasard et de nulle part' that he refers, and to '*nos* difficultés à vivre' (pp.9 and 45 respectively – my italics).

And that these difficulties left scars for life there can be no denying either, since when we meet up with the old boys again years later, none of them (ironically, considering the book's title) is in anything like an enviable position. Desoto is being cocooned – and exploited – by a Doctor Reoyon, who has diagnosed that 'Daniel est resté un enfant... Voilà le problème [...] Tout ce qui lui rappelle l'enfance ou le collège ne ferait qu'aggraver son cas' (pp.102–3); Yotlande has become thoughtful and melancholic, clinging to the Scossa café in which he sees 'un peu le dernier vestige de sa jeunesse, le dernier point fixe dans la débandade générale' (pp.89–90); McFowles has got married because 'il aspirait à un équilibre' (p.54), but will soon die unfulfilled in a bobsleigh accident; Charrell is involved in sordid activities, which result in his being shot; and that just leaves Newman. True to his name, Newman has tried to become a new man, seeking to end his *dérive* through engagement – 'ça représente quelque chose de stable' (p.184) – and calling himself Valvert to show that, as he says, 'je recommence ma vie à zéro' (p.187).[36] But his fiancée and her mother want him to kill a certain Grout de l'Ain,[37] so it is unlikely that things will turn out well for him either. Little wonder, then, that Edmond should observe: 'Le collège nous avait laissés bien désarmés devant la vie' (p.195), and little wonder either that, as ever, 'Patrick' should share in this malaise which afflicts his former schoolmates: 'nous, les anciens de Valvert, des coups de cafard inexplicables nous secouaient, des accès de tristesse que chacun de nous tentait de combattre à sa manière. Nous avions tous [. . .] un "grain"' (p.54).[38]

Yet there is one way in which 'Patrick' clearly differs from his old *camarades de classe*. He may well sometimes get disheartened like them, but having moved on from his unsettled past to a career as a detective novelist, he seems to be the only one of his year to have actually made a success of his life (even Edmond, who has likewise entered the artistic domain, only ever gets bottom billing). In fact, it could now almost be one of his own *polars* that we are reading, for whatever else *De si braves garçons* may contain, it is certainly not lacking in crimes or mysteries. 'Au collège, déjà, Newman s'entourait de mystère', we are informed, 'et quand on voulait en savoir plus long sur lui [. . .] il souriait sans répondre ou détournait la conversation' (p.188). Charrell likewise remains very much in the shadows, constantly promising to explain what he is doing, but never quite getting round to it. And just why is he eventually shot? Once again, we never do find out. Nor do we ascertain if Dr Reoyon is in breach of trust, as he manifestly appears to be, or what is meant by the 'trafic d'influences' that the Karvés are said to be involved in. Yet it is hardly the fault of the narrator that such lacunae prevail, for like a good detective, he is ever ready to investigate, and always pursues his enquiries until the trail runs cold. Sometimes, on good days, he will meet with a measure of success, as when he decides to work on the Karvé 'case': 'J'ai mené une enquête', he admits, 'J'ai questionné des gens et consulté de vieux journaux' (pp.35–6), and as a result he discovers that the Doctor and his wife (formerly 'Andrée la Pute'!) have been in prison for receiving stolen goods. But on bad days, that is to say most days, he will come to a dead end, thwarted by the destructive passage of time: 'Les soirs d'été', he recalls of Mme Portier, 'elle nous emmenait dîner au bord de la Seine. Rueil? Chatou? Bougival? J'ai tenté, à plusieurs reprises, de retrouver cette auberge. Sans succès. Les environs de Paris ont tellement changé' (p.137).[39] In other words, contingency is the bane of his life, and he can no more make discoveries at will than choose which of his old friends he will bump into, and when. The questions raised by his memory, therefore, are insoluble without good fortune.

Time, chance, memory, the past, the novelist as detective – these are all, of course, major features of Modiano's own work as a writer, so the aforementioned links between author and narrator can be extended to their literary practices as well.[40] Indeed, the further this professional comparison (or *mise en abyme*) is pursued, the stronger the similarities seem to assert themselves. Witness the structure of the text that 'Patrick' has produced: once again a vital element is the use of echoes, reflections and contrasts, as the different responses to ageing demonstrate. Some characters, like Mme Portier, are deeply concerned about growing old, with Mickey du Pam-Pam in particular being so obsessed – and trying so hard to look as he did years earlier – that he has become a 'vieux jeune homme de soixante ans' (p.91).[41] Others, on the contrary, have no such problems to preoccupy them: 'A soixante ans', it is noted of Sylvestre-Bel, 'il pouvait prétendre en avoir trente-cinq comme certains américains [*sic*] qui demeurent, à force de bronzage, d'hygiène corporelle et de soins de beauté, momifiés dans leur jeunesse' (p.19). Others still see ageing as something actually to be aspired to, as is the case for Christian Portier who, in feigning maturity, is shown to be 'à l'inverse de ces hommes mûrs qui s'efforcent de rentrer le ventre et de marcher d'un pas leste pour se rajeunir' (p.144). And so we could go on, and not just in respect of the loss of youth. Mme Portier and Newman are both plagued by an old man they would rather see dead; Bijou's mother is as bad a parent as those whose children are at Valvert; Anne-Marie McFowles evokes the eighteenth century, as does Mme Karvé; and this is barely to scratch the surface of the *jeu de miroirs*.[42]

On a more fundamental level, too, the structure of *De si braves garçons* is marked by the concept of the mirror, with its overall guiding principle proving to be that of symmetry. There are, for example, fourteen chapters in all, and the first seven of these are of almost exactly the same length as the second seven. Furthermore, Edmond Claude's two appearances as narrator occur in Chapters II and XIII, while the novel as a whole ends on a note which heralds its start, both in terms of setting (the collège de Valvert) and in terms of its concluding sentence ('Nous étions de si braves garçons . . .' – p.197). In this latter instance especially the sense of going back to square one is acute, for not only are we reminded of the very title of the work, but also, through the use of the *points de suspension*, we are warned that the story is by no means over. It may well, in fact, be about to begin.

This being the case, the problem of interpretation inevitably raises its head. What, we wonder, is the significance of such circularity? Why are there so many echoes and parallels in the text? There are, it would appear, at least two possible answers to these questions. First, the lack of complete linearity helps, as ever, to create an evocative atmosphere: combining with the backwards-and-forwards movement in time, it gives the novel a certain dream-like feel, a feel which itself suggests that, as the back cover of the work announces, the narrator's 'souvenirs rejoignent sans cesse le présent, au fil d'une réalité faite de rêve et de nostalgie'.[43] Second, and somewhat in contrast to this, the mirror technique creates an impression of *order*, the realization that, at some stage, someone has chosen this approach with a specific aim in mind – to turn what could be a succession of short stories into a harmonious entity.[44] On one level, of course, this organizer could be none other than 'Patrick', the main-narrator-cum-novelist. Ultimately, though, it must be Modiano himself who has arranged the text in this way, and this is not merely to state the obvious. There is an important associated point to be made here as well. For as in *Une jeunesse*, the sense of order in *De si braves garçons* is more pronounced than in any of the pre-1980 novels, and once again this prompts the question 'why?', to which we might reply, 'because in addition to the constant structural mastery we now have a chronology that is entirely consistent' – we may well still fluctuate between the past and the present, but the different layers of time remain perfectly distinguishable (thanks largely to a more traditional use of verb tenses). And that is not all; there are no glaring inconsistencies with dates either, nor is the subjectivism of the text quite as strong as in previous works (the use of *je* remains prevalent, but only to tell stories in the third person). In short, then, the narrative has taken a step closer to realism, and if we consider this to be little more than a *symptom*, then its originating cause can relatively easily be surmised: the emotional *stability* which, more and more, is becoming a feature of Modiano's life itself.[45]

Further evidence of this personal development is given by the source material of the novel, for it is no doubt due to a more settled state of mind that the author, finally, has decided to evoke his schooldays. As noted above, this period was an especially troubled time for him, with the awareness of his family problems becoming ever more acute the older he got. And as if that were not enough, he was still, we suppose, trying to come to terms with the loss of Rudy, who had died only two or three years earlier. This latter point, in particular, is hugely significant. All of Modiano's works thus far have been dedicated to his sadly-departed brother, yet never before has he been able to depict – at length – his adolescence. It has obviously proved too painful for him. But with *De si braves garçons* all that has changed. Admittedly, he is still not yet dealing with his moments of intense trauma, but he is getting much closer to them, edging his way forwards from one act of self purging to the next. For there can be no mistake about it – this, too, is a work of exorcism, and a very effective one at that. So effective, in fact, that, with the benefit of hindsight, it can be seen as something of a watershed in the *œuvre*. Never again, from this moment on, will the words 'Pour Rudy' introduce one of Modiano's novels, and this, at the end of the day, can have but one corollary – most visibly, as in *Une jeunesse*, an attempt has been made to break with the past.

A break with the past has been attempted, it is true, but not without a certain cost, since the move towards realism exacts a demanding toll. The author may well treat us to his usual artistry, but he does not challenge us to the same extent he had previously, a development which, in turn, represents another link to *Une jeunesse* – the (at least partial) return to tradition leaves us somewhat dissatisfied and very much *sur notre faim*, with our judgement being coloured accordingly. *De si braves garçons* is not, we decide, as rich or provocative as we might have hoped, nor are its experiments markedly for the better. It is an improvement on its predecessor, granted, but overall this should not obscure the issue – comparatively speaking, the work is not quite up to the standard of the first six novels. It is, in a word – and for all its qualities – one of the lesser texts in the *œuvre*.

Notes

1. Strictly speaking, the award was made not to honour the novel itself, but to recognize Modiano's *œuvre*, the implication being

that *Rue des Boutiques Obscures* is in some way inferior to the preceding works. As may by now be apparent, this is by no means the case.

2. The birth of his first daughter, Zénaïde (evoked in *Livret de famille*), was followed a few years later by that of a second, Marie.

3. Pudlowski, 'Modiano le magnifique', p.28.

4. Contrast p.10 above. Note, though, that his interest in imaginary autobiography is unaltered – it is just that he will henceforth fantasize on his own, rather than other people's, memories.

5. Although trumpeted as an *inédit*, this text is, in fact, based very closely on 'Courrier du cœur'.

6. Despite having Jean-Paul Belmondo as producer and star, this film was abandoned before it ever saw the light of day – see Gilbert Rochu, 'Les Gangsters sont des affreux', *L'Événement du jeudi*, 15–21 August 1991, pp.72–9 (p.79).

7. Modiano, 'Patrick Modiano', p.79.

8. This experiment with the narrative voice seems to have been in Modiano's head since at least 1969, when he confessed that 'il faudrait faire quelque chose sans "je"' (Texier, 'Rencontre', p.8).

9. 'Un livre pour rien', p.61.

10. Pudlowski, 'Modiano le magnifique', p.28.

11. He has, in fact, composed a number of pop songs, one of which has been identified as *Étonnez-moi Benoît*, written in collaboration with Hugues de Courson, and sung by Françoise Hardy. Cf. *Livret de famille*, p.108.

12. 'À bout portant . . . Patrick Modiano', p.28.

13. Note also his admission: 'Il arrive un moment où il faut essayer de faire quelque chose de différent, pour fuir une espèce de routine qui me fait peur, qui est angoissante' (Geille, 'Modiano m'intimide', p.66).

14. 'Un livre pour rien', p.61.

15. As is often the case, Modiano may be alluding to a real-life figure here – see Coenen-Mennemeier, 'Le philtre magique', in Bedner (ed.), *Patrick Modiano*, p.69, n.7.

16. Note that Bauer, through his album, also acts as a sort of archivist, and thereby demonstrates, once again, the ambiguity of photos (and documents in general) for Modiano – evocative, in their recording of what once was, of the

inexorable passage of time (as is the case here), they can simultaneously preserve the past and hence save it from destruction (as when Bauer, again through his album (pp.181–6), is able to give details of Brossier and Bejardy years earlier).

17. This widespread building of castles in the air (often associated with a new start in life) was, of course, very much a feature of the 1960s, as the idealism of May '68 demonstrates. For further proof that Modiano is in tune with his setting here, cf. Georges Perec's *Les Choses* (Paris, Julliard, 1965), which is significantly subtitled *Une histoire des années soixante*: 'Ils rêvaient d'abandonner leur travail, de tout lâcher, de partir à l'aventure. Ils rêvaient de repartir à zéro, de tout recommencer sur de nouvelles bases. Ils rêvaient de rupture et d'adieu' (p.90).

18. In addition to being typically absent, the parents of Louis and Odile possess, individually, a number of other familiar traits, such as the profession of dancer at the *Tabarin*, a dubious past during the Occupation, and links to the Vélodrome d'Hiver (holding centre for Jews after the *grande rafle* of 16–17 July 1942) – for more detail here, see *Une jeunesse*, pp.46, 72.

19. See *Rue des Boutiques Obscures*, p.190. (Note also the persistent theme of dreaming there.)

20. See *Livret de famille*, Chapter V, which deals with Reynolde and his country seat. Cf. also Grosbois in 'Memory Lane' (pp.11–12). (Might Modiano have at the back of his mind here a certain Valbois, the property owned by one of his long-standing influences, Valery Larbaud?)

21. Cf. e.g. *La Ronde de nuit*, pp.43, 78, 156, *Les Boulevards de ceinture*, pp.57, 85, 151, *Livret de famille*, p.174, or '*Les Écrivains de la nuit*, de Pierre de Boisdeffre', p.351.

22. Note that this meeting takes place – predictably – entirely by chance, and in a blatant *lieu de passage* (the Gare Saint Lazare).

23. Cf. Galey, 'Roman: Modiano, l'Hoffmann des villes', pp.30–1, and Lambron, 'Modiano et la mélancolie française', p.92.

24. This inclusion of exploitative sex, and its relatively more graphic (though still allusive) portrayal, represents (yet again) something of a novelty in the *œuvre*. A further aspect of its role in *Une jeunesse* is, in effect, to mark Odile's movement from innocence to adulthood. (In much the same way, non-initiated sex will punctuate Louis's advance to

maturity: Brossier hires a prostitute for him, and Nicole Haas takes him into her bed – pp.25–6, 174–5).

25. Cf. p.25 above.

26. This familiar, all-consuming incertitude derives, as ever, from a no less familiar source – Modiano's technique, which, to echo an earlier point, 'is of the cinema: he passes from sequence to sequence without ever staying to analyse' (Sturrock, 'Past Possibilities', p.506).

27. Ibid.

28. For more on *Memory Lane* and *Poupée blonde*, including the way they are integrated into the *œuvre*, see Czarny, '*Memory Lane*, de Patrick Modiano', pp.13–20, Delbourg, 'Dans le saint des cintres', p.36, and Pudlowski, 'Tout Modiano en 60 pages', p.48.

29. This novelty within a basic framework of recycling is likewise shown by Modiano's two other productions of the period, 'Mes vingt ans' and the preface to a new edition of Cocteau's *Le Livre blanc* (both 1983) – despite the general drift towards self-repetition, no old work is exploited here, unlike Morel's, 'Une dissertation de Modiano', which goes to the very opposite extreme: reproducing one of the author's schoolboy essays, it embodies no new writing at all.

30. '*De si braves garçons*', p.9.

31. This question is all the more pertinent in that Modiano has said little about his schooldays in interview.

32. For apparent confirmation of this, see Rolin, 'Patrick Modiano', p.64 and Audiard, 'Le bal des anciens', p.29. (Modiano no doubt rechristened his *alma mater* Valvert in memory of the nearby Château de Vilvert, the same sense of word play leading him to transform the rue du Docteur-Kurzenne into the rue du Docteur-Dordaine.) Note however that, as usual, a certain ambiguity still exists here – Pierre-Jean Morel thinks Valvert is modelled on the collège Saint-Joseph, near Annecy ('Une dissertation de Modiano', p.37).

33. See e.g. *Rue des Boutiques Obscures*, p.69 and cf. *De si braves garçons*, p.196.

34. Another inference is that Modiano is again unifying his *œuvre*, making one work echo the next. For further examples of this, see *De si braves garçons*, Chapter XI, where the Gare du Nord is associated with sex and menace (cf. *Une jeunesse*), or note that Mme Portier wears a 'parfum poivré' (p.151), just

like Denise Coudreuse (see p.87 above).

35. See pp.86–7 and Note 75 to Chapter 3 above.

36. This idea seems to have obsessed Modiano in the early 1980s. It has already cropped up in *Une jeunesse* (see p.102 above), and features also in *Poupée blonde* (p.22) and 'Mes vingt ans', the whole of which deals with the concept of an *homme phénix* (with the phrase 'je repars à zéro' itself occurring on p.190).

37. Modiano has no doubt based this name on that of Francis Bout-de-l'An, a top-ranking *milicien* during the Occupation.

38. Cf. *Memory Lane*, pp.19–24, where Winegrain and Bourdon (relatively minor characters in *De si braves garçons*) likewise demonstrate this general point.

39. Cf. his interest in his old school, which leads to the discovery that 'Valvert n'existe plus' (p.23).

40. Note also the reappearance of the Occupation (on, say, pp.124–9, 133, 138, 157).

41. This figure of the man who wants to stay young is characteristic of much of Modiano's work at this time. Already seen in *Une jeunesse*, in the form of Brossier (see p.102 above), he further manifests himself in *Memory Lane* (as Claude Delval) and in 'Mes vingt ans' (as Guy Scheffer). Needless to say, perhaps, there is an obvious link here to the theme of the new start, which is also common to most of these texts (see Note 36 above).

42. As ever, this use of reflection goes way beyond the text itself – in addition to the numerous links to the *œuvre* (many of which have been outlined above), there are also *clins d'oeil* to a novel which, from his earliest days (see *La Place de l'Étoile*, p.14), Modiano has openly acknowledged as an intertext: Valery Larbaud's *Fermina Màrquez*. Needless to say, perhaps, this confirms a point already strongly emphasized, namely that none of the author's novels is marked by a sense of closure – any one work constantly alludes to previous works, with reality thereby established as *fuyante*.

43. Regarding the linking of the circle and nostalgia, cf. Warehime, 'Originality and Narrative Nostalgia: Shadows in Modiano's *Rue des Boutiques Obscures*', pp.341, 344. For the ties between circularity and *rêverie*, recall Note 74 to Chapter 2 above.

44. Note also that, although each chapter tends to focus on just one old school member, unifying references are made to

characters from other chapters – see e.g. Johnny (Chapter IX), who is introduced in Chapter V (p.58), or Portier (Chapter X), who crops up again in Chapter XIII (p.188).

45. The same sense of order, significantly, is also visible in the author's two other books of this period: *Memory Lane* and *Poupée blonde*.

5

Tales of Crime and Mystery: 'Quartier perdu' and 'Dimanches d'août'

Modiano [. . .] pratique [. . .] le genre série noire. La répétition, d'un roman à l'autre, des mêmes thèmes, des mêmes obsessions, des mêmes nostalgies, est semblable, finalement, à celle [. . .] des héros favoris de Simenon ou de Chandler.

Antoine de Gaudemar

Mon sort était de ne poursuivre que des fantômes, des êtres dont la réalité, pour une bonne part, était dans mon imagination.

Marcel Proust

As has just been seen, with *De si braves garçons* Modiano closed the door on an important phase in his literary career, finally breaking out of the shadow of Rudy which, like that of his father, had hung over his creative writing since he first put pen to paper. And having closed this door, the question now was where to proceed next. Should there be a radical change of direction? Should previous practice simply be continued? On the face of it, the answer would not be long in coming. 'Je n'ai gratté que trop longtemps mes vieilles cicatrices', the author would soon reveal. 'Assez d'autobiographie romancée! Il me tarde de changer de décors, de parler de choses, de gens "extérieurs".'[1] So, once again, a break with the past is what is announced, and in the following two publications, the aforementioned *Poupée blonde* and 'Mes vingt ans', this does indeed appear to be what happens, with the autobiographical element being barely visible, if at all. Yet in spite of this, as ever, the breaking of new ground cannot really be said to be total, for there are still a good many discernible links with the rest of the *œuvre*. And when Modiano then returns to the novel form, the same sense of continuity and change remains: his next two major works, *Quartier perdu* (1984) and *Dimanches d'août* (1986), may well differ in certain respects from their predecessors, but they clearly have much in common nonetheless, not least their general nature – they too have narrators who act like detectives; they too embody enigmas, and they too, in a word, have their roots firmly embedded in the *polar* genre, as we shall now very quickly discover. For it is on these two tales of crime and mystery, precisely, that the present chapter will concentrate.

After the narrative experimentation of his two previous novels, which saw the use of the third person in *Une jeunesse* and that of (at least) two narrators in *De si braves garçons*, Modiano returns in his ninth major text, *Quartier perdu*, to the single *je* which had been such a feature of his work prior to 1980. Yet despite this turning back of the clock, as it were, we have clearly come a long way since we said goodbye to Guy Roland, for Ambrose Guise, our new narrator, has none of the rootlessness which characterized his amnesiac predecessor. On the contrary, he could hardly be more settled in his life – not only is he a wealthy, best-selling English novelist, but as he himself is the first to admit: 'Tout contribuait à mon bonheur: une femme [. . .] Trois enfants [. . .]; une maison à Londres [. . .]; un chalet à Klosters; et ce vieux rêve que j'avais réalisé l'année dernière: racheter la villa de Monaco qui avait appartenu à la baronne Orczy' (pp.27–8). Or put in more general terms: 'Tout était devenu si cohérent, si solide, si lumineux dans ma vie . . . Plus aucune zone d'ombre, plus de sables mouvants' (p.27).

Be that as it may, a Modiano narrator would not be worth his salt if he were totally unambiguous and respectable, and Guise is certainly no different in this respect, for as his very name implies, he is living under an assumed identity. Twenty years ago, before he fled to Britain, he was a Frenchman called Jean Dekker, and was implicated in the killing of Ludo Fouquet. If he has now returned to his native Paris, it is in order to embark on a typically *modianesque* pilgrimage through memory, that is to say: 'Attendre que la descente à travers le temps soit achevée [. . .]. Reprendre pied dans le Paris d'autrefois. Visiter les ruines et tenter de retrouver une trace de soi. Essayer de résoudre toutes les questions qui sont demeurées en suspens' (p.29).

The image of the descent here is extremely well chosen,

indicating that Guise has gone up in the world (materially, morally, etc.) since he escaped across the Channel. Indeed, so appropriate is it that it is quickly elevated to the status of leitmotif, with numerous other aspects of the text gloriously consolidating its impact. Perhaps the most impressive of these is the constant reference to freewheeling downhill, whether by unknown cyclists, or by the narrator himself, yet hardly any less important is Rocroy's flat at 45, rue de Courcelles, for it was here that the then Jean Dekker concealed himself in 1965, in a sort of secret basement *two floors down*, and it is from here that he is presently conducting his pilgrimage, in an atmosphère which is nothing if not conducive: 'Au moment où j'ai fait claquer la porte derrière moi, j'ai cru que je replongeais dans le passé, à cause de l'obscurité, de la fraîcheur du vestibule qui contrastait avec le soleil de plomb du dehors [. . .]. C'était comme descendre brusquement au fond d'un puits' (p.48).

As this extract explicitly demonstrates, and as may already have been naturally inferred, the relationship between the two main time-blocks in the novel, 1965 and 1984 (again the Occupation has been relegated to the background),[2] is essentially of a contrastive nature, with past and present being linked to a whole host of other opposing concepts such as hot/cool and light/dark. Of the heat/cold polarity, little more needs to be said, the quotation having ably shown how different temperatures pertain indoors and outdoors. The light/dark contrast, however, is much more interesting, for it operates on more than the climatic level of 'obscurité'/'soleil'. It also evokes, for example, the narrator's changing circumstances, his current 'luminous' situation and his 'shadowy' existence twenty years earlier – when Jean Dekker and his colleagues were committed birds of the night.[3]

Fundamentally, of course, as in most of Modiano's novels, what lies behind this binary divide is the question of identity, with the past–present split reflecting a similar fissure between the narrator's current life and his 'vie antérieure' (p.13), between his two irreconcilable names of Guise and Dekker, the one French and noble, and the other of humble, foreign origin.[4] And since, as we have seen, language can contribute to a sense of identity, the separation of Ambrose from Jean is further conveyed linguistically, the former being more at home with English, the latter being totally dependent on French (a fact which, in turn, sets up an additional contrast: French name, foreign language/ foreign name, French language). It is certainly not for nothing, then, that the opening words of the novel are 'C'est étrange d'entendre parler français' (p.9) – the pursuit of a lost means of expression is another key feature of the pilgrimage.[5]

So, too, is the re-creation of a positive relationship with Paris, for when Jean fled across the Channel he palpably severed his geographical roots as well. Prior to his departure, understandably, everything was in perfect harmony: 'Paris était une ville qui correspondait à mes battements de cœur', he recollects. 'Ma vie ne pouvait s'inscrire autre part que dans ses rues. Il me suffisait de me promener [. . .] dans Paris et j'étais heureux' (p.130). Yet since he has arrived back, he has quickly come to realize that 'J'étais désormais étranger à cette ville. Plus rien ne m'y retenait. Ma vie ne s'inscrivait plus dans ses rues' (p.44). Luckily for him, though, this dichotomy, like all the others, only represents the *point de départ*, for as his pilgrimage progresses, his sense of being caught between two stools diminishes, as past and present come together: 'Oui, j'étais à l'étranger', he soon adds to his earlier statement. 'Pourtant, à mesure que mes pas m'entraînaient vers l'appartement de la rue de Courcelles, Paris redevenait peu à peu ma ville' (p.48).

This tendency towards reconciliation would perhaps explain, at least in part, why the aforementioned contrasts within the work seem to be counterbalanced by a no less impressive system of parallels. For a system of parallels there most certainly is. Take, for instance, Carmen's flat, which was such a feature of Jean's life in 1965. It has, we learn, 'une grande entrée au dallage noir et blanc' (p.104), 'une porte si bien encastrée dans le mur qu'on ne la distinguait pas de celui-ci' (p.106), a 'salon [qui . . .] s'avançait en rotonde' (p.107), and drawfuls of old *documents* which are accorded the status of 'archives' (p.137). Now take 45, rue de Courcelles, where Ambrose is currently based when not in his hotel. It too has a 'vestibule au dallage noir et blanc' (p.49) and a secret door (p.48), it too has a 'grande pièce à rotonde' (p.37), and it too has a room set aside for the storing of 'archives' (p.48). Admittedly, Carmen's flat is at street level, whereas Rocroy's is on the second floor, but this perhaps serves better to emphasize the initial discrepancy between the two main time-blocks, as a result of which, as we have seen, the movement from present to past is inexorably *downwards* (the secret room at the rue de

Courcelles, we recall, is also on the ground floor). In most other respects, quite palpably, the comparison holds up well.

Much the same can be said about the amorous attachments formed in the novel, for nearly all of the couples we encounter are, on the whole, incompatible in terms of age. Jean (with Carmen), Maillot (with Drida Bricard), Doris (with Maillot), Carmen (with Farmer and Blin) and Ghita (with Rocroy) each settle down with a partner who is so much older than them, so well established on the far side of the generation gap, that, once again, we can talk about different temporal levels being combined. And if this uncommon pairing already smacks of the typical *modianesque* theme of surrogate parenthood,[6] then the relationship between Jean and Rocroy, in another dazzling *jeu de miroirs*, serves explicitly to confirm this impression. For the latter is very much a father figure for Dekker, being just as able to adopt 'une voix douce et paternelle' (p.125) as to elicit the eloquent response: 'Il m'avait parlé comme un père parle à son fils' (p.151). Indeed, he can even be said to have fostered his young *protégé* in his literary career, advising him first to take up the pen, and then leaving him the legacy of dossiers, notes, and so on from which (with the aid of his memories) he will fashion the novel that we are now reading.

This being the case, it is highly significant that, together with Ghita Wattier, Rocroy should have lived where he did in the rue de Courcelles. The second-floor flat in question, at number 45, was also once occupied by Marcel Proust,[7] and Proust, too, has obviously served as a sort of *parrain* to Guise. Time, memory, the past and identity – key features, as has been seen, of *Quartier perdu* – are Proustian themes *par excellence*, and so is the notion of the journey, which likewise characterizes Ambrose's text: Carmen's flat is described as a ship (pp.106–7, 109, 110); the narrator informs us: 'J'étais comme un voyageur qui vient d'arriver à destination et s'étonne de ne plus être secoué par les cahots du train' (p.80), and this is not to mention numerous other instances of the metaphor, such as the use of the word *pèlerinage* or the already-noted image of freewheeling downhill. In fact, the closer the narrative is studied, the greater the echoes of *A la recherche du temps perdu* become, with Guise experiencing his own equivalent of the *madeleine* sensation – 'Il suffit que je regarde Hayward conduire [. . .] et que je sente l'odeur d'Acqua di Selva, pour me rappeler tous les détails de cette nuit d'il y a vingt ans' (p.161) – and discovering, after Marcel, that the terminus of his journey must lie in literary creation, the pursuit of which will give his life the cohesion it currently lacks: 'Et si le passé et le présent se mêlaient?' he eventually realizes. 'Pourquoi n'y aurait-il pas, à travers les péripéties en apparence les plus diverses d'une vie, une unité secrète, un parfum dominant?' (p.86).

Of course, as we well know, Proust is the avowed literary *parrain* of Modiano himself, so what we patently have here, once again, is an authorial recognition of debt, a sort of 'filial' acceptance of the 'paternal' bequest. And should any doubts about this remain, they can perhaps be dispelled by referring to two other aspects of *Quartier perdu*, both of which similarly allude to the novelist's inheritance as a writer. First, the mention of baroness Orczy, 'ma marraine littéraire en quelque sorte, à laquelle j'avais succédé 19, avenue de la Costa, Monte-Carlo' (p.28), which not only provides us with an *explicit* acknowledgement of the legacy absorbed (that of the inventor of the Scarlet Pimpernel, whose influence will soon be further evidenced by *Une aventure de Choura*), but also with a teasingly *cryptic* one as well (Modiano, we recall, succeeded Maurice Sachs at 15 quai Conti in Paris).[8] Second, there is the nickname which Rocroy gives to Ghita – Gyp – and which was the *nom de plume* of one of Proust's many aristocratic acquaintances, the Comtesse de Martel de Janville (1849–1932), who according to Vivienne Mylne was a best-selling novelist and author of a mass of books, 'the vast majority of [which] were *dialogués*, with many – though not all – laid out like plays. She sometimes used letters, and also quotations, real or invented, from newspapers; her cutting from one scene to another anticipates the technique which Martin du Gard would refer to as "cinématographique".'[9] As may now readily be conceded, there are obvious similarities here with Modiano's own technique. He may not, it is true, use the *dialogué* form for his most important texts, but he *has* clearly set out his previous book, *Poupée blonde*, in the guise of a play. Furthermore, he too includes in his novels all sorts of different *documents* (in *Quartier perdu*, for instance, we find a newspaper advert on p.14, Hayward's card on p.26, Rocroy's letter on pp. 29–31, a newspaper article on pp.31–2, police reports on pp. 52–3 and 54–5, and a note on pp.81–2), and he too employs a distinctively cinematographic style (as when Guise has no sooner booked a taxi for later than it has arrived and is picking him up – pp.154–5).[10]

Thus, as ever, Modiano can be seen to be placing himself in a discernible literary tradition.[11] Yet by keeping his references to his *parrains littéraires* implicit for the most part, he is simultaneously doing something more besides: he is punctuating his text with 'clues' to be interpreted, and thereby helping to establish his book as a sort of informal *polar*. For an informal *polar* is precisely what *Quartier perdu* is, with Ambrose Guise formed in exactly the same mould as most of the author's previous protagonists – that of narrator–detective whose aim is to clarify the past. And to achieve this he must go through the various stages of standard police procedure, that is to say: set up an investigation, exploit his own memories where applicable, question any surviving witnesses, consult relevant documents, and then sit down and write up the results. But whereas real law enforcers are never allowed to fabricate evidence – and this is where the aforementioned informality comes in – he, as a novelist, has no such restrictions to hold him back. On the contrary (as Serge Alexandre also discovered), it is all the better for him if he can let his imagination run wild and actively fantasize.

This freedom to invent no doubt explains the thread of unreality that runs through *Quartier perdu*, a thread which, though sometimes hidden, regularly comes to the surface in a variety of different guises. One such is the depiction of Dekker's old acquaintances as ghosts. 'J'imaginais mal les Hayward, Fouquet et tous les autres à la clarté du jour', we are informed. '[. . .] Je ne les apercevais que la nuit, comme si, déjà, à cette époque, ils n'étaient plus que des fantômes' (pp.162–3). Of all the ghostly apparitions we encounter, though, by far the most striking is the present-day Georges Maillot. White-haired, in a white coat and driving a white Lancia, he regularly makes a late-night journey around Paris, pursued by Tintin Carpentieri and, on one occasion, Ambrose Guise as well. Perhaps his appearance relates to something he said in 1965: 'A Paris [. . .] j'ai l'impression d'être un fantôme' (p.131). Perhaps it shows the dangers of taking too keen an interest in the past (Tintin looks out for the phantom every twenty-four hours, and is so obsessed that 'il avait suffi de prononcer le nom de Georges Maillot et le présent n'existait plus pour lui' – p.59). Or perhaps it just demonstrates that Ambrose, too, is pursuing spectres (his nocturnal drive being a further manifestation of the theme of the voyage).[12] Yet whatever the explanation (or explanations) may be, one thing remains certain – we are much closer here to the world of dreams than to that of traditional reality.

What is more, this impression of *rêverie* is far from being localized; as in virtually all of Modiano's novels, other aspects of the text help consolidate its emergence. There are, for example, the echoes already cited above, and which, in harness with a network of leitmotifs, give the narrative a dream-like, cyclical feel – not for nothing will Ambrose hear the leitmotival tune, *Avril au Portugal*, and remark that it is 'distendu, ralenti, comme dans un rêve' (p.114).[13] Better still, there are countless facets of the work which, if not always overtly contradictory, nonetheless seem to defy the bounds of conscious logic. The chronology is not unquestionably consistent; Jean can have no money (p.109) and then apparently buy a paper (p.110); Maillot's wife is introduced as Maria Giovanna (p.81), but is later referred to as Doris (pp.134, 149–50); and if Guise's British passport actually is as he describes it – pale green with two golden lions – he would never have been allowed back into France at all![14] Thirdly, there is the theme of the oriental, which (in another contrast) subverts the Frenchness of Paris and thereby adds to the sense of unreality, our *dépaysement* starting with the appearance of Yoko Tatsuké, proceeding thanks to the Japanese tourists and the 'quelque chose de japonais chez [Rocroy]' (p.39), re-emerging in Carmen's *meuble* and *paravent* – both Chinese – and reaching its zenith with the pagoda opposite 45 rue de Courcelles.[15] And it is no coincidence that a film crew – complete with Japanese actor – is currently shooting at this selfsame location. Being 'cet univers parallèle à l'espace romanesque',[16] the cinema, too, evokes the imaginary, so much so that when Ambrose meets the crew's assistant director (whose very nickname – Tintin – augments the element of fantasy),[17] he is left reflecting: 'Je sortais d'un mauvais rêve. Tintin existait-il vraiment?' (p.64). Nor is it a coincidence that the film being made is *Rendez-vous de juillet*, for as Guise himself makes clear: 'Moi aussi, sans très bien m'en rendre compte, j'étais revenu à Paris pour un rendez-vous de juillet' (p.73).[18] In other words, once again, we find ourselves faced with a form of self-reference, an echo of the *mise en abyme*, whereby the text openly alludes to its own production, and hence further erodes its links with traditional reality.

This use of the *mise en abyme* suggests, of course, that there are a number of similarities between author and narrator, and as ever

Patrick Modiano

this is certainly the case, although appropriately, given the essentially ludic nature of the device, there are also enough differences to make total identification impossible.[19] For example, like Modiano, Guise was born in Boulogne-Billancourt in July 1945 (but on the twenty-fifth, not the thirtieth); his mother was a music-hall 'girl' (but English and not Belgian); he spent his childhood on the Left Bank and part of his adolescence in Haute-Savoie (but did not subsequently remain in France); he is contented in his family life (but has three children, not two); and he is currently working on his ninth novel (but does not produce works of a high literary standard). This last point, relating to the common ground of fiction-writing, in turn leads on to other areas of overlap between the real-life novelist and his central character, with the narrative that Ambrose 'produces' evoking countless previous texts in the *œuvre modianesque*. The concept of a 'petit groupe' (p.132) of funlovers harks back, through almost every intermediate work, to *La Ronde de nuit* at the very least;[20] the reappearance of Andrée Karvé and the fact that Dekker was 'un si brave garçon' (p.30), 'le seul à [s']être tiré d'affaire' (p.42), remind us inevitably of *De si braves garçons*; the two key spots in the rue de Courcelles – number 45 and the Chinese pagoda – have already cropped up in *Livret de famille*;[21] the frequent mention of a 'start in life' is an old, reworked refrain;[22] and there is much more of this sense of *déjà vu* besides.

In particular, there is the conclusion of the novel, which not only borrows the theme of amnesia from *Rue des Boutiques Obscures*, but also, as usual, brings no tying up of every loose end. We do, admittedly, come to discover how Ludo was killed, but whether it was murder or manslaughter we cannot really say. 'C'est parti tout seul', we are told by the person who fired the gun (p.174), yet the police report states that there were actually three shots, one first of all and then two more shortly afterwards. Was there at least some element of premeditation? We shall never know, and there was never any chance that we would, since by his own admission Modiano is incapable of writing *polars* entirely *à la* Simenon. 'Ce qui m'ennuie', he reveals, 'c'est l'obligation de boucler une enquête. Le climat m'intéresse davantage que l'intrigue.'[23] It certainly does, and this explains why his *dénouement* takes place not on the traditional level of content, but rather on the more suggestive level of form. For by the closing pages, we have palpably reached a state of equilibrium. Guise has tracked down the young woman who provides the missing link between the 1960s and the 1980s, and he has not found her in any old situation. She has just returned from the south of France (thereby offsetting her earlier residence on the avenue du *Nord*), and this serves to emphasize that a journey has been completed – *her* journey, obviously, but another one as well, because: 'Elle revient de plus loin encore. Carmen. Rocroy. La-Varenne-Saint-Hilaire. Toutes ces rues en pente' (p.181). This image of the sloping street, as has been seen, has long been associated with Ambrose's own 'descent' into his 'vie antérieure', and given that he and the woman are now standing 'là où vient mourir la pente du Boulevard Sérurier' (p.181), this can mean but one thing – it is his own voyage, his own pilgrimage that has finally come to an end. Stylistically at least, then, the 'enquête' has been 'bouclée'. And although this final – and skilful – drawing together of themes is by no means new in the context of the *œuvre*, it nevertheless stands out as being particularly impressive, and confirms what might already have been inferred: after the somewhat experimental *Une jeunesse* and *De si braves garçons*, both of which pale in the bright light of his previous novels, Modiano, in *Quartier perdu*, is assuredly back to his brilliant best.

If *Quartier perdu* is one of Modiano's richest novels, then the text which follows it, *Dimanches d'août*, is undoubtedly (and with typical contrariness) one of the sparest. Never before have we encountered so few key characters in a work of this type, and never before have we been so struck by 'une disparition presque complète de l'intrigue, pourtant déjà mince dans un livre comme *Villa Triste*.'[24] Indeed, were a *résumé* of the 'plot' to be requested, it would take little more than a line or two to provide one: Sylvia falls in love with Jean, the narrator, and then runs away with him, stealing her ex-lover Villecourt's diamond in the process; somehow tracked down, she disappears, and neither she nor the gemstone are ever seen again. So, a tangled web of intrigue this most definitely is not.

Yet light though the 'content' of the work may be, there is still enough of it, even in summary, to suggest where the novelist has sought his inspiration: the genre of the *roman policier*, with its concentration on crime and mystery. And that this debt to the *polar* is, in fact, a real one is confirmed by the now-familiar activities of Jean, for like most of his predecessors, he readily slips into the role of amateur detective. He pursues his own *enquête* into his girlfriend's disappearance, asking questions and interviewing witnesses, and when he comes to write down the results, it is with police procedure very much in mind. 'Je voudrais noter les détails [. . .]', he explicitly states at one stage, 'comme si je rédigeais un rapport de police ou si je répondais à l'interrogatoire d'un inspecteur' (p.80).

Thanks to this semi-professionalism, he eventually clears up a good many of the riddles which perplex him, most notably that of the Neals, who claim to be a couple known to have long since died. But his success is far from total. We never do discover, for example, the exact cause of Sylvia's disappearance – she might have been abducted, and the diamond stolen, but this is never said to be the case for sure. Nor, more importantly, do we learn a great deal about Jean. He is prone to anguish and panic, that we do know, and, especially after Sylvia's departure, to feelings of solitude, emptiness and despair. But in terms of his *état civil*, he is a lot less easy to categorize. He seems to have no family ties to speak of and, perhaps because of this, no surname either. Indeed, it is not until page 61 that we are even apprised of his first name (another mystery solved!).[25] And that is not all. Although this profile might suggest that Modiano has taken a step back towards his early narrators – who are also of uncertain identity and out of sorts with the world – he has, if anything, gone back a whole stage further. For Jean, almost impossibly, is much more of an unknown quantity than his already mysterious predecessors: uniquely (and fittingly, given the aforementioned spareness of the work), he is even bereft of those traits which, on the basis of previous practice, we might reasonably have expected him to share with his creator.[26] Without a doubt, then, at the very heart of the novel, at our main point of contact with the text, there lies an enigma, an enigma which, like so many others, is never reassuringly clarified.

Needless to say, perhaps, this lack of certainty with respect to content is aggravated, as in all of Modiano's works, by matters of style and form. The start of the novel raises a series of questions instead of establishing facts (Who are the unspecified *je* and *il*? In what circumstances did they meet before? How can they cause problems for each other? . . .); the final words – 'ces dimanches d'août' (p.161) – typically eschew a sense of closure in favour of a new beginning (we are taken back to the very title-page of the work);[27] and in between, the narrative is conspicuously divided not by numbered chapter headings (as in, say, *De si braves garçons*), but rather (as in *Quartier perdu*) by a succession of long and short gaps, as if to demonstrate, *visually*, that extensive lacunae abound, or, to use Jean's phraseology, that 'tous ces événements récents de ma vie [. . .] me semblaient à moi-même trop fragmentaires, trop discontinus pour être compréhensibles' (p.128).

This reference to the 'visual' aspect of *Dimanches d'août* is by no means ill-founded, for the novel itself actively encourages this response, most notably (as ever in the *œuvre*) by its own constant allusions – if not self-assimilation – to things cinematographic. There are the usual filmic *points de repère*, ranging from the mention of real-life actors (Errol Flynn, René Dary, Raymond Aimos)[28] to the final evocation of the Joinville studios, and whole scenes could again have been written with the cinema specifically in mind, as when Modiano deals with the delicate question of sex: no sooner has Sylvia addressed Jean as *tu* than we get the symbolic appearance of a canoe on the Marne, a gap in the text, and a 'cut' to the two of them much later in his bedroom, where she is in the process of re-dressing (p.155). Now of course, this technique has long been a characteristic of Modiano as a novelist, and can be traced right back to some of his earliest publications.[29] But that said, *Dimanches d'août* is arguably the most film-like of all his writings so far, as two further observations will perhaps illustrate. First, the narrative does not just refer to the seventh art occasionally and incidentally, but, rather, does so *systematically*, thereby prompting the reader to become a sort of 'viewer' of the text, in much the same way as the narrator views – or re-views – the succession of events which he needs to interpret: 'J'ai voulu revisiter tous les endroits où nous étions allés [. . .]: ainsi de ces films que l'on fait revenir en arrière sur la table de montage pour y examiner inlassablement les détails de la même séquence. Mais [. . .] le film se cassait ou bien j'étais arrivé au bout de la bobine' (p.117). Second, there is the dedication of the novel, which is always significant for Modiano, and which, in this instance, clearly hints at the visual aspect of the work to come – not for nothing is one of the two names mentioned that of the recently deceased Marc Grunebaum; Grunebaum was, by the time he died, a well established and experienced *cinéaste*.[30]

The other name cited, Jacques Robert, is not insignificant either: Robert was a professional photographer,[31] and the theme of photography likewise runs the length and breadth of *Dimanches d'août* – witness the key contribution made to the narrative by the seafront 'holiday snaps' man, or the fact that Jean himself once had a 'métier de photographe' (p.29). In this latter instance especially, the deliberate nature of Modiano's ploy is transparent, for if previous practice had been adhered to, the narrator would surely have been a budding writer when he first met Sylvia in La Varenne. That he was not can realistically amount to just one thing: the photographic thread has been introduced advisedly, to support the network of filmic allusions and thereby consolidate the optic impact of the novel.[32]

Yet despite this complementarity of the two visual media, there is also a clear difference in the way in which they are employed in the text. Photography, as always, is seen as a means of preserving the past, a method of freezing reality. Or as Jean says, snapshots are 'les traces qui demeurent plus tard d'un moment éphémère' (p.80), and so 'il ne faut jamais négliger ces sentinelles, leurs appareils en bandoulière, prêtes à vous fixer dans un instantané, tous ces gardiens de la mémoire qui patrouillent dans les rues' (p.80). The cinema, on the other hand, and again as ever in the *œuvre*, is associated with *unreality*, and destroys any documentary qualities the narrative may have had. Thus, when Villecourt is accidentally hit in the face, 'Il n'avait plus beaucoup de réalité. Le sang même qui avait giclé de ses lèvres [. . .] ne paraissait pas être du sang véritable mais un artifice de cinéma' (p.68). Similarly, about thirty pages later we are informed: 'Nous avancions, portés par un tapis roulant et les rues défilaient et nous ne savions plus si le tapis roulant nous entraînait ou bien si nous étions immobiles tandis que le paysage, autour de nous, glissait par cet artifice de cinéma que l'on appelle: transparence' (p.95).

This tension between the real and the unreal is, of course, a feature of all Modiano's writing, and so fundamental is it that, here as elsewhere, it manifests itself in a variety of other forms as well. One of the most visible of these is the depiction of the two principal settings of the text, Nice and La Varenne.[33] Nice, to judge by the places Jean visits there, is unquestionably the same town as the one mapped out on the street plans of today. The public gardens, the main buildings and the major thoroughfares (apart from the occasional confusion of Boulevards and Avenues) – everywhere that is mentioned is instantly and blatantly recognizable. Yet hardly has this note of realism been struck than it is immediately muffled and suppressed. For as in *Rue des Boutiques Obscures*, the city is presented as a 'ville de fantômes' (p.96),[34] and this ghostliness does not just afflict the minor, background characters, but also the key figures of Villecourt (p.68), the Neals (p.76) and the narrator himself (p.36).

La Varennne, on the face of it, contrasts totally with the city of Nice in real life – it is in the north, not the south; it is inland, not by the sea – yet Modiano encourages us to ignore these contrasts and concentrate instead on a certain parallelism between the two sites, a parallelism which he is obviously at pains to stress. 'Il me semblait', Jean remarks of his time on the *bords de Marne*, 'que nous déjeunions dans une enclave de la côte d'Azur transportée en banlieue' (p.145), and this is by no means the only time he connects us to the south of France. The photos he takes around the Villecourts' are modelled on those of a certain Vennemann, whose principal subject was Monte-Carlo; when he sees Sylvia wearing a pareo he thinks of Saint Tropez (p.134); one of the roads he once walked down was the Promenade des Anglais (p.135); and so on and so forth, until the assimilation is complete. And when it is complete, we realize why it was attempted in the first place – to emphasize the fact that, in essence, the two settings have a tremendous amount in common, both being, as Jacques Pécheur has observed, '[des] lieux d'apparence, de trompe-l'œil: l'un, Nice, où les identités sont en transit, l'autre, les plages de la Marne où l'apparence respectable des villas bourgeoises sert à dissimuler l'argent salement gagné, "l'argent des filles"'.[35]

This reference to respectable fronts and 'identités en transit' is an important one, and finds an echo (typically) in the major characters of the novel. Take, for example, the Neals, who, as already mentioned above, are anything but the reputable couple that they claim to be – they are simply hiding behind a mask. And when this mask slips, as it sometimes does, a troubling reality can be glimpsed through the pure façade: 'Brusquement', Jean informs us at one stage, 'j'avais senti flotter, chez Neal, des relents de la Canebière et de Pigalle' (p.105), and this is not mere imagination on his part. His 'ghostly' acquaintance is, in fact, one

Paul Alessandri, a criminal and ex-convict. And as if this 'slippage' between identities were not perplexing enough, it becomes even more so when the Neals are then portrayed as mirror images of Sylvia and the narrator (p.90). So, character merges into character, and identity (as ever for Modiano) becomes an unstable concept.

Yet the problem here is not just one of *fusion*; it is also one of *divergence*, for both Villecourt and Neal, despite their apparent unity, are shown to be different people at different times. 'Cet homme ne ressemblait pas à celui d'il y a sept ans', we are told in respect of the former (p.15), and with the latter (as befits a man living in a house numbered 50*bis*)[36] the metamorphosis can take place at much greater velocity: 'Neal était un homme différent de celui de l'autre soir' (p.82).[37] Indeed, not even the narrator can escape from this rapid changing of role. When he tries to be a detective, making enquiries, he suddenly realizes that, rather like a criminal, '[sa] démarche semblait tout à fait indiscrète – et même suspecte' (p.70), and no sooner has he thought about abandoning the Neals than they do exactly the same to him (pp.110–12). Once again, then, we find ourselves faced with a system of parallels and contrasts, the ultimate aim of which can leave little room for doubt: 'L'interversion et la substitution des rôles [. . .] dissipe[nt] les contours entre rêve et réalité, vérité et mensonge.'[38]

This erosion of frontiers certainly is a key feature of the work, and can similarly be seen in the rejection of linear chronology. From what appears to be the present to a period situated only seven years earlier (the 'only' here suggesting the novelty of this relatively small *décalage* – further proof that Modiano is taking an ever more contemporary focus, even if references to the Occupation still occur), the narrative oscillates backwards and forwards in time, exploiting the now usual technique of the flashback through memory. Occasionally, this oscillation establishes yet another evident contrast within the text, as when Jean avows: 'Au début, quand Sylvia m'a rejoint ici, je voyais les choses d'une manière différente que je ne les vois ce soir' (p.35). But more often than not, the two different temporal levels are fused into one, thanks to a series of statements such as: 'Ma chambre d'aujourd'hui ressemble à celle de la pension Sainte-Anne [. . .]. Il y flotte la même odeur' (p.42). And it is this fusion of past and present which, perhaps more than anything else, gives the 'reality' of the narrative the texture of a dream, all the more so in that the words *rêve* and *rêver* are applied leitmotivally throughout the text (pp.15, 79, 94, 147, etc.). And that is not all. Jean actually does have a dream at one stage, and describes his experience thus: 'Tout finit par se confondre. Les images du passé s'enchevêtrent' (p.46). Significantly, this comment might just as easily have been used to describe *Dimanches d'août* as a whole.

In fact, it might also have been uttered apropos of Modiano's entire *œuvre*, for the extensive network of echoes is not confined to the work we are currently studying. On the contrary. It stretches outwards and backwards (as ever) to take in virtually all of the novels which have gone before. The aforementioned themes of identity and memory, for instance, are nothing if not typically *modianesques*, and it is no surprise either that Jean formulates statements such as: 'L'hôtel Régina [. . .] est l'une de ces rares habitations particulières qui demeurent dans le quartier. Mais sans doute ces vestiges disparaîtront-ils à leur tour' (p.69) – the ravages of time have long preoccupied the author as well. So, too, has the concept of chance, which is likewise taken up again here, with coincidence piling upon coincidence,[39] and the stolen diamond (la Croix du Sud) plainly symbolizing a heartless Fate.[40] A Fate which, for the most part, alights on the shoulders of Sylvia, who (in yet another internal echo) has a somewhat duplicating role to play: inseparably bound to the sought-after jewel (Jean runs off with, and then loses, both of them simultaneously), she, like it, can additionally be seen in symbolic terms – as happiness in the abstract, as joy incarnate, or, more pointedly, given that she has now disappeared, as an enchanting *paradis perdu*,[41] a *paradis perdu* which, once again, links us back to the rest of the *œuvre*.

Even on a less thematic, more detailed level this sense of *déjà vu* is intense. Jean and Sylvia's wish to 'tout recommencer à zéro' (p.36) harks back to *Une jeunesse* and *Poupée blonde* (amongst others); the pension Sainte-Anne resembles that of Mme Portier in *De si braves garçons*;[42] la Croix du Sud was the name of the chalet in *Rue des Boutiques Obscures*; the setting of La-Varenne-Saint-Hilaire is shared with *Quartier perdu*; the reappearance of Pagnon takes us back to *Les Boulevards de ceinture*; the concern with non-human 'pedigrees' ties in with countless previous works;[43] the leitmotival phrase, 'aucune importance' (pp.18, 26, 36, etc.), does anything but innovate; and so the similarities go on, locking *Dimanches d'août* into the pattern set by its pre-decessors, and bestowing on the *œuvre* a character that is manifestly cyclical – as if all of Modiano's output derived from the same, single, protracted bout of *rêverie*.

Yet this repetition from book to book does more than just generate an atmosphere akin to that of a dream world. It provides an opportunity for playful humour as well. When Villecourt and Sylvia disappear, for instance, Jean tries to track them down, but finds himself thwarted in both cases. 'Vous n'êtes même pas de sa famille' (p.33), he is told in respect of the former, as explanation of why his old rival's employers will refuse to tell him anything. And as for the latter, he contacts the police only to discover that their unique concern is with 'recherches dans l'intérêt des familles' (p.124), and that his girlfriend is accordingly deemed unworthy of even the merest investigation on their part. Now obviously, one aim of this double failure is to create an additional parallel within the work, and hence reinforce the *jeu de miroirs* that is constantly taking place there. But a supplementary effect is to evoke Modiano's previous pursuit of his father in his fiction, and thereby emphasize, ludically, that he has abandoned his old obsession with his family and moved on.

Not that *Dimanches d'août* relies entirely on external relation-ships for its humorous element. Far from it. It provokes a considerable number of wry smiles in its own right. For how can we fail to be amused when, say, Jean stares into a car expecting to find Sylvia, only to disturb an amorous couple and be called a *voyeur* (pp.114–15)? And then there is the constant irony of the narrative, evident both in the network of echoes and contrasts and in individual comments such as: 'Nous avons rompu le cercle magique qui nous isolait' (p.57), which, in actual fact, marks the first step on the road to abandonment and solitude. Finally, and fittingly, considering this is the point at which we began, there is Modiano's treatment of the *polar* genre, which is almost ludic in the extreme. Mysteries proliferate at an amazing rate; the detective-hero is as disoriented as everyone else; the traditional recapitulation scene leads nowhere (pp.122–5); the need for precision is taken to excessive lengths;[44] keys open doors way outside the book itself;[45] and other cultural formats (the cinema, the ghost story, etc.) incessantly, if subtly, impose themselves upon the text. In other words, what we are dealing with here is not so much a true detective novel as an affectionate, parodic exploitation of the form – nothing less, in the final analysis, than a *pastiche* of the tale of crime and mystery.

Notes

1. Rolin, 'Patrick Modiano', p.63.
2. Apart from the brief details of Farmer (pp.52–3), the *années noires* crop up mainly allusively, through the use of such words as *bombardement*, *exode*, *décombres* (p.9) or *blackout* (p.18).
3. The words *luminous* and *shadowy* here derive from Modiano's own usage – see p.121 above. For more on the use of black and white in the novel, see Josselin, 'Méfiez-vous du Modiano qui dort', p.57, or Bony, 'Suite en blanc', pp.654–60.
4. The Dukes of Guise have been famous throughout French history, with their role in the religious wars of the sixteenth century bringing them into especial prominence. Dekker clearly brings back to mind the oriental Deyckecaire (du Caire?) of *Les Boulevards de ceinture* (although the author may also be thinking of the Hollywood film actor, Albert Dekker). For more on the possible significance of the narrator's names, see Bony, ibid., p.657.
5. Note also the implicit link here to the familiar (see Note 36 to Chapter 4 above) concept of starting again from scratch, a link soon to be made explicit by Modiano himself: 'C'est une obsession de tout recommencer à zéro. [. . .] Pour recommencer sa vie, le seul moyen c'est de ne plus parler sa langue maternelle' (Chapsal, '10 ans après: Patrick Modiano', p.58).
6. It is also, of course, the latest example of a tendency seen earlier in Brossier (in *Une jeunesse*) – a middle-aged person consorts with someone years younger and, thereby, seeks to cling on to an ever more distant youth.
7. See Philippe Michel-Thiriet, *The Book of Proust*, translated by Jan Dalley (London, Chatto and Windus, 1989), p.94. This work also contains a ground plan of the flat (p.376), to which Modiano's descriptions can usefully be compared.
8. See Note 114 to Chapter 2 above.
9. 'Martin du Gard, the *Roman dialogué*, and Gyp', *French Studies Bulletin*, 38 (Spring 1991), pp.3–5 (p.3). Gyp's Proustian

connections and the fact that Ghita lives at 45 rue de Courcelles suggest that Modiano has not stumbled on his character's nickname by accident. Indeed, it is possible that he was first drawn to the Comtesse de Martel's work by her renowned anti-Semitism, for we know that he devoured anti-Semitic literature prior to composing *La Place de l'Étoile*.

10. Note that this 'cut' is signalled to the reader by a gap in the text – yet another example of how even the blank spaces are meaningful in Modiano's work (cf. Note 63 to Chapter 3 above). For more on the novelist's cinematic style, see p.34 (including Note 76) above. Note also the authorial admission: 'Je désire laisser des silences. Au cinéma et dans tous les arts, j'ai toujours été obsédé par ce qui est suggéré' (Montaudon, 'Patrick Modiano', p.15).

11. Note also that the promiscuous Carmen has something of Mérimée's heroine about her, while the title of Guise's *Jarvis Who Loves Me* palpably derives from Ian Fleming's *The Spy Who Loved Me*.

12. Cf. Martinoir, 'Sur le cadastre de la fiction': '[Maillot] est une figure métaphorique du désir et de la maladie [...] de l'impossible retour' (p.5).

13. Note also, apropos of this mention of leitmotifs, the familiar 'aucune importance' (pp.51, 67, 69, 75, 114, 126 and 150).

14. For more of Modiano's liberties here, see Joye, *Littérature immédiate*, p.95.

15. Incongruous as it may seem, there is indeed a *pagode chinoise* across the road from Proust's old flat – the ultimate clash of eastern and western cultures.

16. Martinoir, 'Sur le cadastre de la fiction', p.5. Note that Modiano is well aware of this parallelism – see Maury, 'Patrick Modiano', p.104.

17. Tintin is, of course, the hero of Hergé's famous comic strips.

18. Note also that *Rendez-vous de juillet* is a real-life movie (made by Jacques Becker in 1949). This allusion to the cinema, when added to the earlier *clins d'œil* towards literature (Proust, Gyp, etc.), popular song (*Avril au Portugal*) and strip cartoons (Tintin), serves to demonstrate, once again, the amazing breadth of Modiano's cultural references.

19. This playfulness of the text cannot be overemphasized. Already seen in the cryptic allusions mentioned above, it is further conveyed (and, indeed, symbolized) by the key

character in Guise's past – a certain *Ludo* Fouquet.

20. In addition to the gangsters of 3*bis* square Cimarosa, see, most strikingly, the baron's *bande* in *Villa Triste* (p.145), or the group depicted in *Memory Lane* (pp.9ff.).

21. See *Livret de famille*, pp.26, 76. Marignan's 'new life' writing a series of books in English (p.26) further highlights the precursive nature of this work *vis-à-vis Quartier perdu*.

22. See *Quartier perdu*, pp.31, 77, 88, 103 and cf., say, *Memory Lane*, p.69.

23. Rolin, 'Patrick Modiano', p.63.

24. Czarny, 'Patrick Modiano: *Dimanches d'août*', p.76.

25. This late naming of the narrator may, of course, be another 'borrowing' from Proust, all the more so in that, as we shall see, other such 'borrowings' are discernible in the text.

26. There is one possible exception here: the fact that he is called Jean – Jean is Modiano's second forename (a point not without significance for *Quartier perdu* and, as we shall see, subsequent works in the *œuvre* as well).

27. Note also that the phrase itself, as Gerald Prince points out ('Patrick Modiano (30 July 1945–)', p.152), is typically ambiguous, additionally suggesting 'dimanches doux'.

28. René Dary (1905–74) started out as a child actor and remained in the profession for the rest of his working life. Raymond Aimos (1889–1944) died, as Modiano rightly suggests (pp.21, 154), in the heat of the Liberation, and is perhaps best known today for his role in Julien Duvivier's *La Belle Équipe* (1936). For brief details of Errol Flynn, see Note 11 to Chapter 3 above.

29. A more recent comparison is *Quartier perdu*, p.118, well analysed by Jean-Claude Joye (*Littérature immédiate*, p.110).

30. He was also, no doubt, a family friend – see *Livret de famille*, p.46.

31. He was, it seems, the 'photographe des Editions Gallimard', and had died in a car crash in July 1985 (see Audouard, 'Modiano: il n'y a pas beaucoup d'écrivains de sa hauteur . . .', pp.52–3).

32. Note also the purely practical point, which Modiano himself will later stress – a writer or a photographer, for him, 'c'est la même chose. Comme j'écris des romans à la première personne [. . .], j'essaie [. . .] de trouver quelqu'un qui ait une activité proche de la mienne, [. . .] pour lui permettre de

formuler certaines choses' (Montaudon, 'Patrick Modiano', p.16).

33. Note also the aforementioned reference to real people such as Raymond Aimos, the appearance of whom in the text makes the reader (as usual) unsure of the exact, overall status of the book – are the characters being drawn from life or invented?

34. See also p.35 and cf. *Rue des Boutiques Obscures*, p.42.

35. 'Patrick Modiano: *Dimanches d'août*', p.18.

36. This use of *bis* is significant on at least two counts. First, it embodies, just like Neal, a same/different dialectic – 50*bis* is *like* 50 (being an 'encore' of that number), yet it is plainly quite *distinct* (being an entirely separate residence). Second, having no independent identity of its own (it defines itself in relation to number 50, and, furthermore, is situated where no house is normally to be found), it evokes a sense of indeterminacy, and so symbolizes the uncertainty of both Neal and the settings in general. (For other examples of this use of *bis* and, accordingly, proof that the ploy is of wider applicability, see *La Ronde de nuit, passim* (3*bis* square Cimarosa), *Les Boulevards de ceinture*, p.70, *Rue des Boutiques Obscures*, pp.86–7, 99, 107, 150, *Une jeunesse*, pp.79, 177, *Quartier perdu*, p.54, or, to look forward to a future text, *Voyage de noces*, p.153.)

37. See also pp.17, 20, 34, 107. This multiplicity of the self over time is, of course, like so much of Modiano's work, eminently Proustian. Cf. e.g. *A la recherche du temps perdu*, II, p.228 ('après cette première métamorphose, Albertine devait changer encore bien des fois pour moi'), or II, p.16 (where we see 'la transmutation de M. de Charlus en une personne nouvelle'). For a further nod in the direction of Proust, see later on p.15 ('Peut-être avait-il oublié des pans entiers du passé ou fini par se persuader que certains événements, aux conséquences si lourdes pour nous tous, n'avaient jamais eu lieu') and cf. *A la recherche du temps perdu*, IV, pp.549–50 ('Non seulement certaines gens ont de la mémoire et d'autres pas [. . .], mais même à égalité de mémoire, deux personnes ne se souviennent pas des mêmes choses').

38. Clerval, 'Patrick Modiano: *Dimanches d'août* (Gallimard)', pp.89–90.

39. See e.g. the photographer who knows Alessandri (p.120), or the fact that Neal and Villecourt happen to meet up with Jean

and Sylvia again.

40. For other examples of fate in *Dimanches d'août*, see pp.129, 149. For more on the symbolism of la Croix du Sud, see Poirot-Delpech, 'Un diamant gros comme le Négresco', p.14.

41. See e.g. p.161: 'Jamais nous n'avions été aussi heureux qu'à ces moments-là'. Note also that Sylvia's surname, before she takes on Villecourt's, is Heuraeux (a slight elaboration of the adjective *heureux*).

42. See *De si braves garçons*, pp.152–4 and cf. *Dimanches d'août*, pp.38–44.

43. The pedigree in question here is that of the diamond – see *Dimanches d'août*, pp.126–7. Cf. the earlier interest in the life histories of, say, dogs (*Livret de famille*, p.154) and horses (*Quartier perdu*, p.144). Note also that, as with so much else in Modiano's books, this concern is palpably double-edged – on the one hand, it acts as a parallel, reflecting the obsession with people's *état civil*, and on the other, it serves as an ironic contrast, with more often being known about the animals and objects than about the individuals who surround them.

44. See Jean's obsession with finding the *mot juste* (pp.46, 49, 58).

45. See e.g. Neal's comment on p.93 ('Je n'ai aucun mérite à cela: je ne me suis donné que la peine de naître et d'hériter beaucoup, beaucoup d'argent de mon père'), which is clearly an allusion to Beaumarchais's Figaro (see Beaumarchais, *Œuvres*, edited by Pierre Larthomas (Paris, Gallimard, Bibliothèque de la Pléiade, 1988), p.469: 'Noblesse, fortune, un rang, des places; tout cela rend si fier! Qu'avez-vous fait pour tant de biens? Vous vous êtes donné la peine de naître, et rien de plus').

6

Childhood to the Fore: 'Remise de peine' and 'Vestiaire de l'enfance'

Un écrivain pense et repense toujours à ce qu'il a vu dans son enfance.

Patrick Modiano

Son enfance, c'est la clef de Patrick [. . .]. Pour lui, c'est le paradis perdu, l'âge d'or, un monde d'hier à la Zweig.

Dominique Modiano

As the last two chapters have endeavoured to show, the 1980s saw a marked progression in Modiano's approach to his writing. At the start of the decade, in *Une jeunesse* and *De si braves garçons*, he is undoubtedly in a somewhat experimental mood, and seems to be moving closer to the more traditional, 'story-telling' type of novel. Then, having thus taken one step backwards towards the past, he rapidly takes another two forwards, refining his original interest in the detective novel, and producing the unquestionably modern *Quartier perdu* and *Dimanches d'août*. These two developments, taken together, are immensely significant, demonstrating, quite manifestly, that the author's pre-1980 *angoisse* has slowly been alleviated, and that he is now trying to find the correct form and style for a less emotionally driven type of fiction. Indeed, his next series of publications – from 1986 to 1989 – will provide further evidence of this increased stability, for they relate almost entirely, and virtually without exception, to a topic that has proved too painful for him even to contemplate addressing in his writing before: his childhood.[1] *Une aventure de Choura* (1986), *Une fiancée pour Choura* (1987) and *Catherine Certitude* (1988) are all written, by his own admission, not just for his two young daughters (and, by extension, for all French children), but also because: 'Il n'y a pas tellement de différence entre un livre pour enfants et un autre. On écrit d'abord pour soi. On ne pense pas que c'est pour les enfants. On songe à sa propre enfance, c'est une nostalgie. Parce qu'au fond les lectures enfantines sont les premières qui vous ont frappé.'[2] And this pursuit of 'sa propre enfance' becomes even more evident in his two major works of the period, *Remise de peine* (1988) and *Vestiaire de l'enfance* (1989), as the pages which follow will now seek to confirm.

Merely to glimpse the cover of *Remise de peine*, which sports the red and white livery of Le Seuil rather than the hitherto omnipresent buff of Gallimard, is to realize that Modiano, like so many of his characters of the 1980s, has now reached a point in his career where, quite visibly, he can no longer advance without forcing himself, as it were, to 'repartir à zéro'.[3] 'Ce livre', he obligingly confirms, 'il fallait [. . .] une espèce de changement pour que je l'écrive. [. . .] j'avais commencé à l'écrire [. . .] avant mon premier roman. Mais je n'y suis pas arrivé. [. . .] En fait, c'est un peu le livre que j'aurais voulu comme mon premier livre.'[4] And it is not hard to see why – this work is clearly his most confessional piece to date, and deals with what is perhaps the most important period of his entire life: that time in the mid-1950s when, in the company of his younger brother Rudy, he lived out the late childhood that was to mould him and persecute him for countless years to come. Not that he admits to having written a formal autobiography – what he has produced, he argues, is 'quelque chose de romanesque avec des éléments autobiographiques'.[5] In the minds of most of the critics, though, there was little doubt at all. The book was 'un récit autobiographique',[6] and as such its significance was all too glaringly obvious: '*Remise de peine* [. . .] est le creuset des romans antérieurs [. . .] de Patrick Modiano, où l'on pourra découvrir, à l'occasion, des clés.'[7] This talk of revelations is justified, so much so, in fact, that it is from this precise angle, at least initially, that Modiano's eleventh major work can most fruitfully be approached.

Of all the various insights provided by *Remise de peine*, arguably the clearest – and the best – relate to the (comparatively small) number of characters who animate its pages. And prime amongst these, in terms of importance, are the parents of the narrator, the now grown-up Patoche, for the depiction of this couple complements what Modiano has already said elsewhere in respect of his own particular mother and father. *Le père*, for example, now seems to have been arrested not once during the troubled years of the German Occupation, but rather twice:

> Il avait été arrêté un soir de février dans un restaurant de la rue de Marignan. [. . .] Il avait profité de la pénombre et d'un instant d'inattention des policiers [. . .] pour s'enfuir.
>
> L'année suivante, on l'avait appréhendé à son domicile. On l'avait conduit au Dépôt, puis dans une annexe du camp de Drancy, à Paris, quai de la Gare [. . .].
>
> Une nuit, quelqu'un était venu en voiture [. . .] et avait fait libérer mon père. (pp.116–17)

This second detention certainly comes as something of a surprise to us (although it would, of course, further explain why the young Modiano was to become so obsessed with the unsavoury *années noires*).[8] Less unexpected yet just as resonant (we have already encountered this point in the pages above), is the behaviour of the father after the war, once he has married and started a family – from French Equatorial Africa to Colombia in South America, he is almost constantly away from home travelling, abroad on exotic business trips. And as if that were not bad enough, what we are told about *la mère* is hardly any more reassuring either – a working actress prone to going off on tour (and leaving her two boys in the care of female friends), she, too, is regularly separated from her sons for extensive periods of time (pp.11, 142). So, to the blight of the much-publicized paternal absence, Modiano now seems to be adding the regular 'disappearance' of his mother.

This mention of maternal 'abandonment' marks a vital new development in the *œuvre*,[9] and as such is eminently noteworthy for two major reasons. First, it helps throw light on the string of actress-model-chorus girls who adorn the pages of Modiano's fiction,[10] for where must these creations have their roots, if not in the person of the novelist's *comédienne* mother?[11] And that is not all. Once this initial inference has been made, it is possible to proceed further down the same path and make another, of much greater consequence this time since it suggests *why* the link between parent and characters should exist: just as paternal surrogates are used to stand in for the missing father, so too, it can be argued, is the mannequin-starlet figure deployed to counteract maternal absence.[12] This being the case, the author's early comment on his literary practice (see p.42 above) is an unhelpful guide to his work as a whole, for as can now confidently be asserted, once he begins to move his focus away from the *années noires* and their 'impureté', he comes, most markedly, to evoke *both* of his parents in his creative writing.[13]

The second reason why this 'motherlessness' is important has already been touched on above – coupled with the long-known lack of a father, the want of a mother ensured that Modiano was, along with his beloved brother Rudy, transformed into a sort of quasi-orphan as a child. 'Nous n'avions plus de nouvelles de nos parents', we are now confidentially informed. 'La dernière carte de notre mère était une vue [. . .] de Tunis. Notre père nous avait écrit de Brazzaville. Puis de Bangui. Et puis, plus rien' (p.94). This near-total solitude could not, of course, fail to have severe repercussions, and repercussions there most certainly were. Not for nothing does Patoche quickly find himself in trouble at school, being expelled on more than one occasion (pp.32, 142), and not for nothing does he immerse himself in a substitute family either – the author is clearly evoking his own experiences here, experiences which, fascinatingly, throw an entirely new light on to much of his earlier fiction.

Take, for example, the 'drôle de famille' (p.33) formed by Annie F., her mother Mathilde, Hélène Toch and a young child-minder dubbed Blanche-Neige: the real-life individuals they are based on have obviously served as models for previous characters as well. Annie F., the stand-in mother,[14] is a notable case in point. In her mid-twenties, blonde, 'le visage doux et délicat' (p.16), exuding 'tant de douceur féminine, une si grande fragilité' (p.113) and favouring 'une robe bleu pâle' as evening wear (p.16), she has clearly been echoed in many of Modiano's earlier female figures, the majority of whom similarly combine femininity and vulnerability.[15] Furthermore, she has the undoubted ambiguity of her predecessors too, for in counterpoint to her somewhat tender and delicate side, she has 'quelque chose de brutal' about her (p.16), and a good many more 'masculine' traits besides: her hair is cut short; her daytime costume is 'un blouson d'homme' with 'pantalons noirs très étroits' (p.16), and she regularly visits the dubious 'Carroll's' club in Paris.[16] Thus, effectively, Annie is two different women in one, and just as her 'womanly' aspect seems to have gone into many of Modiano's insecure *jeunes premières*, so too does something of her 'virile' personality appear to have fed into the other key type of female character found in the *œuvre* – the supremely confident, sexually uninhibited (and often self-prostituting) figure.[17]

Another substitute relative who creates an impression of *déjà vu* is 'la petite' Hélène Toch, the narrator's makeshift aunt.[18] 'Une brune d'une quarantaine d'années, avec un front large et des pommettes' (p.15), Hélène immediately reminds us of, say, our old acquaintance Denise Dressel (*Livret de famille*), not to mention the countless other high-cheek-boned women who, like her, possess this distinctive 'air mongol'.[19] What is more, when the spotlight is switched from Miss Toch's face to her apparel, our sense of familiarity increases: 'Hélène s'habillait d'une drôle de manière [. . .]: un pantalon de cheval avec des bottes, des chemisiers aux manches bouffantes [. . .], un fuseau de ski noir, ou même un boléro incrusté de nacre' (pp.33–4). Now, such an extravagant dress sense – a relic of her days in the circus – might not in itself seem widely significant (although exoticism in general is often a feature of Modiano's women), but one element in this list of accoutrements most definitely is: the boots and the riding breeches, for the preceding texts are, quite visibly, dotted with women who share this love of things equestrian.[20]

Moving away now from the 'drôle de famille', and on to the other characters in *Remise de peine*, the resonant drawing from life can be seen to continue. Frede, as *patronne* of 'le Carroll's' and wearer of 'des vestes d'homme' which look like 'des vestes de cavalière' (p.19), plainly provides an artistic link between Annie and Hélène (combining the presumed lesbianism of the one with the equestrian impact of the other), and hence seems, in turn, to evoke further memories of Modiano's 'horsewoman' figures (all the more so in that the sexuality of these *amazones* tends, on the face of it, to be no more conventional than hers apparently is).[21] Yet of all the people we are introduced to in the book, she is the one who can most easily be traced back to her model.[22]

Harder to identify historically, yet no less important for that, are Jean D. and Roger Vincent,[23] with the former in particular striking a chord. Consider, for example, his physical appearance in the 1950s: 'grand et mince [. . .]. Des cheveux noirs et un visage aux traits réguliers [. . .] yeux marron [. . .] sa coupe de cheveux: une brosse longue' (pp.69–70). Add in 'un regard affectueux et naïf' (p.101), and the fact that 'il s'habillait d'un blouson de daim

[. . .], de chaussures à semelles de crêpe' (p.69), and what we have here is clearly one of Modiano's male archetypes.[24] Indeed, when he turns up again in the 1960s, our feelings of preacquaintance intensify, for he has 'à peine vieilli' (p.97) and as if to emphasize this constant youthfulness, he has acquired a girlfriend about ten years his junior.

Strangely enough, much the same could be said here of Roger Vincent, for he shares this ability to withstand time: 'Ses cheveux étaient blancs', we are apprised, 'mais il n'avait pas l'air vieux' (pp.62–3). Given such an early (and joint) example of agelessness to ponder, it is hardly surprising that, once he took up the pen, Modiano should make the theme of eternal youth a key leitmotif of his work.[25] Nor is it surprising, in retrospect, that he should pepper his *œuvre* with American convertibles,[26] for they no doubt derive from exactly the same source: the man who served as model for Roger Vincent, one of whose prized possessions, it just so happens, was a 'voiture américaine décapotable' (p.59).

If Jean and Roger would appear, like their leading ladies, to evoke the 'keys' behind so many of Modiano's previous characters, then so, too, do members of the supporting cast in *Remise de peine*. To begin simply with the paternal acquaintances acknowledged in the work, Sacha Gordine has already been mentioned in *Villa Triste*; Fly has turned up in '1, rue Lord-Byron';[27] Geza Pellemont has featured in *Villa Triste, Livret de famille* and, presumably, '1, rue Lord-Byron' (in the guise of Geza Belmont); and as for Stioppa de D., can he realistically be anyone other than the Stioppa de Djagoriew of *Rue des Boutiques Obscures*? It is unlikely, to say the least. Just as unlikely as our failing to put a name to Andrée K.: thanks to the revelation that she is 'la femme du grand toubib' (p.58), we can instantly identify her as Andrée Karvé, the Andrée Karvé of *De si braves garçons* and *Quartier perdu*.[28]

Thus, without a doubt, *Remise de peine* provides great insights into Modiano's choice of characters in his fiction, and serves to confirm something he said about them way back in 1975. When asked if they were mere figments of his imagination, he dissentingly replied: 'Non, je les ai rencontrés quand j'étais petit. Je les ai décrits tels que je les ai connus.'[29] So, the existence of real-life 'keys' seems indisputable.

This historical base might, in turn, help shed light on some of the other features of the *œuvre modianesque*, and most notably on its cult of marginality. For example, quite apart from the models for Annie and Frede (who, as has been seen, lived on the fringes of 'conventional' *sexual* behaviour), nearly all the adults evoked in *Remise de peine* seem, to a greater or lesser extent, to be involved in another, more embracing form of marginal activity: crime and illegality. Witness the dubious company that they are revealed to keep. Jean D., we already know (from Note 23), is acquainted with a lead player in the Ben Barka Affair, and Andrée Karvé (definitely) and Hélène and Roger (possibly) are connected to the now infamous 'bande de la rue Lauriston' (pp.87–8).[30] In this latter instance especially, the effect on the young Modiano can be seen to have been immense, for as he concedes through his narrator: 'J'ignorais que "la bande de la rue Lauriston" me hanterait si longtemps' (p.88).

Part of the reason for this is that, as he makes clear at the same time, his father would also, later, talk about the rue Lauriston, so the French Gestapo would for ever be associated with his search, through his fiction, for his filial identity. Now admittedly, this point is hardly a novel one, having already been made, quite forcibly, in Chapter 2 above. But this is not to say that *Remise de peine* simply goes over well-trodden ground again. On the contrary. As in so many other areas, it throws a brand new light on Modiano's treatment of the Occupation, for it makes explicit, for the first time, exactly why Eddy Pagnon should constantly crop up in his work: the author believes that it was Pagnon, in person, who freed his father from jail during the *années noires*, and that, since such a favour would presuppose an already established friendship, to find out more about the French *gestapiste* is to fill in a huge gap in the paternal past. This view, which has underpinned the *œuvre* from the start, is now finally articulated, then.[31] And as page after page of *Remise de peine* attests to the depth of the novelist's research here (research so diligent that it produces a much fuller biography of Pagnon than most of those found in the history books on the period),[32] two details imposingly stand out: the disclosure that 'Pagnon [. . .] avait acheté un cheval de course [. . .] et [. . .] fréquentait [. . .] les manèges de Neuilly, Barbizon' (pp.119–20), and the further revelation that, before the war, when he probably met Modiano senior, he was employed in a garage. Could this be why jockeys and racehorses punctuate the author's pursuit of his father in his fiction? Could this be why garages act as *points de repères* throughout the quest as well? The contentions are arguable, to say the least.

This is especially true of the second suggestion, for the weight of evidence behind it seems irresistible, as when we are informed: 'Le garage du XVIIe où travaillait Pagnon? Si je parvenais à le découvrir, un ancien mécano me parlerait de Pagnon et – je l'espérais – de mon père et je saurais enfin tout ce qu'il fallait savoir' (p.121). More tellingly still, the narrator then goes on to talk of another such establishment, 'peut-être le même que celui de Pagnon' (p.123), and the location of which is decidedly full of portent: 'Cette zone où Neuilly, Levallois et Paris se confondent [...] une rue bordée d'arbres dont les feuillages formaient une voûte. Pas d'immeubles dans cette rue, mais des hangars et des garages' (p.106). What is revealing here, we realize, is that not only is this instability of setting – as already noted – a hallmark of the *œuvre* as a whole, but so, too, is the road with its trees 'en voûte'.[33] In other words, Modiano's acknowledged aim in writing (to search for his father) has, quite tangibly, had a profound effect on his literary technique – it has influenced not just his choice of characters (based, more often than not, on paternal acquaintances), but also his typical décors.[34]

That this is so can further be seen from another of his constant backdrops – the château. For as *Remise de peine* again suggests, the father knew a man (referred to here as Eliot Salter) who, until he had his property requisitioned and (typically) disappeared at the end of the war, was most unashamedly a *châtelain*. And not the *châtelain* of some obscure estate at that. Quite the opposite. His now abandoned house and gardens are, we note, naggingly familiar to us, probably because we have already encountered them countless times before.[35]

Apart from the garage and the country mansion, there is a third, and final, resonant setting in *Remise de peine*: the actual town itself. From the early clue that we are in 'un village des environs de Paris' (p.11), on through the mention of the rue Docteur-Dordaine (p.12), to the appearance of the nearby 'hameau des Mets' (p.38), river Bièvre (p.39) and Villacoublay aerodrome (p.51) – not forgetting our old friend, the adjacent château – the picture being painted is an emphatic one: we are in the same locality as in *De si braves garçons* – Jouy-en-Josas.[36] But if the locality is plainly identical, the chronological setting most definitely is not. As we have seen, we have moved back in time to the mid-1950s, and this is eminently noteworthy for two vital reasons. First, because it fills in a gap in Modiano's public biography (up until now, he has said relatively little about this early period of his life). And second, because it explains the centrality of Jouy-en-Josas in his fiction – having apparently lived in the village on two different occasions, and for a number of years in total,[37] he is bound to have been influenced by his protracted residence there. For as we all know, nothing is as formative as the experience of childhood.

Childhood – the importance of this word cannot be overemphasized as far Modiano is concerned, and certainly not in respect of *Remise de peine*, for one of the other great revelations of this work, in addition to those listed above, is that the author's previous texts contain far more *souvenirs d'enfance* than had hitherto been suspected.[38] Not for nothing, therefore, should Modiano's early narrators be so *enfantins* in outlook – the author is doing more than simply seek out his father in his fiction; he is delving back into his own childhood as well.

Be that as it may, the fact remains that, within the *œuvre*, it is *Remise de peine* that best highlights this leitmotif of *l'enfance*, for the good reason that, quite manifestly, the very form of the work has now been geared to encapsulate the concern. Never before, in a major text, has Modiano penned a narrative whose perspective is so intrinsically naive: the syntax rarely reaches any level beyond the simple; characters are assimilated to comic-book heroes (Blanche-Neige, Buck Danny);[39] leitmotifs create a sense of child-like repetition;[40] the information divulged is highly fragmentary; and the dominant tone is one of confusion, with the young protagonist being excluded from every adult *confidence*. Without a doubt, then, the world-view we are given is that of an immature child.[41]

But only in purely formal terms, for ultimately, as the text itself reveals, the book is the work of a grown-up, a grown-up who, as writer and narrator, is looking back to his early years and reliving them in one of the most treasured of all his faculties: the faculty of remembrance. Such recourse to memory is, of course, one of the staples of Modiano's technique, and here, as elsewhere, it helps explain the many uncertainties of the narrative (recollection being, in practice, non-chronological and somewhat less than complete). But it also has added significance besides. By establishing a link between young boy and mature man, it helps show how the one grew into the other, that is to say how the novelist was already present, in embryo, in the small child, as a number of the points made above ably demonstrate: the awareness that the world is full of mysteries; the readiness to adopt a substitute family; the tendency to turn people into 'legends' – all these attributes of the young hero of *Remise de peine* reappear in Modiano's *œuvre* as a whole. And so, too, do many of his other characteristics, such as his unwillingness to pursue things to their conclusion (pp.54, 94), his proclivity to indulge in *rêverie* (pp.50–3, 95), and his basic lack of inner security (p.126). Of all the revelations produced by this double perspective of man and boy, though, one of the most striking must surely relate to the question of crime and detection, for if, as has been seen, the child is surrounded by criminals and mysteries, to such a degree that he becomes, unwittingly, a sort of background *witness* to a felony, then the adult writer is the very opposite – a pseudo-*detective* who, thanks to his investigations, has managed to resolve some (though not all) of the enigmas of his past. Once again, therefore, the events of childhood explain the deeds of maturity.

And there is one final way in which this is true, for *Remise de peine* is much more than a simple attempt, on Modiano's part, to clarify the uncertainties of his youth; it is, additionally, an endeavour to face up to the pain of the past, the pain that is so poignantly brought into focus at the end of the work: abandoned by his temporary guardians, his mother and father still absent in Africa, the narrator is left all alone, an 'orphan', with no source of comfort except his brother Rudy. Henceforth, we assume, his life will be marred by suffering, as one interpretation of the work's title confirms – his 'peine' has been handed over to him, to be kept in his possession for many years to come. Yet this is by no means the only meaning of the term 'remise de peine'; there is (typically) a second connotation to it as well,[42] one which is equally, if not more, appropriate in the present context – the phrase is regularly used in legal circles, to refer to a reduction of sentence. So it could very well be that, by writing this book, Modiano has reduced his own emotional 'imprisonment', and freed himself, a degree or two more, from the heavy shackles of his past.[43] After all, has he not now verbalized what he, himself, describes as 'une période de ma vie dont je ne pouvais parler à personne' (p.141)? And has he not chosen also, for the first time, to give Rudy more than a passing mention in his writing?[44] Such evidence, on reflection, seems totally conclusive: *Remise de peine* is a work of exorcism – the author's most radical act of self-purging thus far.

If childhood has been seen to be the prime focus of *Remise de peine*, then its centrality to Modiano's next work is undoubtedly – and instantly – even more apparent, encapsulated by the author's very choice of title: the highly expressive *Vestiaire de l'enfance*. Indeed, this link between the two texts is not just confined to their common theme, but also extends to the way in which they depict it, for the narrators of both books clearly have backgrounds that are similar, if not identical. 'Notre mère nous emmenait, quand nous étions petits, dans les loges et les coulisses des théâtres', we have already been informed,[45] and the same experience is alluded to in this new work: once again we encounter the actress mother taking her son into her dressing-room backstage – and leaving him there while she performs in her play (p.70). And the father is no more present than he was in *Remise de peine* either, for he turns up only briefly – in the typical no-man's-land of a café (p.109) – and is otherwise never more than merely glimpsed – vicariously – behind the appearance of a relatively minor third party: a certain Beauchamp, who, we learn, shares 'le charme louche [. . .] de mon père et de ses amis' (p.137), and has a number of other key features in common with them besides: 'mêmes gestes, même voix, mêmes cheveux noir aile-de-corbeau plaqués en arrière, même désinvolture, mêmes expédients, même vie incertaine' (p.136).

As may already have been inferred, such details suggest that the parents in question are based very heavily on Modiano's own, and that this autobiographical strand in the text is important can be seen by the countless additional links that bind the narrator of *Vestiaire de l'enfance* to his creator. An entry into the world in July 1945, in Boulogne-Billancourt (p.96); early days spent 'sur la rive gauche, à Saint-Germain-des-Prés' (p.69); schooling at a *collège* reachable by bus from the Porte d'Orléans (p.70); a subsequent career as a Paris-based novelist (p.19) – all of these aspects of the protagonist's life are applicable to the author as well. However, it would be wrong to conclude from this that, following *Remise de peine*, the *je* who addresses us is once again in large part the writer himself, for this is most definitely not the case. There are numerous areas in which such a close identification irrevocably breaks down. For example, it is revealed that the main character was born on the *twentieth* of July 1945, not on the thirtieth (p.96); that he has now turned his back on his native France completely (p.29); that he has only been writing for a period of ten years at most (p.81); and that he no longer produces top-quality novels (p.49), preferring instead to churn out a worthless radio serial, *Les aventures de Louis XVII* (pp.9–10).[46] As a result of all this – and as always in the *œuvre* – the central 'I' of the narrative must be seen as ambiguous: part author, part creation, he is of at the very least *dual* status.

This basic ambivalence is further implied by his name, or rather his names, for in true *modianesque* fashion, he actually has an identity that is double: at present, he is living under the (fictitious) 'nom d'emprunt' of Jimmy Sarano (p.19), but he has also led a 'vie antérieure' (p.39) – as the aforementioned novelist in Paris, where (in another, more subtle link to his creator) he was known to the world as Jean Moreno.[47] Jean was, of course, the *prénom* of Dekker in *Quartier perdu*, and of the narrator of *Dimanches d'août*, and this serves to confirm what may, by now, have become obvious, namely that *Vestiaire de l'enfance* does not maintain the highly autobiographical approach of *Remise de peine*. On the contrary, it finds the author returning to the two works which immediately precede it, and (as explicitly indicated by the title-page) to his preferred format of the *roman*.

In particular, it finds him returning to *Dimanches d'août*, for, as in his tenth novel, he manages to work wonders with the absolute minimum, producing a text which, from the word 'go', is remarkable for its spareness. Plot has been so reduced as to be virtually non-existent (Jean meets a young girl called Marie, wonders if he knew her in his 'vie antérieure', but reaches no definite conclusion). Characters are so vague (being, for the most part, exiles with unknown pasts) that they are barely deserving of the title. And as for setting, the lack of precision here is, if anything, even worse: we are presented with 'une ville morte' (pp.95, 96), whose main characteristics are silence and oppressive heat, but, apart from that, we can be sure of very little. Geographically speaking, we could be almost anywhere in the western Mediterranean, as Carlos Sirvent rightly observes: 'On finit par douter de la réalité de cette ville et par se demander où elle se trouve exactement sur la carte: Espagne? Afrique? Méditerrannée?' (p.127). We never do find out, although the reason for this uncertainty is much less obscure. 'J'avais envie', Modiano has confessed, 'que le décor soit en harmonie avec l'état d'esprit du personnage',[48] and in harmony it most certainly is. Prone to feelings of apprehension and solitude (p.29), 'détaché de tout' (p.45) and permanently wracked by 'une sensation de vide' (p.29), Jimmy is typically hard to pin down, his life full of mysteries. Exactly why did he uproot himself and become an exile, like all of his colleagues? 'Pour m'alléger d'un poids [. . .]', he says, 'et d'un sentiment de culpabilité que j'essayais d'exprimer dans mes livres'. But as he himself immediately adds, he is 'coupable de quoi?' (p.48). Might his guilt have something to do with the mysterious car accident (or was it a crime?) which he evokes (pp.48, 93)? Predictably, we are never told. Not for Modiano, then, a well-defined, reliable narrator. Like concrete settings, intricate plots and detailed characterization, this key aspect of traditional fiction has been totally abandoned as well.

So too, true to form, has classical chronology, for, as in each of the preceding texts, past and present coalesce as memory works its magic. Thus, although we can distinguish three main temporal planes in the novel (the now, which sees Jimmy 'in exile' and intrigued by Marie; twenty years earlier – probably 1965 – when, as Jean, he was friendly with the young daughter of an actress called Rose-Marie; and five years before that, when he was still at school and used to visiting his mother's *loge*), none of these levels is presented integrally, as a block, in its rightful place in time, but rather in a series of overlapping fragments, often linked (as ever) to a chance event or a coincidence. In fact, even if the narrator does not initially realize it, this discontinuity of time provides a whole new meaning to the 'présent éternel' in which he claims to live (pp.37, 40).

It also does something else besides. It embodies that binary relationship – difference–sameness – that is the most vital structuring device within the novel, and the key to a complete understanding of its status. For the essence of the work, it is clear, lies not in its overall content (which, as has been seen, is virtually non-existent), but rather in its form, and in particular in its succession of contrasts and parallels.

On the disjunctive side, the series of oppositions help us to see how past is separated from present, to gauge just how well Jimmy has detached himself from Jean; and, as implied above, the basic conflict here is that of the real and the invented. The décor within which Serano moves is, as previously noted, entirely imaginary, having no clear model in the world of geography, whereas Moreno's stamping-ground is the city of Paris, in all its realistic glory. And that is not all. The same antagonism exists with regard to some of the characters. From Sirvent through to Mercadié, all of the narrator's current associates are plainly creatures of fiction, while a good number of his old acquaintances, such as the actor Max Montavon, are most demonstrably not.[49] Not for nothing, then, has *Vestiaire de l'enfance* been said to be 'semblable à un diptyque';[50] this is precisely the form that it evokes.[51]

All the more so in that, in addition to these patent contrasts, a network of parallels is deployed within the work, parallels whose aim is to counter the effect of the oppositions (yet another contrastive feature!) and destroy the frontiers between the three main time-blocks in the novel. Witness the way in which the narrator's memories of his mother reflect those he has of Rose-Marie and her daughter. Not only does an actress with her child figure in both cases, but Jean finds himself, uncannily, revisiting exactly the same places – places such as the film studios at Saint-Maurice, of which he enlighteningly remarks: 'Nous avons déjeuné avec Rose-Marie à la cantine [. . .], la petite et moi. J'y ai si souvent accompagné ma mère que je crains que les souvenirs ne se superposent et se mêlent dans mon esprit' (pp.134–5). In this final comment especially, the point could hardly be more explicit.[52]

The greatest merging of temporal planes, however, involves not two bygone eras, but rather, more strikingly, the normally separate levels of past and present. For as mentioned above, Jimmy, in his exile, bumps into a young girl called Marie, and wonders why she seems so familiar to him; it is, significantly, at roughly the mid-point of the novel, while he is lost in a 'demi-sommeil' (p.67),[53] that he finds the answer to his question: her face, he convinces himself, 'est celui d'une enfant que j'ai connue il y a longtemps. Son prénom n'était-il pas: Marie – comme l'autre?' (p.68). This 'enfant' is, of course, the daughter of Rose-Marie, and very quickly, a whole mass of additional links cement the two characters to each other. The current Marie, although older than her predecessor, still comes across as being very much a child (pp.32, 33, 36, 58), and just as Jean, twenty years ago, had adopted 'le rôle d'ange gardien' (p.78), 'à la manière d'un père ou d'un grand frère' (p.78), so too does Jimmy watch over *his* 'ward', most notably by paying her hotel bill when she gets into arrears. Indeed, the room she occupies at the Alvear proves to be yet another parallel to the past, since the narrator's early musings on this *chambre* – 'Telle que je l'imaginais, elle était en tout point semblable à celle que louait Rose-Marie, et l'hôtel Alvear se confondait pour moi avec le Moncey Hôtel, rue Blanche' (p.98) – are ultimately shown to be well founded: he actually sees for himself that 'La chambre était semblable à celle du Moncey Hôtel' (p.144). And that this discovery should be made in the final pages of the work is no coincidence, because it is here, quite manifestly, that the temporal slippage is at its most acute. Having, back in the Sixties, taken the younger 'Marie' to her uncle's flat at the Porte Dorée, 'au troisième étage droite' (p.140), and not joined her there as he had promised, the narrator now finds himself in the hotel room of her older namesake – again on the 'troisième étage . . . première porte à droite' (p.144) – and *he* is the one who, in a reversal of the original situation, is expectantly waiting for *her* to appear, as her brief note to him (p.120) suggested that, sooner or later, she would. 'Peut-être allait-elle apparaître', he speculates, looking out of the open window. But the reflections which follow bring no resolution, serving, instead, simply to increase the sense of *déjà vu* that abounds:

> C'était la même lumière de fin de jour, en été, lorsque je surveillais, de la fenêtre de chez sa mère, la petite [. . .].
> Tout se confondait par un phénomène de surimpression [. . .] et devenait d'une si pure et si implacable transparence . . . La transparence du temps, aurait dit Carlos Sirvent. (p.145)

Everything certainly is becoming confused, so much so that, with these penultimate words, we are taken right back to the beginning of the text, for we already know that, at the start, Jimmy's world is a world where 'le temps s'est arrêté' (p.22), a world where everything is repeated from day to day, from week to week (pp.9, 13, 18, 33), and where life is lived, as has been seen, 'dans une sorte d'intemporalité [. . .] de présent éternel' (p.37). In short, a world characterized by the selfsame 'phénomène de surimpression'. And the general corollary of this is quite clear: as ever in Modiano's fiction, it is the circle, and not the straight line, that rules supreme.

Given this active promotion of circularity, it is a measure of the author's great achievement that, quite apart from the merging of the three main time-blocks, and of start and finish, almost every other aspect of the novel becomes an echo in its own right as well. The chauffeur, who, according to the bizarre terms of a will, has constantly to watch over Jimmy, represents a sort of *dédoublement* of his 'ward', acting as his guardian angel, yet keeping him under surveillance, just as Sarano himself 'protects' Marie and disturbingly spies on his neighbour (pp.66, 80);[54] the statue of Javier Cruz-Valer, with its displacement enshrined in song – 'De socle en socle | Tu te promènes | Javier Cruz-Valer' (p.62) – becomes a reflection of the transplanted narrator, while its old, abandoned plinth, as Sirvent more explicitly suggests, 'est à l'image de cette ville, [. . .] de notre vie à tous ici' (p.127); Paris, by narratorial accord, seems to be the very embodiment of symmetry, its eastern section forming simply 'une réplique, en plus trouble et en plus triste, de l'ouest' (p.136); phrases and details, such as 'aucune importance' (pp.18, 25, 31, 58, 137), the distinctive taste of the water (pp.12, 33, 95, 115) or the *sac de paille* (pp.11, 26, 52, 54, etc.), recur so often that they are raised to the status of leitmotifs; and so the list goes on.

In fact, this provision of mirror images is not limited to the confines of the text itself, for time after time we are subtly reminded of previous works in the *œuvre*. Is it in *La Place de l'Étoile* that we read: 'Peut-être, si je sortais de l'hôtel, me retrouverais-je non plus Mariahilfenstrasse mais à Paris'? Could it be *Quartier perdu* that informs us: 'Je n'avais pas entendu depuis longtemps quelqu'un parler vraiment français'? Might it be in *De si braves garçons*, or in 'La Seine', that we find an actress abandoning her young daughter to the care and attention of a boy of nineteen? No. Despite appearances to the contrary, it is in *Vestiaire de l'enfance* that all these events and statements occur.[55] It is just that they evoke a strong sense of *déjà vu*.

On the level of its major themes, too, the novel seems to be insistently familiar. The instability of identity; the omnipotence of chance; the interaction of past and present; the elusiveness of reality; the recourse to memory and/or *rêverie*; the centrality of the cinema; the cult of enigmas – these key aspects of the work, which have already been encountered, either directly or indirectly, in the analysis above, are concerns which are patently quintessential, both for the author and for his *œuvre*.[56] And so is the one main thematic strand that underpins them all, and which it will now be useful to discuss rather more fully: the irrevocable, steady-paced onward march of time. For the basic law of *Vestiaire de l'enfance*, as for all of the previous texts, is that, whatever people may ideally desire, 'le temps poursuivra son travail d'usure' (p.47). So the vital question is how to react, and Jimmy presents us with one – but by no means the only – solution to the problem: he produces *Les aventures de Louis XVII*, the premiss of which is 'la survie des personnes disparues, l'espoir de retrouver un jour ceux qu'on a perdus dans le passé' (p.10).[57] And that is not all he does. As we are reminded by the regular *mise en abyme* – through comments such as 'à l'instant où j'écris ces lignes' (p.114) – he is also the source of the prose we are reading, which is not without considerable significance, since it shows us that, just as he did with his musings on Louis XVII, he is once again resuscitating the past, his own past, and this in two obvious ways: first, by noting down his memories and linking them to the present, and second, by ostensibly cultivating literariness, the quality he claimed to have left behind when he packed his bags and fled Paris.

Yet this recuperative work can achieve only so much, with the result that, throughout the novel, as has been seen, we remain firmly fixed in the world of the possible, never in that of the definite. Marie may well look a lot like Rose-Marie's daughter, but certain identification is never forthcoming. Quite the opposite in some respects, as when Sarano remarks:

> Cette fille de l'hôtel Alvear était-elle l'enfant que j'avais connue rue Fontaine? En dépit du front et du regard, l'âge ne correspondait pas exactement et la coïncidence aurait été trop romanesque . . . Mais la vie ne vous réserve-t-elle pas des surprises encore plus grandes que celles qui vous attendent dans le prochain chapitre d'un roman? (p.122)

This playful confusion of reality and fiction is quite typical of the book as a whole, and the principle it embodies is most manifest – no sooner has one thing been asserted than (as in many a New Novel) it must instantly be discredited, and other avenues quickly opened up. For to be true to its antithetical structure, the text must constantly self-destruct, and leave nothing in its ever-increasing wake but a void – a void which Jimmy, with a measure of ludic self-consciousness, will then, once again, inevitably try to fill.

It almost goes without saying, of course, that, behind Sarano, it is Modiano himself who is responsible for this teasing ludism, Modiano who, more or less directly, is commenting on his own outlook and position as a writer, and nowhere is this game-playing better illustrated than in the following declaration: 'Ici rien ne m'évoque mon passé ni celui des quelques personnes dont je m'inspirais pour mes livres, du temps où j'habitais la France' (p.37). As may readily be conceded, it could almost be the author himself talking here, for he too, in many ways, is breaking with his previous literary practice. For the first time, in one of his major works, he has set his narrative outside France,[58] and hand in hand with this development goes the abandonment of all the old, familiar faces. Max Montavon has, it is true, already featured in *Poupée blonde* (but only as a name in the cast list),[59] and Julien Blin does, admittedly, evoke the Lucien Blin of *Quartier perdu*, but these characters, like those – far better established – of the mother and the father,[60] are now well and truly associated with *the past*; the figures who currently surround the narrator are entirely new creations, and have no outward links to the rest of the *œuvre* at all. Thus, the exorcism pursued in the preceding text, *Remise de peine*, seems to have proved refreshing. Modiano, it would appear, can now distance himself from the one sorry period of his life that has regularly fuelled his fiction: his unhappy childhood.

Yet if he has managed to place his own early years more firmly behind him, he has most definitely not, as indicated above, abandoned *l'enfance* as a literary theme. For the key to the book is, without a doubt, Jean Moreno's experience as a child, and, more specifically, his relationship with Rose-Marie's daughter. Or rather, his lack of a relationship with her, because, having had a crush on her mother, and focusing simply on that, he was guilty of selfishly neglecting his young companion. But now that he has become Jimmy Sarano, things have considerably changed. 'Je regrette que les choses ne se soient pas déroulées autrement', he confesses at one stage (p.109), and it is not difficult to see why: 'Ce qui était resté à l'état d'ébauche chez Rose-Marie atteignait son point de perfection chez cette petite' (p.138). So, the ideal was at hand, but he did not realize it – and now that he does, it is far, far too late: 'Elle marque une cassure dans ma vie, cette journée passée pour la dernière fois avec Rose-Marie et la petite . . . Après, je suis passé dans ce qu'il faut bien appeler l'âge adulte' (p.134). This, then, is why he tries to turn Marie into Rose-Marie's grown-up daughter – he is seeking to recapture a time which, perhaps, is not so much a paradise lost as paradise not seen as such in the first place.[61]

Yet whatever his actual intentions, the outcome of his venture is predictable, as the final pages of the novel plainly demonstrate. Having, inadvertently, locked himself out of his room – and thereby escaped from the close surveillance of the normally present chauffeur – he decides to go for a stroll, and finds the experience most liberating: 'J[. . .]'éprouvais une sensation de légèreté, comme après avoir rompu une dernière entrave' (p.128). Even when his 'guardian angel' discovers him, the signs are still undeniably positive:

> L'air me semblait d'une légèreté qu'il n'avait pas habituellement. L'avenue était déserte [. . .], mais cela ne me causait pas la moindre sensation de vide ou d'angoisse. La journée allait commencer, une journée d'été splendide et pleine de promesses. [. . .] Pour la première fois depuis longtemps, j'assistais au début de quelque chose. (p.132)[62]

However, as we have seen, this optimism quickly gives way to disenchantment. Marie has apparently abandoned him, and with her has gone the sole, vital connection to his past. Henceforth, his childhood, like the outgrown *blouson* he left in the wardrobe, and which 'achève peut-être d'y pourrir aujourd'hui' (p.73), will for ever be the prisoner of time. Darkness now falls, silence reigns, and all expectation disintegrates. We are left, fittingly, at virtually the selfsame point we came in: with Jimmy figuratively at sea, swamped by 'ce sentiment familier de vide' (p.145). And who can blame him? His *vestiaire de l'enfance* seems to have been locked tight.

Notes

1. *Paris* (1987), his choice of texts and paintings to evoke his home city, would appear to be an exception within this general trend, although it could, of course, be argued that Modiano is evoking his childhood *indirectly* here, as he does more explicitly in his preface to Pierre Le-Tan's *Paris de ma jeunesse* (1988): 'Chacun de nous, à sa manière, tente de retrouver le Paris de son enfance et de sa jeunesse' (p.9). Much the same

might also be said of 'Les livres de Julien Gracq' (1989), in which the novelist praises an author he has no doubt read as a youngster.

2. Montaudon, 'Patrick Modiano', p.17. One of the 'lectures enfantines' to which Modiano alludes here was, no doubt, Baroness Orczy's Scarlet Pimpernel stories – see *Une aventure de Choura*, pp.20–30, and cf. *Quartier perdu*, p.28 (or pp.121 and 125 above). This establishment of an outward link to the *œuvre* is typical of all three of the so-called 'children's books', and confirms that Modiano approaches his 'livres pour enfants' in much the same manner as the rest of his fiction.

3. As suggested, this theme of a new beginning is a vital one for Modiano after *Rue des Boutiques Obscures*. Already highlighted in Chapter 4 above, it further manifests itself in the only self-penned text included in the author's *Paris*.

4. Josselin, 'Mondo Modiano', p.59. The opening words of this quotation notwithstanding, cynics would, no doubt, assume that there was also a strong financial incentive for the change of publisher.

5. Ibid., p.60.

6. The phrase is used both by Josselin ('Patrick tel qu'en Patoche . . .', p.61) and by Grainville ('Patrick Modiano: retour aux sources', p.vii). Note also the view of the less forthright Czarny: 'même si Modiano récuse le terme d'autobiographie, on doit considérer que ce livre est celui qui se rapproche au plus près de ce projet' ('La Trace douloureuse', p.176).

7. Josselin, 'Patrick tel qu'en Patoche . . .', p.61. Cf. Nourissier, 'Modiano: souvenir d'en France, souvenir d'enfance', pp.72, 73.

8. For a previous, and slightly fuller account of the father's first arrest, see *Livret de famille*, pp.105–6. (But note that, typically for Modiano, the two versions of the event are not entirely consistent. For more on this discrepancy, see Czarny, 'La Trace douloureuse', p.176. Note also that this lack of consistency, which confuses the informed reader, points to another possible interpretation of the 'revelation' in *Remise de peine* – Albert might just have been picked up by the authorites *once*, with this sole arrest, like so much else in the *œuvre*, now being *dédoublé* by the author in the aim of creating uncertainty.)

9. In *La Place de l'Étoile*, there is, admittedly, a reference to an actress mother 'qui faisait souvent des tournées en province'

(p.38), but as has been seen, none of Schlemilovitch's declarations is in any way definitive. Other than this, Modiano has previously only mentioned his mother's theatrical tours in interview (see e.g. Jamet, 'Modiano s'explique', p.32).

10. See e.g. Yvonne Jacquet (*Villa Triste*), Denise Coudreuse (*Rue des Boutiques Obscures*), Maddy Contour (*Memory Lane*), the nameless addressee of 'Le Courrier du cœur'/'Lettre d'amour' and, we assume, Arlette d'Alwyn ('1, rue Lord-Byron').

11. This suggestion that the characters derive from the same basic source – and are therefore linked – can perhaps be substantiated by referring to *Villa Triste*, which informs us that Yvonne's surname is 'très suave, très français, quelque chose comme: Coudreuse, Jacquet' (p.23). Coudreuse will, of course, be the name given to Denise in *Rue des Boutiques Obscures*. (There will also be a Mlle Coudreuse in *Livret de famille*, and while it may be true that this character is involved neither in the world of high fashion nor in that of show business, she nevertheless still has a job – governess – which instantly marks her out as a substitute mother – see *Livret de famille*, p.77.)

12. From a psychoanalytical point of view, it might also be said that, as the leading ladies tend to be romantically involved with the narrators-cum-'authors' of their respective texts, they allow the novelist, through the medium of his fiction, to displace his father in his mother's affections, and thereby consolidate the Œdipal killing that is such a feature of his earliest work. For more on this subject, see Bedner, 'Modiano ou l'identité introuvable', p.59.

13. The two film stars who *are* associated with the Occupation and its decadence – Annie Murraille (*Les Boulevards de ceinture*) and Betty Beaulieu (*Lacombe Lucien*) – are based not on his mother, it may be recalled, but rather on Corinne Luchaire. Interestingly enough, the more the *œuvre* progresses, the more his mother comes to feature *openly* his work, whether simply as 'ma mère', as in the autobiographical *Livret de famille* and *Remise de peine*, or as Luisa Colpeyn, as in *Poupée blonde*. (According to Nettelbeck and Hueston, she even appeared in 'Un Innocent', the television programme which Modiano scripted.)

14. Already the narrator's *marraine* (p.62), and now filling the maternal role while his parents are away, she will actually claim that he is her son on p.28. Note also that, given her position as Patoche's godparent, and given that the *extrait de baptême* in *Livret de famille* (p.94) is, apart from the blanks, apparently Modiano's own (see Assouline, 'Lieux de mémoire', p.42) Annie can (somewhat tentatively) be traced back to her historical source – a certain Madeleine (Maddy?) Ferragus.

15. The partnerless (and no less blonde) bride in *Rue des Boutiques Obscures* even shares the taste for light blue dresses with her – see *Rue des Boutiques Obscures*, pp.18, 19, 22–3.

16. Modiano describes 'le Carroll's' only as a 'boîte de nuit' in the rue de Ponthieu (pp.19, 21). There is no mystery for Jean-François Josselin, however: we are dealing with the 'célèbre night-club des Champs-Elysées fréquenté par des lesbiennes' ('Patrick tel qu'en Patoche . . .', p.61).

17. This recourse to the wife/lover, mother/whore cliché by Modiano may appear somewhat offensive, but it should not be judged in isolation from its context. The novelist's male creations are, after all, just as hackneyed as their *consœurs*, and stereotypes in general are an integral part of *l'univers modianesque* – witness *Livret de famille* and its depiction of Switzerland (see Chapter 3, Note 44 above). Note also the predictable nature of Britain – mist and fog, tweeds and pipes – in *Une jeunesse* (pp.135–54).

18. For her own acknowledgement of this role, see *Remise de peine*, p.38. The woman on whom Hélène is based (a retired trapeze artist) seems to have been the lover of real-life circus-boss Mustapha Amar (see ibid., p.137).

19. See p.87 above and cf. both the girl in *Quartier perdu* (p.166) and Charrell's wife in *De si braves garçons* (p.167).

20. See e.g. Sylviane Quimphe (*Les Boulevards de ceinture*), Nicole Haas (*Une jeunesse*), or Suzanne Charrell (*De si braves garçons*).

21. See e.g. Nicole Haas, who is said to have '[des] allures garçonnières' (*Une jeunesse*, p.115).

22. According to Josselin ('Patrick tel qu'en Patoche . . .', p.61), she derives from the real-life boss of 'le Carroll's', Frédé. (Presumably, Frédé was also a source of inspiration for Maud Gallas, who likewise 'fut gérante d'un établissement

Patrick Modiano

nocturne du quartier de la Plaine Monceau où ne fréquentait qu'une clientèle féminine' – *Les Boulevards de ceinture*, pp.76–7).

23. Jean D. can, with some detective work, eventually be unmasked. Thanks to the allusion to his small role in the Ben Barka Affair – he is said to have been the last person to see Georges Figon alive – he can be seen as the literary counterpart of Jean Vignaud (see *Remise de peine*, pp.98–9 and cf. either, *passim*, Roger Muratet, *On a tué Ben Barka* (Paris, Plon, 1967), or Philip Williams, *Wars, Plots and Scandals in Post-war France* (Cambridge, Cambridge University Press, 1970), pp.78–125). Roger Vincent, for his part, cannot as yet be identified (unless, of course, Modiano has not disguised him in the slightest – a Roger Vincent is mentioned (once) in Bernard Violet's *L'Affaire Ben Barka* (Paris, Fayard, 1991), p.374, but with so little detail that a link to *Remise de peine* cannot automatically be established).

24. Cf. e.g. Henri Marignan in *Livret de famille* (p.24).

25. See again *Livret de famille*, p.24. See also p.112 above (including Note 41) and cf. *Dimanches d'août*, p.13.

26. See e.g. *Une jeunesse*, p.193, or *Villa Triste*, pp.68–76.

27. He will also turn up again later, in *Paris Tendresse* (p.54).

28. Despite this emphasis on her individuality, *Remise de peine* also shows her to be of *typical* appearance: 'Des pommettes, des yeux verts, des cheveux châtain clair' (p.79).

29. Bosselet, 'Patrick Modiano: "J'ai un petit talent d'amateur"', p.17. Note that Modiano adds to these two sentences the important recognition: 'Mais peut-être étaient-ils différents.'

30. The allusion here, of course, is to the group of French *gestapistes* headed by Bonny and Laffont – see p.40 above. Note also that the singer with the 'voix rauque' whom we encounter elsewhere (p.82), and who is presented as the friend of Roger and Hélène (p.95), is in all probability Edith Piaf, whose association with the Paris *milieu* is legendary (for fuller details, see Edith Piaf, *My Life*, translated by Margaret Crosland (London, Peter Owen, 1990), or Margaret Crosland, *Piaf* (Sevenoaks, Hodder and Stoughton, 1985)).

31. To discern how this belief has coloured the earlier fiction, see e.g. *De si braves garçons*, pp.138, 157.

32. Cf. p.79 above.

33. See e.g. *Les Boulevards de ceinture*, p.195, *Livret de famille*, p.22,

Quartier perdu, pp.103, 170, or (looking ahead now), 'Polar à huit mains: L'Angle mort: Chapitre 3', p.86.

34. For more garages in Modiano's work, see *Villa Triste*, pp.118–42, *Une jeunesse*, pp.79–80, 119, *Dimanches d'août*, pp.27-8, and *Rue des Boutiques Obscures*, p.204. Note also that *Remise de peine* (p.122) 'borrows' the Garage de la Comète from this last text, and suggestively adds: 'ces années n'auront été, pour moi, qu'une longue et vaine recherche d'un garage perdu' (p.123).

35. See *Remise de peine*, pp.41–2, 45–7, and cf. *Rue des Boutiques Obscures*, pp.69–70, 73–5. Cf. also (if somewhat less strikingly) *Dimanches d'août* (pp.69–70, 77–8), *De si braves garçons* (pp.13–14, 24) and *Quartier perdu* (pp.141–6).

36. See p.109 above, and note the connection with *Rue des Boutiques Obscures*. (For further comparisons, see Note 33 to Chapter 4 and cf. *Remise de peine*, pp.11–14.) See also *Livret de famille*, with its mention of Jouy-en-Josas and 'la paisible et mystérieuse rue du Docteur-Kurzenne où nous avions vécu, mon frère et moi' (p.91). As we have seen (Note 32 to Chapter 4 above) the rue du Docteur-Kurzenne is the true name for the rue Docteur-Dordaine, and the house where Modiano lived there has since been identified as Number 38 (Assouline, 'Lieux de mémoire', p.37).

37. 'Nous sommes restés beaucoup plus d'un an rue Docteur-Dordaine', we are told in *Remise de peine* (p.91), and in *De si braves garçons* the information is even more specific: 'J'avais habité ce village pendant trois ans', at the age of 'neuf ou dix ans' (p.106). Pierre Assouline, however, will put the length of this first stay at about two years ('Lieux de mémoire', p.36).

38. See e.g. *Rue des Boutiques Obscures*, pp.128–9, 156, and cf. the apparently autobiographical trip to Versailles in *Remise de peine* (pp.81–6).

39. Cf. Roger Vincent's 'legendary' quality on p.65, and note how this use of legend as a reference point is echoed in l'école Jeanne-d'Arc and l'auberge Robin des Bois.

40. See e.g. the repeated phrase, 'mon frère et moi' (pp.11, 15, 17, 20, 22, 23, 38, 42, etc.).

41. Although this naivety is new in a major text, Modiano has, of course, already taken this stance in his two works targeted at children, *Une aventure de Choura* and *Une fiancée pour Choura*. It is the adoption of this stance which makes *Remise de peine*

'novelistic' in the author's eyes, 'les impressions d'enfance, [étant], d'une certaine manière, des transpositions roman-esques' (Josselin, 'Mondo Modiano', p.60).

42. For further recognition of the title's ambiguity, see Petit, 'Modiano, Patrick: *Remise de peine*', p.408.

43. Such a reading would, of course, tie in nicely with the focus on crime and criminals within the text.

44. Note also the overt allusion to Rudy's death (p.102) – another new development.

45. *Remise de peine*, p.96.

46. Louis XVII (1785–95) was the son of Louis XVI and Marie-Antoinette, and Dauphin from 1789 onwards. Imprisoned in 1792, he was said to have been killed in jail, although rumours circulated that he had managed to escape. It is on this assumed break-out that *Les aventures de Louis XVII* are based.

47. As we have seen (Chapter 5, Note 26 above), Jean is the author's second forename. In respect of the surname, Modiano, Moreno, 'admirez l'à-peu-près', as Bertrand Poirot-Delpech has remarked ('Charmes de l'imprécision', p.15).

48. Montaudon, 'Patrick Modiano', p.15.

49. As Montavon is linked to the narrator's mother, and is situated in the earliest temporal block recalled, he seems to provide further proof, if any were needed, that the author's *rêverie* is constructed on a distinctly autobiographical bedrock. Note also that Mercadié's past similarly includes concrete elements, such as 'Pierre Sandrini, le patron du Tabarin' (p.119).

50. Alhau, 'Patrick Modiano: *Vestiaire de l'enfance*', p.103.

51. Note also the poles of light/dark, clarity/*ombre* in the work (e.g. pp.11, 65, 113–14).

52. Even when past events cannot be ascribed to a time-block, the same associative thrust is often in evidence – see e.g. p.109.

53. This indeterminate state – and the *rêverie* that goes with it – is, of course, an ideal context for the process of conflation being depicted (which, in turn, is doubtless why it is invoked insistently in the text – cf. e.g. pp.65, 68, 129).

54. See also the close of the novel, where the chauffeur, we are told, 'attendait, comme moi' (p.144).

55. The quotations come from pp.60 and 30 respectively.

56. Note also the (almost obligatory) reference to the Occupation (pp.38–9).

57. Cf. the 'appels dans la nuit' (pp.48–50) or the man at the club Brooks (pp.84–5). (Note also how this adds to the aforementioned parallelism in the novel.)

58. *Catherine Certitude*, published the year before, had been set *outre-Atlantique* in New York. (Most of the text deals with memories of Paris, however.)

59. Modiano used his credits page deliberately to have close contacts 'contribute' to his mock play. Alongside Montavon, for example, we find Hugues de Courson (see Chapter 4, Note 11), and Luisa Colpeyn (cf. Note 13 above).

60. And, it might be added, Beauchamp, who, if not already known to us by *name*, nevertheless is by *type*: the has-been who 'avait connu une période plus brillante' (p.136). (Cf., say, Meinthe (*Villa Triste*), Le Gros and Bourlagoff (*Livret de famille*), Blunt (*Rue des Boutiques Obscures*), Bellune (*Une jeunesse*), Doug (*Memory Lane*), or Mickey du Pam-Pam (*De si braves garçons*). Note also Modiano's own comment on his characters: 'ce sont tous des *has-beens*. Je les ai choisis ainsi pour qu'ils donnent la mesure du temps' (Ezine, 'Sur la sellette', p.5).)

61. Note also that, when taken with Jean's aforementioned need to flee France (see p.154 above), this nostalgic thrust sets up a telling contrast in the work, and douses the past with typical ambiguity. As Jean-Claude Bologne has helpfully said: 'Les deux passés qui obsèdent Modiano sont réunis dans ce roman: celui que l'on veut retrouver, enfance, amours malheureuses, et celui qu'il faut oublier, le drame qui a brisé le cours de la vie et des souvenirs' ('Le nouveau piège de Modiano', p.102). (For more on the import of 'le drame' in Modiano's fiction, see Prince, 'Re-Membering Modiano, or Something Happened', pp.35–43. To appreciate how this sense of *fêlure* is evoked stylistically in the *œuvre*, see Martinoir, 'Sur le cadastre de la fiction', p.5.)

62. Again there is a link to the *œuvre* here – note the final sentence of this quotation and cf. *Livret de famille*, p.22.

7

Towards a Final Exorcism: 'Voyage de noces', 'Fleurs de ruine' and 'Un cirque passe'

A chaque œuvre, Patrick Modiano s'écorche un peu plus. Égratine un peu plus son intimité et ses plaies.

Philippe Lacoche

Looking back over Modiano's works prior to 1990, it becomes clear that, whatever else they may represent, they embody a movement towards an enduring, authorial exorcism. From the early confronting of the *années noires* in *La Place de l'Étoile*, *La Ronde de nuit*, and *Les Boulevards de ceinture* (not to mention *Lacombe Lucien*), on through the filial respects paid to a newly deceased father (in *Rue des Boutiques Obscures*) to the subsequent descent – ever more probing – into the depths of a painful childhood (*De si braves garçons*, *Remise de peine*), the self-purging has been protracted, but most obviously effective. So effective, in fact, that, as we approach the 1990s, we might expect Modiano to carry on down the same path, and provide even more evidence that he is finally coming to terms with his past.

Not surprisingly, perhaps, this is precisely what transpires. Out goes the old, draining gestation period for each successive novel, and in comes the establishment of a more regular rhythm of production, the yearly cycle already presaged by *Vestiaire de l'enfance*. And if this change of rhythm suggests, in itself, a less emotionally inhibited creative process (and, of course, the perfecting of the novelist's literary technique), then so, too, does the *content* of the texts of this period, whether these texts be the relatively brief *Paris Tendresse* (1990) and 'Polar à huit mains: L'Angle mort: Chapitre 3' (1991),[1] or, as this chapter will now endeavour to show, the author's three most recent books – *Voyage de noces* (1990), *Fleurs de ruine* (1991) and *Un cirque passe* (1992).

After even the most cursory of initial glances, what immediately stands out about *Voyage de noces* is the sense of freshness that is emitted by the text, the impression that, without ever abandoning his most distinctive obsessions, Modiano has found a variety of ways to serve up something new to his readers.[2] Consider, for example, our point of entry into the novel, the first-person narrator.[3] He may very well be called Jean, have been born (we deduce) around 1945, and have suffered from 'de drôles de parents qui avaient toujours cherché un pensionnat [. . .] pour se débarrasser de moi' (p.38), but this typically autobiographical side to him is quickly undermined: he is also, we learn, married to a Dane (Annette), completely childless, and, more strikingly, an (albeit indifferent) cuckold. Thus, in terms of their eventual impact, the discrepancies with the author are far, far greater than ever before.

This uncertain relationship between character and creator can further be seen in the area of literary production, for although Jean is a self-confessed 'greffier incorrigible' (p.96), and has already composed an article on Henry Stanley,[4] he is not, by profession, really a writer at all. He is an explorer. But his career, like his marriage, has started to get stuck in a rut, to such a degree that, when he stumbles across a *fait divers* – the suicide, in Milan, of one of his old acquaintances, Ingrid Teyresen – he is ready to embark on a new adventure, an adventure which, perhaps not surprisingly (being the latest manifestation of our old friend, the quest), takes on an all-too-familiar form: he decides to act as the dead woman's biographer, and in the process to write what will become, more or less, his own (self-reflexive) memoirs.

Before he can make this *emotional* break, however, he has to escape on the *physical* level as well: instead of setting off on another mundane expedition, as planned, he returns to Paris, books into a hotel, and cuts himself off from his family and his friends. And having in this way, as it were, detached himself from his inhibiting present, he is free to journey back into the past, and to pursue his inquiries about the unfortunate Ingrid.

This use of the phrase 'to pursue his inquiries' is made quite deliberately, for as may by now be obvious, Modiano has, once again, turned his hand to the genre of the *roman policier*. Or at least this is the impression we get in the opening pages of the work. There, we quickly learn of the suicide (the 'crime'), and in next to no time the narrator seems to be playing the role both of witness (although an undeniably poor one), and of (frustrated) detective (pp.9, 13). Yet, as ever, Modiano's appropriation of the genre is far from total. Whole aspects of the enigma remain unresolved at the end, and certain 'traditional' elements (such as the secret staircase) are so self-consciously exploited that they become virtually parodic. Not for nothing, then, will Ingrid, like so many of her predecessors, exhibit a penchant for detective fiction (pp.37, 43)[5] – this, too, is typical of the author's ludism, of the playful way in which his texts acknowledge their debts.[6]

Yet this is not to say that the failure to exploit, in full, the form of the *roman policier* can be ascribed solely to a desire, on Modiano's part, to lighten his text through humour. This is most manifestly untrue. The lack of closure in the work, especially, has other determinants besides, most notably the uncertainty imposed by those two ubiquitous *modianesque* obsessions: time and memory.

Of these twin concerns, it is the former which, as ever, is the greater source of incertitude in *Voyage de noces*, its onward march again tending to leave nothing of substance in its wake. Dusting and painting may put off this inevitable destruction (pp.82–3),[7] but they will never prevent it, as we are constantly reminded throughout the text: the voice on the wartime radio (a collaborator's, we assume)[8] is said to be doomed in advance (p.83), and at the close of the novel the point is made even more forcibly, with Ingrid, her old surroundings and, ultimately, Jean himself all displaying a distinct lack of immortality:

> J'arrive devant [le] cinéma que l'on a transformé en magasin. De l'autre côté de la rue, l'hôtel où habitait Ingrid [. . .] n'est plus un hôtel [. . .]. Le café du rez-de-chaussée [. . .] n'existe plus. Un soir, elle était retournée elle aussi dans ce quartier et, pour la première fois, elle avait éprouvé un sentiment de vide.
>
> [. . .] Ce sentiment de vide et de remords vous submerge, un jour. Puis, [. . .] il se retire et disparaît. Mais il finit par revenir en force et elle ne pouvait pas s'en débarrasser. Moi non plus. (p.157)

So, the narrator does finally come up with some sort of explanation of Ingrid's suicide, despite the fact that he has had relatively few *documents* to work on.[9] The ravages of time may well have been wrought, but he has rescued something from the destruction all the same.

Part of the reason for this, quite evidently, is that he has been able to fall back on his own recollections. Yet as mentioned above, memory is not a real source of certainty for him either, and this on a number of very different counts. First, like everything else, it has been gradually eroded over the years: the present, which finds Jean setting off in search of Ingrid, is situated twenty-three years after he first met her in the company of her husband Rigaud, twenty years after he met her for a second, and final, time, and fully eighteen years after she sadly committed suicide; needless to say, perhaps, in the intervening period, much has been forgotten. Second, there is the added problem that the narrator is not simply trying to recall his own first-hand experience; much of his key information is made up of Ingrid's memories (recounted to him on the night they met up again by chance), so the unreliability factor is doubled. Third, and finally, it is hard for us to decide, given the aforementioned loss of details, whether it is pure mental effort that is hauling the past out of oblivion, or whether imagination is being called on to help fill in the gaps; it is all very well for Jean to make statements such as: 'Je ferme les yeux et je tente de reconstituer mon itinéraire' (p.111), but how are we to interpret *reconstituer* here? Reconstruction through knowledge? Or reconstruction through fantasy? Typically, we are never entirely sure where we stand.[10]

All the more so in that, quite apart from the problematics of time and memory, numerous other aspects of the text intensify our uncertainty. Aspects such as the constant reference to dreaming (an alternative form of invention) and its consequent subversion of reality. 'Tout à l'heure', the narrator admits in a key passage in this respect,[11] '[. . .] j'ai eu la sensation d'être dans un rêve' (p.96), and after considerably emphasizing the point, he continues:

> J'ai fini par m'endormir et j'ai rêvé pour de bon: Une nuit d'été très chaude. J'étais à bord d'une voiture décapotable. [. . .] Du centre de Paris, nous roulions vers [. . .] la Porte d'Italie. Par moments, il faisait jour, nous n'étions plus dans la voiture, et nous marchions à travers de petites rues semblables à celles de Venise ou d'Amsterdam. Nous traversions une prairie vallonnée à l'intérieur de la ville. La nuit, de nouveau. (p.98)

This quotation, with its blatant contradictions *à la nouveau roman*,[12] is highly significant in the context of *Voyage de noces*, for the use of incongruity here is far from being unique. It is, in fact, a feature of the text as a whole, with the chronology of the work, especially, failing to prove entirely consistent.[13] Now such naked inconsonance, of course, is not all that surprising in the light of what was said earlier, for it can be taken, on the one hand, as further proof that the author is acting ludically, pushing the conventions of his genre to their absolute limits, if not beyond. Or, on the other hand, it might be said to confirm that the text is largely *imagined*, a fictional world in which real-life logic plays no automatic part. Indeed, it is in this latter perspective that the quotation above comes into its own, for if the main characteristic of Jean's dream is incoherence, and the narrative itself is regularly contradictory, would this not tend to support the view that the text is just one long *rêverie*?

Whatever the case may be, one thing seems certain: there is an inbuilt tension in the novel between sets of polar opposites – between dream and reality, and imagination and fact. And that these oppositions are intentional, and not fortuitous, can be seen by the existence of yet another antithetical strand within the work: the conflict between truth and illusion, *l'être et le paraître*. Witness the Rigauds on the Côte d'Azur, in 1942:

> Ces gens [. . .] leur semblaient maintenant irréels: des figurants qui faisaient partie d'une tournée théâtrale que la guerre avait bloquée à Juan-les-Pins, et qui étaient contraints de jouer leurs rôles de faux estivants sur la plage et dans le restaurant d'une fausse Princesse de Bourbon. Le Provençal lui-même, dont la masse blanche se devinait au fond des ténèbres, était un gigantesque décor en carton-pâte.
>
> [. . .] ils entraient dans le hall. La lumière étincelante du lustre leur faisait cligner les yeux. [. . .] Les choses reprenaient un peu de consistance et de réalité. Ils se trouvaient dans un vrai hall d'hôtel, avec de vrais murs et un vrai concierge [. . .]. Puis, ils montaient dans l'ascenseur. [. . .]
>
> Au terme de leur lente ascension dans l'obscurité, ils accédaient à un palier et à un couloir qu'éclairaient faiblement des ampoules nues. C'était ainsi. Ils passaient de la lumière à l'ombre et de l'ombre à la lumière. (pp.60–1)

This extract, with its movement from *faux* to *vrai* (not to mention its metaphor of the theatre, that generator of illusion *par excellence*) could scarcely illustrate the conflict between truth and falsity more explicitly.[14] Nor could it provide a better demonstration of the way in which, with a masterful flourish, this particular conflict is linked up to the others already mentioned above (note the opposition of 'le réel' and 'l'irréel') in the aim of producing a whole *network* of contrasts.

Indeed, the passage also presents us with two new antitheses – light/dark, white/black – which similarly interlock throughout the book. 'Les contrastes d'ombre et de soleil', the narrator remarks on page 37, 'se sont accentués au point que je revois tout en noir et blanc', and he certainly does see everything in these opposing terms, especially as far as 1942 is concerned – his depiction of events then is positively monochrome.

The first signs of this *monochromie* appear when Ingrid and Rigaud decide to change flats. It is winter, snow lies on the ground, and having earlier noted, from their luxurious abode at 3, rue de Tilsett, 'la grande tache de l'Arc de Triomphe, plus sombre que la nuit, et la place que la neige rendait phosphorescente' (p.107), they set off across Paris for the spareness of 20, boulevard Soult. Outside, in the dark, they stumble upon a most amazing scene: 'un traîneau attelé à un cheval noir [. . . qui] avançait [. . .] à une allure de corbillard' (p.144). Now from this, already, we can appreciate the range of contrasts being developed. Yet the technique becomes even more flagrant once the couple leave the capital and turn up on the Côte d'Azur, for there it is summer, a hot sun beats down upon them, and almost everything emits an aura of brilliant whiteness,[15] as is entirely appropriate, given that they are on their 'voyage de noces'. Furthermore, to emphasize just how things have changed since they crossed over into the Free Zone, no sooner do they arrive in Juan-les-Pins than they encounter 'un fiacre noir attelé d'un cheval blanc' (p.55).[16]

Looking back over all these details, it becomes clear that any one pair of opposites is supported, and reinforced, by a whole plethora of others, the full catalogue of which seems to be virtually endless. To highlight simply the more obvious, we might wish to note disjunctions such as: occupied Paris/*zone libre*, town/coast, winter/summer, cold/heat, restrictions/freedom, spareness/luxury, *corbillard/noces*, and this is barely to scratch at the surface of the list. So as stated above, the contrasts are nothing if not extensive.[17]

Yet despite this sustained emphasis on *difference*, there is, strangely enough, also a tendency towards *conjunction* being implemented here, for the same binary conflicts (that of black and white, say) often recur on different time levels in the work, with the result that one historical period, by a process of comparison, is being subtly connected to another.[18] And this associative thrust is by no means coincidental, for just as a series of contrasts is developed into a network, so, too, in a final explosion of dissonance (that of similar/dissimilar), is parallelism raised to the status of system, with echoes reverberating around the text virtually unabated.

At their most basic, these echoes can be traced back to the key settings of the novel, which in actual fact are quite few – the action is restricted to the Côte d'Azur and to Paris, with the odd excursion into Italy. Yet if these décors are limited in number, they are not at all limited in time. They reappear as the years move on, with the operative figure, more often than not, being that of the mirror-image: two. Jean goes to Milan twice, the Riviera twice, flees central Paris twice, and so the text continues, with the Rigauds clearly 'doubling up' as well.

One of the corollaries of this is that the characters quickly start to merge into their past selves, and repeat their previous actions, as when the narrator recalls his early days with Annette: 'Nous avions habité l'Hôtel Dodds quelques semaines mais [. . .] j'ai oublié le numéro de notre chambre. Celle que j'occupe aujourd'hui? En tout cas, ma position n'a pas changé: je suis étendu sur le lit' (p.96). Ingrid and Rigaud, too, patently demonstrate this tendency, still playing dead at the first signs of danger a full twenty years after the war has ended (pp.40, 41, 54, 84).

Granted, this oneness with a former self may not, as things stand, be all that startling – we have, no doubt, all had similar experiences of *déjà vu*. But what is unusual is the fact that, systematically, different characters begin to blend into each other as well, with the narrator most strikingly setting the tone. From Rigaud to the man dubbed 'la tache sombre', from Ben Smidane to Fawcett and Mauffrais, the number of 'twins' that Jean possesses is absolutely incredible.[19] Yet of all his various 'doubles', one, undoubtedly, stands out head and shoulders above the rest – Ingrid Teyresen, for his merging with her is almost total: the two of them visit Milan, arriving, apparently, at the same station and on the same platform (p.13); they book into the same hotel, and drink the same drink there (p.12); they experience the same emptiness and the same world-weariness (pp.54, 92, etc.), and they both live their lives as a permanent *fuite*.[20] Jean does not, it is true, go so far as to emulate his predecessor's suicide, but as the last sentence of the text suggests, this may well be on the cards in the future.[21] For the work ends in precisely the same way that it began – on a note of *rapprochement* between the two characters, and this return to square one, in turn, confirms that, once again, the basic movement of Modiano's prose is overtly non-linear. It is, rather, the figure of the circle that shapes the narrative.

Further evidence of this is given by the leitmotifs that run through *Voyage de noces*, leitmotifs such as, most notably, the making of a journey.[22] Visible when the Rigauds change flats in Paris – they take a few things packed in a 'sac de voyage' (p.142), and travel in the horse-drawn *traîneau* – this theme persists as they subsequently head south, ride in the *fiacre* at Juan-les-Pins, and thereafter enjoy themselves on their much-announced 'voyage de noces' (pp.56, 57, 58, 63, 65, 67).[23] Even when Ingrid is encountered, years later, alone in Paris, she will say that her husband is away 'en voyage' (p.113) . . . as, of course, Jean himself often is as well, being an explorer by profession. Indeed, it is perhaps because he has chosen this particular career (and, no doubt, because of his general liking for *fuites*) that he has decorated his flat to look like a ship, the 'illusion d'être toujours en croisière' (p.46) which this produces finding an echo (typically), in the nearby place Blanche (p.47), the more distant Champs-Elysées (p.51), the remoter still Altitude 43 in Saint-Tropez (p.57).

Now this is all very well, it might be said, but it does rather beg the question why. Why this insistence on travelling? And, ultimately, why all these parallels and contrasts? To help us to answer the first of these questions, we have, fortunately, two vital clues to guide us. First, the large number of *rues en pente* which crop up in the novel (pp.38, 55, 98, etc.), and which, as in *Quartier perdu*, clearly serve as a prolonged metaphor for time: 'Je comprends', Jean remarks at the end of his quest, 'pourquoi il suffisait de me laisser glisser en roue libre sur ce vélo rouge: je remontais le temps' (p.156). Second, there is the dream we have already had cause to consider (p.171 above), and which, quite obviously, also takes the form of a journey; if, as has been proposed, this *rêve* is a reflection of the book as a whole, then the natural inference to draw is that the novel, as its title suggests, is itself an extended voyage, the type of voyage involved here hardly giving rise to doubt – we are dealing with an excursion through time, using the vehicle of remembrance and/or imagination.

This leads us on to our other niggling question – why so many oppositions and echoes? – the reply to which would appear to be relatively simple as well: as ever, this is the ideal way for Modiano to express (in all their ambiguity) his perennial, personal obsessions. For on the one hand, the conflicts emphasize the destruction wrought by time, the lack of continuity it imposes, while on the other, the parallels convey a sense of endurance, and highlight the ability of memory (supplemented, where necessary, by invention) to ensure that 'il n'existe plus de frontières entre les saisons, entre le passé et le présent' (p.124). And what this comes down to, ultimately, as Robin Buss has observed, is the articulation of perhaps *the* key theme of *l'œuvre modianesque*: 'the nature of individual identity, the continuities and disjunctions of the self'.[24]

This merging of epochs, and the access to past selves which goes with it, in turn links into another of the novelist's preoccupations: the return to the long-lost days of childhood, for thanks to the conflation of temporal strata, *l'enfance* can instantly be recaptured, as Rigaud discovers – fittingly – at the end of his wartime voyage. Having abandoned Paris and sought safety on the Riviera, 'Il se demanda s'il n'avait pas choisi pour refuge Juan-les-Pins car cet endroit était lié à son enfance' (p.71). Admittedly, his childhood was a distinctly unhappy one, but the fact remains that his journey (through time as well as through space) has led him to 'revenir au point de départ, sur les lieux de son enfance' (p.79). And the full import of this emerges when, in another *jeu de miroirs*, Jean is led to make exactly the same confession (pp.18–19), only this time, despite his own troubled upbringing, he regards the return to his youth as a much more positive achievement. On several occasions he says that the 1960s, when he was yet to become an adult, were the happiest days of his life (pp.32, 86), and adds that, when he took up the outmoded career of explorer, it was precisely because it represented 'une manière de poursuivre les rêves de l'enfance' (p.16), which is perhaps also why he now searches so hard for

Ingrid – thanks to his self-assimilation to his predecessor, his recording of *her* formative years is a vicarious re-embracing of *his own*.[25]

But he cannot, of course, turn the clock back with any degree of permanency. At the end of the book, his wife will not help him re-create their happy past (p.150) and the Ingrid he is identifying with is not the child, relatively safe, on the Côte d'Azur, but the fully-grown woman, soon to die, as her spirit already has done. Time, as has been seen, is inexorably moving on . . . as it does in all of Modiano's works, we might add, and this is by no means a negligible point, for what the preceding paragraphs demonstrate, through their mention of the author's recurrent themes, is that, as ever, the system of parallels being employed is not limited to the confines of the immediate text, but extends, instead, way out beyond them, and into the recesses of the *œuvre* as a whole.[26]

However, as we have seen, internally there are no echoes without compensatory contrasts, and the same applies in this wider context too, for despite its similarities with the preceding texts, *Voyage de noces* clearly, and distinctively, sets itself apart from its forerunners as well. Some good examples of this break with the past have already been noted, in the introduction to this section above, but it will be appropriate, now, to finish with what is arguably the most important and telling illustration of them all: the treatment of the early 1940s. For from the opening lines of the text, when the hotel evokes a 'blockhaus' (p.9) and Milan a 'ville ouverte' (p.11), the war takes on a key role in the narrative, the largest role, in fact, that it has played for some time. But the striking thing is that, unlike previously, the narrator now is detached from the period. It is the Rigauds' experience of wartime France, and not his own, that he is (imaginatively) recalling; it is Ingrid, not he, who is Jewish and under threat; and it is she, not he, who adopts a false identity. In short, from their earlier, privileged position, the war years have been reduced to a level of time like any other, and this, together with the aforementioned biographical disjunctions between Jean and his creator,[27] would appear to suggest but one thing: Modiano's drive towards exorcism, if not complete, is at least progressing by leaps and bounds.

Like *Remise de peine* before it, *Fleurs de ruine* again finds Modiano temporarily switching from Gallimard to the Editions du Seuil, and his reason for so doing would appear to be much the same as it was before: to become more confessional, and to address his troubled past more directly.[28] Not that we have moved into the realm of pure autobiography, though – the personal revelations are given no special prominence in the work, and, indeed, as will shortly be demonstrated, are often tied into fictitious 'facts' from which, in status, they are virtually indistinguishable. In short, we are dealing not so much with a succession of *confidences*, the detail of which is the be-all and end-all of the work, as with the *process* by which such details are presented – the way in which memories, whether real or invented, can be triggered by external objects.[29]

The starting-point of this mental peregrination, fittingly, is a another form of meandering, a physical one this time – a stroll through the streets of Paris. And as in *Voyage de noces*, this journey is quickly linked to a suicide, an event from which (ironically, considering it represents a form of closure), the main body of the text will subsequently grow. The suicide in question is that of Urbain and Gisèle T., and goes back almost sixty years to 24 April 1933. On that distant night, the doomed couple went out, took part in an 'orgie tragique' and then, 'pour des raisons mystérieuses' (p.13), returned home and took their own lives. Needless to say, perhaps, these 'unclear reasons' for the crime come to fascinate the narrator, and he determines, like his immediate predecessor, to try to elucidate what they might have been.

To do this, again like Jean in *Voyage de noces* (and any number of other precursors), he sets himself up as a sort of detective, and embarks on his own, personal investigation of the case. Retracing the T.s' footsteps prior to their deaths, consulting the newspapers of the day and re-examining the statements of witnesses, he unearths, unusually for a *modianesque* 'hero', a great deal of undeniable facts – never before have we been presented with so many precise dates and addresses. However, predictably (and ludically), the essential clues remain undiscovered, and by the end of the *enquête* we are left with more questions really than answers. Exactly why did the couple commit suicide? What happened to them during their night out? Why should the narrator delve into an old *fait divers*? We can provide intelligent guesses in reply here, but the text itself does not tell us *explicitly* what to conclude. In fact, it does the very opposite, ensuring that, as ever, the sense of mystery actually deepens as the narrative progresses.

There are two obvious reasons for this. First, the investigation constantly loses its focus. As the narrator proceeds, retracing the steps of the T.s, a string of extraneous, personal memories are evoked (or *rêveries* provoked), and the suicide seems forgotten. And it is not so much this side-tracking itself that is the problem (for as we shall see, tenuous links with the crime are often established), as the fact that, quite often, the characters thus introduced intensify our initial uncertainty – characters such as Duvelz (or should that be Devez?), of whom the narrator himself declares: 'Très vite, je m'étais rendu compte qu'il ne me disait pas la vérité: [. . .] il demeurait vague. Et il se contredisait' (p.19). And this brings us round, opportunely, to the second source of confusion in the work: the protagonist-author's technique, for the above judgement of Duvelz can be applied equally well to the first-person 'hero' himself. He, too, mixes the true and the false, the real and the dreamed; he, too, piles contradiction upon contradiction; and he, too, overtly cultivates vagueness.[30] Add to this his abandonment of chronology and his fragmentation of the narrative, and what we have left, at least in the first instance, is a form designed to create, rather than to forestall, a sense of disorientation.[31]

The end result of this, as ever, is to make us aware of the onward march of time, for if there is a lack of certainty in the work, it is almost entirely due to the havoc wrought by the passing of the years. Not for nothing does the text open (practically) with the two T.s' suicide – this emphasis on death sets the tone for what is to come.[32] Characters will enter the narrator's life and then totally disappear, while the settings, although apparently stable, will prove to be equally prone to temporal attack. Witness the decline that has afflicted Montparnasse, 'un quartier qui [. . .] pourrissait doucement, loin de Paris. [. . .] La fête, ici, était finie depuis longtemps' (pp.16–17). The party most certainly does appear to be over, and not just in this particular instance – the whole book is a litany of decay and degradation.[33]

It is in the context of this irrevocable erosion that, arguably, the narrator's interest in the T.s can best be explained, for he is perhaps not interested in them *specifically*, as a true detective would be, but rather as the manifestation of something more general, namely the ravages of time and the mysteries they create. After all, it is not just the clues to the suicide that he seeks to (re)discover and note down; any detail is deemed worthy of recording by him, whether it be a simple name and phone number (pp.34-5) or a list of long-vanished shops (p.29). In other words, his main concern, it would appear, is a retrospective act of *rescue*, and a key ally for him in this endeavour is his memory. 'Je fais un effort de mémoire pour rassembler le plus de détails possible', he admits at an early stage in the proceedings (p.23), and his stance barely alters in the slightest thereafter. Admittedly, his imagination does, quite regularly, fill in where recollection proves to be deficient or impossible (pp.30, 75, 131, etc.), but this is not seen in terms of failure. On the contrary, any resurrection of the past, whether real or imaginary, is considered preferable to oblivion, as the very title of the work suggests: the 'ruins' may well be extensive, but anything emerging from them (the vital, beautiful 'flowers') will at least in part manage to offset the decay.[34]

This attempt to thwart time, as usual, cannot be divorced from the prizing of childhood. 'Pour Zina | Pour Marie | Pour Douglas', we learn as early as the dedication page of the text, and from this choice of dedicatees (the author's two daughters and the family dog)[35] we infer, immediately, that *l'enfance* will again prove essential for Modiano. And as we read on, our expectations are more than fulfilled. Juvenile pastimes vie with a schoolday *fugue* as the narrator regularly returns to his long-lost youth, and amongst these most poignant of memories, one in particular tends to stand out: his reference to the days when, along with his brother, he used to play in the jardins du Carrousel, in sight of an old clock on the wall of the Louvre.[36] 'Les aiguilles de l'horloge ne bougeaient pas', he informs us. 'Elles indiquaient pour toujours cinq heures et demie. Ces aiguilles nous enveloppent d'un silence profond et apaisant. Il suffit de rester dans l'allée et plus rien ne changera jamais' (p.91). It is no coincidence that, in the course of this statement, the verb tense suddenly switches to the present, nor that the clock seems to inform us, as will later be confirmed, that 'le temps s'est arrêté' (p.123) – Modiano's attempt to abolish time, in *Fleurs de ruine*, is another attempt to recapture his childhood.

The means he adopts to do this are also quite familiar to us – he skilfully links events from different eras so that time, as it were (and as in *Vestiaire de l'enfance*), becomes conflated. 'Les années se confondaient et [. . .] le temps devenait transparent', the narrator observes during his stroll around Paris (p.43), and the further he goes the more parallels emerge between the various layers of the past. Part of this mirroring, of course, can be ascribed to the fact that, for much of the time, he is following in the footsteps of predecessors, most notably the tragic T.s. But this is not always the case. Often, the *dédoublement* in the text has other origins. There are, for example, two Jacquelines, one from the Occupation, and one from the 1960s; the protagonist will twice consume whisky, once as a schoolboy, and once as a budding author (pp.39, 106); and so we could go on, almost *ad infinitum*. In fact, so extensive is this use of echoes that, despite appearances to the contrary, the text is not really fragmented at all. There is a subtle harmony about the work, to such an extent that, quite easily, each portion of it can be linked to one or more others. To begin where Modiano himself begins (more or less), the unfortunate T.s feed in both to Duvelz, thanks to the Montparnasse connection and their apparent promiscuity,[37] and to Claude Bernard, whose house, with its red lift, might have been visited by them on the night of their deaths; Claude Bernard then connects with the Gestapo, Simone Cordier, Jacqueline and the marquis, via a shared association with the XVIe *arrondissement*; Simone ties in with the narrator's father (she was his secretary), who in turn ties in with his son (as does Jacqueline), Pacheco and Pagnon; Pagnon is going out with Sylviane; and Sylviane, it is said, might be involved in the T.s' suicide. Thus, at the end of the day (almost inevitably), we have actually come full circle. And this circularity (which is far more extensive than illustrated here) turns fragmentation into order.

This brings us back, once again, to the role of imagination in the work, for if the various characters and events overlap with one another, it is not because they are all interconnected in real life, but rather because the narrator, mentally, creates hypothetical links where none exist. Time and again he admits to using *rêverie* to supplement fact and, indeed, to improve upon it, 'la contagion du rêve sur la réalité' being a tendency he overtly recognizes in himself (p.41). And ultimately, of course, as suggested above, this 'contagion' derives from his attempt to combat time, since one obvious way to thwart temporal erosion – and the fragmentation and confusion it generates – is, precisely, to reimpose a long-lost harmony on the past, to substitute, no matter how fleetingly or inaptly, a sense of order for uncertainty.

This drive to produce unity from chaos (which, as ever, sets up a clear antagonism in the work) is not directed wholly *inwards*, that is to say confined to the pages of *Fleurs de ruine* itself. Much of the information we are given has an *external* relevance as well, echoing outwards (again quite typically) to form links way beyond the boundaries of the text, and in two (often inter-related) areas in particular: the preceding works in the *œuvre* and the author's personal past.

To illustrate the tie-in to Modiano's earlier books, we need look no further than the character of the marquis, who almost constantly gives off an aura of *déjà vu*.[38] Distinctively attired 'en veste de chasse' and with 'un château et des terres' (p.130) in Sologne, he could have stepped right out of the pages of *Livret de famille*, all the more so in that, yet again, he is associated with a 'chasse à courre' there (p.131).[39]

Philippe de Pacheco is not new to us either, having already appeared under the same name in *Dimanches d'août*, *Voyage de noces* and, we assume, *Une jeunesse*.[40] However, up until now, we have been given relatively little detail about him. We have learnt that he was born in Paris on 22 January 1918, that he was really called Philippe de Bellune, and that he was engaged in dubious activities during the Occupation;[41] but that is about all. *Fleurs de ruine* confirms each of these points (pp.73–4) and does a good deal more besides, filling in whole sections of the character's life history. Yet for all this additional information, our understanding scarcely improves. On the contrary, the man becomes harder than ever to pin down – rumour has it that he died just after the war (p.66), yet he is alive in 1955 (p.83),[42] and, more confusingly still, his identity seems to have been usurped by one Charles Lombard, who is himself an ambiguous man of mystery.[43] Thus, quite manifestly, the erstwhile Bellune is irrevocably 'fuyant' (p.61), the very epitome of a *modianesque* creation.

If Pacheco takes us back to previous texts, though, it is, self-evidently, only because of the way he is presented to us, only because, initially, he is deemed worthy of mention by the first-person *je*. Or, to put it another way, it is the narrator who, in the final analysis, gives rise to this sense of continuity, as a whole variety of other points illustrate. A childhood on the Left Bank of Paris, in Saint-Germain-des-Prés (pp.38, 89); schooldays marked by *fugues*, 'orphanage' and surrogate parents (pp.38, 95–7, 115, 116); later experience as a pseudo-student (pp.55–6); time spent away in Vienna (pp.37, 123, 142); a professional career as a writer(-cum-detective); and the fathering of daughters (pp.111, 122) – this background is typical, in part if not in whole, of all previous leading characters in the *œuvre*.

It is also, of course, very much the background of Modiano himself,[44] and this brings us on to the confessional element in *Fleurs de ruine*. 'Les fantômes ont aujourd'hui un nom, et l'écrivain une histoire', the headline to one review broadly proclaimed,[45] and whilst this statement needs to be kept in some sort of perspective, it is, nevertheless, essentially true: there *are* sections of the work which are autobiographical and which, as a result, throw light on the rest of the *œuvre*.

This is particularly applicable where the Occupation is concerned, for the spotlight again focuses on the seminal figure of Eddy Pagnon. Based at 48*bis* rue des Belles-Feuilles (p.127), soon to move out to Barbizon (p.49), a frequent visitor to riding schools (p.127), and having worked in a garage before the war (p.48), the Pagnon we encounter is our old friend from *Remise de peine*, albeit more fully described thanks to the narrator's (and no doubt the author's) disclosure of the 'nouvelles bribes de renseignements que je viens de rassembler sur lui' (p.48).[46] Part of this new information – new to us at least – relates to two of his acquaintances, both of whom, on reflection, seem to be almost as familiar to us as he is. The first of these is Jean Terrail, whom he apparently swindled out of 300,000 marks in 1943 (p.134), and who has already appeared in *Quartier perdu* and *Dimanches d'août*.[47] The second is his mistress, Sylviane, who is presented in far greater detail. Of modest background and a keen player of billiards, 'cette Sylviane à la chevelure auburn' (p.48) would not remain obscure for long. 'Au début de l'Occupation', we learn, 'elle épouserait un soupirant sans fortune mais qui portait un titre de marquis d'Empire' (p.45), and by the Liberation, she would have become interested in horse-riding, linked up with Pagnon, moved out to Barbizon with him, stayed in a room, above a café, on the quai d'Austerlitz, and, we might add, generally lived the life that, years later, would inspire a veiled reincarnation – as Sylviane Quimphe in *Les Boulevards de ceinture*.[48]

In addition to Terrail and Sylviane, there is, perhaps

predictably, a third acquaintance of Pagnon's to whom reference is made – the narrator's father. And here, too, the sense of *déjà vu* is intense, for once again, we are faced with a man (tellingly identified as Albert) who is nothing if not ambiguous. We learn, for instance, that he arranged to meet people neither on home ground nor away, but on the neutral territory of 'le hall du Claridge' (p.103); that his office was situated at 1, rue Lord-Byron, and was probably chosen 'à cause de sa double issue' (p.104); and that, finally, he suddenly vanished into thin air, leaving his son full of unanswered questions and unsure of whether in fact he existed at all (p.139). He did, of course, actually exist; he was Modiano's own father, and this is why the above details, although apparently minor, are in reality highly significant – they confirm, retrospectively, that most of the *pères* in the earlier fiction are drawn from the real-life model.[49]

The reason for this paternal portraiture can, as ever, be summed up in two immensely portentous words: the Occupation. Or more specifically, it can be traced back to Albert's constant predicament then, a predicament which crystallized when he was arrested – as *Remise de peine* had already suggested, and as is now apparently confirmed – on two entirely different occasions: the first, 'un soir de 1942, près du cinéma Biarritz' (p.103), when he was able to escape (if earlier works are to be believed) entirely by his own devices, and the second, during 'l'hiver de 1943', when he was interned in 'cette annexe du camp de Drancy' (p.48), the Magasins généraux, and could only get out thanks to the intervention of a *gestapiste* friend, the all-powerful Eddy Pagnon.[50] Indeed, such was Pagnon's status then that, it is suggested, he drove Albert away from his captors in an impressive *voiture de luxe* – the Lancia which he had stolen from Erich Maria Remarque (p.113). And this is not mere name-dropping on Modiano's part; not in the slightest. It is an important revelation, for as Jean-Louis Ezine rightly observes,[51] this detail gives a whole new meaning to the oneiric Lancia hunt in *Quartier perdu*, all the more so in that, just prior to the disclosure in *Fleurs de ruine*, the connection between dream, son, father and cross-Paris journey had been emphasized. 'Dans mes rêves', we had been told,

> je fais souvent ce trajet: je sors d'un lieu de détention [. . .]. Il fait nuit. Quelqu'un m'attend, dans une grande automobile [. . .]. Nous

quittons ce quartier [. . .] pour nous diriger vers la Seine. A l'instant
où nous atteignons la Rive droite après avoir franchi le pont du
Carrousel et les guichets du Louvre, je pousse un soupir de
soulagement. Je n'ai plus rien à craindre. Nous avons laissé derrière
nous la zone dangereuse. Je sais qu'il ne s'agit que d'un répit. Plus
tard, on me demandera des comptes. J'éprouve un sentiment de
culpabilité dont l'objet demeure vague: un crime auquel j'ai
participé en qualité de complice ou de témoin, je ne pourrais pas
vraiment le dire. Et j'espère que cette ambiguïté m'évitera le
châtiment. A quoi correspond ce rêve dans la vie réelle? Au souvenir
de mon père qui, sous l'Occupation, avait vécu une situation
ambiguë elle aussi: arrêté dans une rafle par des policiers français
sans savoir de quoi il était coupable, et libéré par un membre de la
bande de la rue Lauriston? (pp.112–13)[52]

'Yes', we immediately reply to this question, 'most definitely', for
everything else in the *œuvre* tends to corroborate this fact.
Modiano is, and always has been, haunted by the wartime arrest
of his father.

This being the case, it is clear that, like so many other texts
before it, *Fleurs de ruine* is a work of self-purging. However,
despite what has just been said, it is not simply the *années noires*
that the author is getting out of his system; he is targeting his
own childhood as well.[53] 'Le monde auquel appartenaient ces
gens', we are informed as we meet Jean Terrail and his
companions, 'réveillait des souvenirs d'enfance: c'était le monde
de mon père. Marquis et chevaliers d'industrie. Gentilshommes
de fortune. Gibier de correctionnelle. [. . .] Je les tire une dernière
fois du néant avant qu'ils y retournent définitivement' (p.134).
'C'était le monde de mon père' – this relatively brief phrase
clearly says it all. Never before has the exorcistic, autobiographical strand in the *œuvre* been better demonstrated. And
never before has anything quite struck us like the final
'définitivement', especially when viewed alongside another
childhood memory. 'A vingt ans', we had earlier been apprised,

j'éprouvais un soulagement quand je passais de la Rive gauche à la
Rive droite de la Seine [. . .]. Je me demande aujourd'hui ce que je
fuyais [. . .]. Peut-être le quartier que j'avais connu avec mon frère et
qui, sans lui, n'était plus le même [. . .]. Longtemps, j'ai ressenti un
malaise à marcher dans certaines rues de la Rive gauche. Maintenant
le quartier m'est devenu indifférent. (pp.88–9)

For years and years, as has been seen, Modiano had great difficulty in accepting the loss of his brother, and this is why the above comment seems to be so meaningful. His new-found indifference to streets which evoke Rudy, added to his aforementioned use of 'définitivement', would appear to signify but one thing: exorcism is proving productive; the ghosts of his past are slowly being laid.[54]

Having once again purged himself in the confessional *Fleurs de ruine*, Modiano, as is his wont, immediately embarks on something of a *volte-face*, switching back to Gallimard from Les Editions du Seuil, and returning to his favoured format of the novel. The result of this double about-turn is *Un cirque passe*, which is, perhaps, the author's most refined book to date, for in it he manages to work his usual wonders with a raw material that has never been sparer. A mere handful of characters; an empty flat; regular silences;[55] no real action – not even the stripped-down earlier texts were ever as bereft as this! Yet not everything has been pruned away and cut back to almost nothing. The stock of the *œuvre*, predictably, has barely been touched at all.

This continuity with the past can be seen, first and foremost, in the abiding influence of the *roman policier*, an influence which, in this particular work, is of virtually paradigmatic proportions. The text opens with the narrator being questioned by the police (not because he has committed a crime, but because his name figures in somebody's diary),[56] and thereafter the theme of the *polar*, if anything, goes from strength to strength. A chance meeting with a co-suspect, Gisèle, creates a clear opening for suspense to come (anything can happen in a world where *le hasard* is king), and almost everything else in the narrative would be quite at home in the *série noire*. The physical settings, for example, are typical of the genre in that, as ever, they represent dubiety, the impersonal and a distinct lack of permanence. From the streets of Paris to a strip joint to other *lieux de passage* (such as restaurants, cafés and hotels) we are whisked through a succession of backdrops that are essentially faceless to say the least – and none more so than the protagonist's flat on the quai Conti. Cleared of most of its furniture, soon to be moved out of completely, this *appartement* (like its bedroom, which 'n'avait jamais eu d'usage bien déterminé' – p.56) is the very symbol of the ephemeral and the uncertain. Add to these troubling décors the aforementioned silences, and what we have is an intention plainly shared with the writers of *romans policiers* – the deliberate creation of mysteries.

This is all the more evident in that, as usual, the key figure of the narrator is the ill-defined incarnate. Abandoned by mother and father alike, he is, appropriately, never said to have a surname at all. Indeed, he is only given any true identification (as opposed to the sobriquet of Obligado and the role-play persona of Lucien) once, on page 137, when we learn (predictably perhaps) that he is in fact called Jean. And as if this vague background were not indefinite enough, after he bumps into Gisèle at the police station she and her friends visibly add to the uncertainty which surrounds him. His co-suspect appears to have no serious family ties either (p.59), nor does she ever disclose her full name, let alone talk about the intricacies of her past. 'Avec elle, je n'étais sûr de rien', he is quickly forced to concede (p.62), and only slightly fewer doubts hang over Jacques de Bavière and Pierre Ansart.

Quite apart from this dearth of relational definition, Jean is hard to pin down in terms of his exact role within the novel. When we first meet him, as noted above, he is helping the police with their enquiries, and as the narrative progresses we come to realize, more and more, that there is perhaps a lot more to this questioning than he himself admits. For we quickly discover that, despite his claims of innocence, there is a distinctly unsavoury side to his nature. He has a marked affinity for deception, whether dealing with friends, acquaintances or complete strangers (pp.9, 12, 19, 36–7, 42–3, 54, 124, 133, 136, 142); he bats not an eyelid when told that Gisèle, with whom he has been sleeping, is both married and a prostitute (pp.59, 139); and worst of all, he thinks nothing of helping Ansart to meet a man and then drive him away, perhaps to make him disappear for ever. Admittedly, we never learn whether a murder subsequently takes place or not, but we do ascertain that Jean is indifferent to this possibility (p.140). We also discover that he has no doubts whatsoever about his own role in the affair – he is not just a key witness, but an actual accomplice as well (p.100).

Now if all these points seem to establish him as being very much on the wrong side of the law, there is, confusingly, another side of him which suggests the very opposite, for by trying to find out about Gisèle and her past, he assumes the mantle of amateur detective – *amateur* not just because he has no formal status, but also because he proves to be somewhat ineffective here. Failing, like so many of his predecessors, to probe sufficiently deeply (pp.48, 50, 53, 64, 102), he manages to unearth little of any importance, the result of which is that, at the end of the day, we rely on the real police for our concrete information. It is they, for instance, who reveal the secret of Gisèle's prostitution, and they who inform us – in a typically *modianesque* blurring of identity – that her real name is Suzanne Kraay (p.130). Yet ineffective or not, Jean remains, at heart, a sleuth, and this, quite manifestly, increases our bewilderment. For how can we call him a criminal if he has the outlook of a detective?

This problem we have in defining him is all the more acute in that, in addition to starring in the narrative, he is apparently producing it as well, and producing it with an obvious aim in mind – eschewing mere presentation of the mysteries that he, in the past, has endeavoured to solve, he does his utmost, stylistically, to create enigmas where none exist. He refuses to state exactly when the action is set, preferring to give a series of allusions suggesting it is sometime in the early 1960s (1963?). He makes no use of hindsight, even though he is writing about thirty years after the events he describes. He glosses over certain aspects of his past, of which he ought to be able to say a good deal more.[57] He throws in details which conflict with others, and hence raise questions rather than clarify.[58] He appears to enlighten, only to backtrack immediately.[59] And most important of all, he deliberately parcels out his revelations, passing on his information steadily, bit by bit – characters (like himself) are introduced and not identified on the spot; past lives are divulged in fragments (and not entirely at that); the title promises us a circus, of which no mention is made for ages; and so we stutter along, with one door closing as another one opens.[60] In this way, then, things which are already intrinsically mysterious are given an additional veil of secrecy, and as this (essentially ludic) technique is more refined here than ever before, further weight is given to the contention implicitly stated above – namely that, in the context of the *œuvre* (with the possible exception of *Rue des Boutiques Obscures*), *Un cirque passe* perhaps owes most to the established genre of the *polar*.[61]

So, Modiano pursues his interest in the *roman policier*, and thereby creates a certain unity with his preceding texts. However, if we are looking for *all* the sources of continuity with the past, there is much more to consider in the work than simply this. The great *modianesque* themes have been retained and re-utilized as well, with time, for one, again reigning supreme, erasing everything and everyone before it, such as the family friend whom Jean recalls, and who, even then, was very much a has-been, 'un homme [. . .] auquel il ne restait, d'une période plus faste de sa vie, qu'une pelisse et un blazer [. . .] usés [. . .]. Qu'avait-il bien pu devenir? Il avait certainement disparu' (pp.100–1).[62] Jacques, Ansart, Gisèle: they, too, will all likewise disappear, leaving behind them nothing but unanswered questions and half-solved mysteries – and a string of perplexing memories.

The use of the word 'memories' here suggests, in turn, yet another link back to the rest of the *œuvre*: recollection. Like all of its predecessors, *Un cirque passe* is retrospective in essence, the main action of the work (in so far as there is any) having taken place much earlier, and now being *remembered* at some years' remove. Furthermore, there is a distinctly Proustian side to this process which is not unfamiliar to us either. The theme of the journey punctuates the text, underlining the mental voyage that is being pursued (pp.22, 64, 141, etc.), and *souvenirs* are frequently triggered, involuntarily, by anything (although normally a setting) which provides enduring ties between past and present,[63] ties which, perversely, are simultaneously *dissociative*, carrying within them the measure of time. 'Les détails topographiques', Jean himself observes, 'ont un drôle d'effet sur moi: loin de me rendre l'image du passé plus proche et plus claire, ils me causent une sensation déchirante de liens tranchés net et de vide' (p.41).

And because memory itself, as ever, is subject to this selfsame erosion (not to mention distortion and incompleteness), once again, imagination has to be called in to remedy its deficiencies, the end result of this being that, in *Un cirque passe* as in the previous novels, a manifest tension exists in the text between fact and fiction, between dream and reality. 'Tu es réveillé?' Jean is asked at one point, and his reply quite manifestly says it all: 'Je ne sais pas [. . .]. Je préfère rester dans l'incertitude' (p.111). We, too, are dragged into the same incertitude, for if things seem relatively straightforward at first, more and more, as the narrative progresses, the concept of *rêverie* asserts itself (pp.40, 85, 99, 110–12, 133, 137, 146), thereby undermining our earlier inferred 'certainties'.

A key role in this development is played by the city of Rome, which, idealized in the extreme, and invoked with ever greater insistence, rapidly takes on an overtly symbolic function – as the antithesis to, and therefore escape from, the constraining environment of Paris. By fleeing to the Italian capital, Jean believes, all his problems will be resolved.[64] Once there, he need have no worries about military service (p.113); his sense of menace will disappear (pp.84–5); he can rediscover, as it were, part of his childhood (pp.126–7); and, best of all, he will have Gisèle entirely to himself. In a word, then, Rome is that typically *modianesque* device: the haven. However, as has been seen, earlier *asiles* have proved far too good to be true, and, not unexpectedly, exactly the same applies here. At the end of the novel, the narrator is still in France, with his dreams in tatters before him. Fate, which had fortuitously given him Gisèle (another symbol of future happiness), has just as abruptly removed her.[65] We are, quite palpably, more or less back where we started.[66]

This final comment, taken with the earlier mention of tensions in the work, would appear to suggest that, once again, we are faced with a narrative which is binary in nature, that is to say constructed upon the basis of circularity and contrast, and when we delve deeper into the matter, we find that this does, indeed, actually prove to be the case.

As far as the contrastive element is concerned, what immediately strikes us, above all else, is that the Rome/Paris opposition is supported by that of Spring/Autumn, and that, in a fateful premonition of their ultimate destiny, our two 'heroes' are constantly shown to be anything but united: Gisèle is at first indifferent to the dangers which preoccupy Jean (p.53), while by the end of the novel their positions have visibly been reversed (pp.137, 141, 142, 148).[67]

The use of parallelism, too, is very much in evidence throughout the book. Words, phrases and ideas are regularly repeated;[68] locations already frequented are visited again later (pp.55, 75, 77, 109, 120, 146); and, as befits a novelist whose style is distinctly visual, dashes of colour are used like a leitmotif in painting.[69] By far the best example to take here, though, is that of another old friend of ours: the substitute family. As has been seen, both the narrator and Gisèle are effectively orphans, and yet, like any number of their predecessors, they are not totally deprived of relations, for where nature has proved deficient, a sort of surrogacy compensates. They readily act as brother and sister for each other (pp.34–46); Ansart is viewed paternally on more than one occasion (pp.42, 46, 68); Ellen James, through a series of links, is established as maternal (pp.82–4); and then, in pride of place, there is Henri Grabley, who is a sort of reflection of Jean's father incarnate (pp.22–3, 103, 107–8). Thus, just as the same notions and the same colours are encountered at different moments, and the same paths retrodden in different epochs, so too does the same 'family' extend to different generations, and what this comes down to, ultimately, is perfectly clear: as implied by the very use of same/different in all these cases, the novel is essentially binary in conception.

This point, like most of the preceding ones in this section, has, of course, already been made umpteen times before, in the context of any number of previous works in the *œuvre*, and while this is not particularly astounding – any author would be loath to change a winning formula – it does, nevertheless, raise certain questions, which it will perhaps now be appropriate to answer: why, if we know what to expect from Modiano, are we never bored by any of his novels? What holds our attention when everything seems so predictable? There are, it would appear, from what has been said above – in this and in earlier chapters – a whole host of possible answers to these questions. To give only some of the more obvious, we might wish to note: the masterful way in which the works are composed, their moments of sheer poetry, their readability, their hidden depths, their unity, or perhaps just their focus on mystery and suspense, which, by their very nature, are automatically intriguing. Of all the explanations we might choose to highlight, however, one would seem to be as convincing as any: the fact that we, as readers, are allotted – and willingly take on – an active role in the proceedings. For we, too, like the respective narrators, soon find ourselves playing the detective.

This 'detection' on our part expresses itself in more than just one way. On the most basic level, that is to say within the confines of any one text, we are led to link up the snippets of information we are given and build up a picture of what actually happened, normally by reimposing chronology and by putting incidents back into their 'original', historical order. Granted, there is less encouragement for us to do this in a relatively spare text like *Un cirque passe* – the much more complicated narrative of, say, *Voyage de noces* presents a far greater incentive – but as long as there are any flashbacks at all to consider, the principle remains the same. Alternatively, if this approach is deemed unsuitable,[70] we might choose to home in on the various textual allusions, and decide on possible 'keys' behind such references.[71] Alternatively still, we could simply try to spot the internal echoes, and use them as sorts of 'clues', directing us, at the very least, towards an overall pattern, if not total solution, for the novel that we are 'investigating'.[72] This final possibility – the pursuit of resemblances – likewise fuels our *enquête* on its other, more demanding level, but here the links are a good deal more widespread, stretching far out into the *œuvre* as a whole, and, indeed, beyond.

These broader, external ties – which now relate not to the aforementioned *grands thèmes*, but to the less visible, and therefore harder to detect, recurrence of detail – tend to be of two quite different types. First, those which are restricted to the fiction which gave rise to them, and second, those which are more autobiographical in nature, and which hence seem to provide insights into the author's life and background. Appositely, *Un cirque passe* provides good illustrations of both.

To begin with the former, the choice is so rich that even the worst sleuth could not fail to find at least one *piste* to follow. Gisèle's marriage to a circus boss evokes Hélène in *Remise de peine*,[73] while her very name reminds us of Mme T. in *Fleurs de ruine*; the reference to 'Charrell et Karvé, des camarades de collège' (p.77) harks back to *De si braves garçons*; the father's obsession with diplomas (p.20) is reminiscent of *Les Boulevards de ceinture*; the car drive across Paris (pp.69–71) is just one connection to *La Ronde de nuit*;[74] the dog as a mirror to humans finds its model in *Villa Triste*;[75] and there are umpteen additional links to *Livret de famille*, prime amongst which is the flat at 15 quai Conti.[76]

This address was, of course, for a good many years Modiano's own, so now is perhaps the right time to move on to the second set of outward *indices* in *Un cirque passe* – those which are more clearly autobiographical in origin. And here, once again, the profile we get of the author is very much a familiar one. There is mention of his various schools (pp.29, 106), of his early wish to be a writer (pp.123, 131), of his short flirtation with university (p.9), and of his two parents, the actress and the businessman, both of whom, as usual, are frequently absent abroad (p.10).[77] Yet within this basic repetition, we are given snippets of new information. To the knowledge (gained from *Vestiaire de l'enfance*) that the mother once played the Théâtre Fontaine in Pigalle, we can now add that she performed there in 'un vaudeville: *La princesse parfumée*' (p.88), while to the earlier descriptions of the quai Conti flat, we can annex details about its previous occupant, the ubiquitous Maurice Sachs (pp.20, 144).[78] In other words, revelations are drip-fed not just within the confines of any one novel, but across the length and breadth of the *œuvre* as a whole – a further challenge to us in our role as reader-detective.

This extended focus is noteworthy for another reason as well: it augments our impression of outlines being blurred, of boundaries being eroded, for if 'clues' are being scattered across every single text, we might choose to conclude that just one, long (and as yet unfinished) monograph is actually being written, with each successive publication being part of this *magnum opus*. Accordingly, total output becomes book, and book becomes chapter, no matter what our initial reaction may be.

This urge to assimilate part to whole is further induced by the fact that, like most of his individual works (and the tendency to self-echo notwithstanding), Modiano's *œuvre* deliberately subverts its own 'realities', as when Jean, the narrator of *Un cirque passe*, informs us that his father ran the *Société civile d'Études de Traitements de Minerais*, located at 73, boulevard Haussmann (p.24) – previously, as we have seen, the paternal business was the *Société africaine d'entreprise*, sited at 1, rue Lord-Byron. Now admittedly, there may not be an *automatic* contradiction here, but this is not always the case.[79] And anyway, the basic point is unaltered – the discrepancy between texts (even if more apparent than real) renders what we read untrustworthy.

This untrustworthiness has, of course, up until now been linked to the cathartic element in Modiano's work, his compulsive attempt to assuage his own ambiguities. So we might expect the same to apply to *Un cirque passe*, and, indeed, it most obviously does. In fact, the sense of exorcism which greets us is at its most intense for some time, so much so that, had the phrase not been used already, we might be tempted to subtitle the work

Patrick Modiano

'Goodbye to All That'.[80] The empty flat on the quai Conti, soon to be abandoned; the familiar techniques of *distanciation* (pp.28, 58, 89, 130, 131); the explicit mention of the end of an era (pp.98, 108, 110, 153) – all of these are suggestive of closure, of a line being drawn beneath the past, and as to exactly where this line is situated, there can be little room for doubt. 'Pour mes parents', reads the dedication of the work, and this is more significant than one might think – not because it implies that, as ever, it is the author's family background that is going to be purged, but because it narrows the target down even further. Apart from *Rue des Boutiques Obscures*, this is the only text which is addressed to the father, so it is his ghost, we assume, which will principally be laid to rest – and the more we delve into the narrative, the more we realize that this is the case, for significantly, 'le père', too, is evoked in terms of definitive departure. Plagued by mysterious 'ennuis' in France (p.59), he has left the country and fled to Geneva (p.20), 'pour y finir sa vie' (p.14).[81] And when his son saw him off at the station, the writing was very much on the wall: 'Mon père m'avait paru brusquement vieilli et las, comme quelqu'un qui, depuis trop longtemps, joue "au chat et à la souris" et qui est sur le point de se rendre' (p.20).[82] Not for nothing, then, do we focus on this final meeting of parent and child, and not for nothing does Switzerland – hitherto the haven which could not be reached – represent the site of the paternal retreat.[83] This is no doubt Modiano's own way of saying 'goodbye to all that', and of conducting an ultimate, unshackling exorcism of his past.[84]

Notes

1. *Paris Tendresse*, a collection of photographs by Brassaï, with an accompanying text by Modiano, finds the novelist doing in real life what he does so well in his fiction – commenting on old photos and noting what they evoke for him. Significantly, the tone is frequently confessional and personal, a clear sign that, as in *Remise de peine*, the author can now slip into autobiographical mode with relative ease. 'Polar à huit mains: L'Angle mort: Chapitre 3' is somewhat different in nature, but basically similar in import. Constituting part of a *polar* written, as its title implies, by eight different authors, this chapter

allows Modiano, yet again, to evoke the wartime arrest of his
father, though in a context which, revealingly, is now one of
virtual self-parody – further proof of the exorcism that has
been achieved.

2. Cf. Buss, 'Fresh, familiar trail', p.1215.
3. Alternatively, note the relatively more complex nature of the
narrative, with its increased movement between different
times, different places and different people.
4. Sir Henry Morton Stanley (1841–1904) is, of course, the man
who, amongst other exploits, managed to find Doctor
Livingstone in Africa.
5. Cf. e.g. Denise (*Rue des Boutiques Obscures*, pp.99, 179), or
Sylvia (*Dimanches d'août*, p.44).
6. For more on this topic of generic *clins d'œil*, see Kaminskas,
'Quête/enquête – à la recherche du genre: *Voyage de noces* de
Patrick Modiano'.
7. Cf. *Rue des Boutiques Obscures*, pp.75–6, or *Vestiaire de l'enfance*,
pp.84–5.
8. The broadcaster seems to be Jean Hérold-Paquis – see *Voyage
de noces*, p.83 and cf. Pascal Ory, *Les Collaborateurs 1940–1945*
(Paris, Seuil, 1976), pp.81, 83. Note also that, predictably
perhaps, this allusiveness is by no means unique – Ben
Smidane's 'visage de pâtre grec' (p.47) is adapted from
Georges Moustaki's 1969 song, 'Le Métèque' (the first two
lines of which are: 'Avec ma gueule de métèque ǀ De juif
errant de pâtre grec'), while the mention of the 'rayons
meurtriers du soleil' (p.11) smacks distinctly of Camus's
L'Étranger (for more on the author's links to Camus, see
Modiano, 'Je me sens proche de lui', p.7, or Coward, 'What
might have been', p.482).
9. One of these *documents*, a cutting from an old newspaper, is
actually based on a real-life *entrefilet* (see *Voyage de noces*,
pp.152–3, and cf. Assouline, 'Lieux de mémoire', p.41) –
further proof that Modiano's technique is grounded in *le réel*.
10. Cf. the 'facts' presented on pp.142–3, which, if p.121 is to be
believed, are probably imaginary.
11. See also pp.72, 77–8, 106–8, and cf. Jean's tendency towards
'demi-somnolence' (pp.27–8, 32–3).
12. Cf. e.g. the start of Alain Robbe-Grillet's *Dans le labyrinthe*
(Paris, Minuit, 1969): 'Je suis seul ici, maintenant, bien à
l'abri. Dehors il pleut [. . .]; dehors il fait froid, le vent souffle

entre les branches noires dénudées; le vent souffle dans les feuilles [. . .]. Dehors il y a du soleil, il n'y a pas un arbre' (p.9).

13. See e.g Jean's renting of Rigaud's old wartime flat in Paris and note the months mentioned (pp.104, 110, 124). Note also the incredible nature of other aspects of the text – the secret staircase, the excessive appearance of chance and coincidence, etc. (for more on this subject, see Buss, 'Fresh, familiar trail', p.1215).

14. Note also that, like the Princesse de Bourbon mentioned above (whose real name is the humorous Mlle Cotillon), Ingrid (a Jewess) is living under a false identity. For more instances of pretence and disguise, see pp.56–7, 78, 91, 95, 102, 119.

15. See e.g. the buildings (pp.60, 71), the bedroom walls (p.80), the bathing huts (p.62), or even the *concierge*'s hair (p.72).

16. Cf. p.68. To underline the contrapuntal intention here, Modiano states that the black horse in Paris normally pulls a *fiacre* instead of a *traîneau* (p.144).

17. For further contrasts relating to Ingrid and to Rigaud, see pp.131, 133, 134.

18. For *monochromie* in the post-war era (and hence a link to the 1942 version outlined above), see e.g. pp.23, 110, 120.

19. Like Rigaud, Jean is French, 'orphaned', has a foreign wife, is currently missing/presumed dead somewhere in Paris, and has rented the flat at 20, Boulevard Soult; like 'la tache sombre' (who, incidentally, is an embodiment of the black/ white opposition – see pp.61–2), he is conducting an investigation of direct concern to Ingrid; like Ben Smidane (with him and Annette), he was the young *protégé* of an older couple (the Rigauds); and like Fawcett and Mauffrais, he disappears whilst on an expedition. (Percy Harrison Fawcett (1867–1925) vanished in the Mato Grosso in Brazil. Years later, Raymond Maufrais (1926–50) did the same in French Guyana.)

20. For example, Ingrid runs away from her father (and possibly Rigaud) while Jean tries to hide from Annette. For more on this typically *modianesque* theme of flight, see pp.17, 94–5.

21. The relevant quotation has already been given – see p.170 above. (Note also that, on pp.45–8, Jean's disappearance is presented as a death.) For additional similarities between

Ingrid and Jean, see pp.130 and 133, and cf. pp.117 and 108 respectively.

22. See also the various objects left in drawers (pp.64, 69, 77, 91, 106), or the regular descriptions of Ingrid's eyes (pp.33, 42, 44, 54, 119).

23. Although the *voyage de noces* of the book's title may seem to apply solely to Ingrid and to Rigaud (as the evidence here suggests), a closer reading of the text shows that this is not so – true to the mirror principle exploited in the work, it additionally applies to Annette, who always wore the *robe de mariée* when she was a model (p.96), and whom Jean now imagines on honeymoon with Cavanaugh (p.18).

24. 'Fresh, familiar trail', p.1215.

25. Cf. his *parrainage* of Ben Smidane, who could be his younger self incarnate – a would-be *explorateur*, full of dreams, and with a place in Annette's bed to boot. (Note also that, as Cavanaugh is Annette's lover as well, Jean is cuckolded twice over – a further example of the *dédoublements* in the work.)

26. Other broad echoes include Rigaud's accumulation of *attestations*, the concept of a haven during the war (p.81), and the adoption of young, child-like characters by their elders (pp.16, 38, 47, 71, 118).

27. Part of the reason for this disjunction would appear to be that, more obviously than ever before, and totally in keeping with the binary nature of the text, Modiano has spread his autobiographical references over two characters, instead of combining them in one. For example, having given certain of his own traits to his narrator (see p.169 above), he then attributes others, such as schooling at 'un collège des Alpes' (p.70), to Rigaud. Similarly, the established starlet/ mannequin figure, a reflection of the novelist's mother, is split up into its twin component parts, with Ingrid being a *figurante/danseuse*, and Annette being a model.

28. Ultimately, of course, this equates to another attempt by the novelist to examine his identity. (Note also that this move back to Le Seuil would harden cynics in their belief that financial factors are at work here – cf. Note 4 to Chapter 6 above.)

29. For specific examples here, see pp.19–20, 52–3, 93–4, 111, 123, and 133. Note also that the haphazard nature of this (eminently Proustian) trigger effect shows, once again, the

importance of chance in Modiano's universe.

30. This vagueness has been exemplified by the questions of the preceding paragraph. The interaction of the historical with the invented, and the use of contradiction, will both be illustrated below.

31. See e.g. the early avoidance of the marquis (p.12), an action not explained until pp.127–39, or the account of the narrator's *fugue*, which is divided between pp.38–9 and pp.114–21.

32. Cf. the even earlier mention of the Hôtel de l'Avenir. Now run down, the establishment provokes the comment: 'Quel avenir? Celui, déjà révolu, d'un étudiant des années trente' (p.12).

33. Cf. e.g. pp.28, 33, 36, 134. Note also that, owing to a typically *modianesque* confusion of tenses, different elements of the text seem to have been written at different moments – a further evocation of the passing of time (see e.g. pp.11, 16, 41, 140).

34. Cf. Bona, 'Géographie du passé', p.4. For other interpretations of Modiano's (typically evocative) title, see Joye, 'A propos de *Fleurs de ruine*', in Bedner (ed.), *Patrick Modiano*, pp.73–84.

35. Ezine, 'La Légende Modiano', p.67.

36. Cf. *Paris Tendresse* and its mention of 'les jeudis où je traversais la Seine pour aller jouer dans la cour du Louvre et dans les petits squares du Carrousel', events which are said to take place 'vers 1953' (p.85).

37. Devez's fondling of his girlfriend (someone else's wife) in front of the narrator and Jacqueline (p.22) is suggestive of the T.s' 'orgie tragique', especially as the hair colours of the two couples are identical, if inverted (pp.18, 21).

38. Alternatively, see *Fleurs de ruine*, pp.55–6, 114–15, 118–19, and cf., respectively, *Une jeunesse*, pp.89–98, *De si braves garçons*, pp.9–15, 25, 44–5, and *Rue des Boutiques Obscures*, pp.54–6.

39. See also p.105 (including Note 20) above.

40. See also 'Mes vingt ans', in which there is a *Pierre* Pacheco.

41. See *Dimanches d'août*, p.127 and *Voyage de noces*, pp.137–42.

42. Cf. Henri Marignan in *Livret de famille* – see Note 48 to Chapter 3 above.

43. The ability of Lombard (as Pacheco) to disappear for long periods and then re-emerge, rejuvenated, does not just emphasize his inherent elusiveness; it provides a further link

to 'Mes vingt ans', which likewise deals with an *homme-phénix*.

44. It is not certain that Modiano ever went to Vienna, but the insistent claims of his narrators to have been there suggest that he did – see, in addition to the pages of *Fleurs de ruine* cited above, *Vestiaire de l'enfance*, pp.59, 63, *Voyage de noces*, pp.25, 27, 35, and (if somewhat less reliably) *La Place de l'Étoile*, pp.102ff.

45. Ezine, 'La Légende Modiano', p.65.

46. This ongoing research perhaps explains why we learn more about the ex-*gestapiste* from Modiano than from historians of the period. Cf. his comments about the former *planton* of the Bonny–Laffont gang (correctly identified as either Jacques Labussière or Jean-Damian Lascaux) on pp.98–100.

47. See pp.162 and 127 of these works respectively. Frustratingly, there appears to be no external, historical confirmation that Jean Terrail ever existed, even though we assume that he did.

48. Compare the above details to, say, *Les Boulevards de ceinture*, pp.47–8, 54, 78–82. Note also that the love of billiards and the stay on the quai d'Austerlitz have, in part if not in whole (recall p.144 above, and cf. *Paris Tendresse*, p.32), additionally fed into Denise Coudreuse in *Rue des Boutiques Obscures*. Finally, note that, unlike Jean Terrail, Sylviane can be traced back to a real-life figure, thanks to Modiano's clue that she became marquise d'A (p.49) – one of the 'associates' of the Bonny–Laffont gang was, precisely, the 'marquise d'Alès, une rousse somptueuse à la chevelure abondante. Issue d'une modeste famille, elle épouse le marquis d'Alès, divorce, exerce de nombreux métiers et échoue rue Lauriston' (Aziz, *Tu trahiras sans vergogne* (Paris, Fayard, 1970), p.144).

49. See e.g. *Les Boulevards de ceinture*, where Deyckecaire/papa has a big office in the rue Lord-Byron (p.161), and arranges meetings in hotel lobbies (p.101). Cf. *Villa Triste*, pp.55, 151, *Livret de famille*, pp.50, 166, and, implicitly, *La Place de l'Étoile*, pp.40–1 and the whole of '1, rue Lord-Byron'.

50. For previous mention of these arrests, see p.144 above. See also Note 8 to Chapter 6, and note, with respect to the comment about one possible arrest becoming two, how this *dédoublement* is now repeated and hence *dédoublé* in turn.

51. 'La Légende Modiano', p.65.

52. Regarding this sense of guilt, cf. p.42 above. Note also the

way in which Paris is said to be split into two 'zones' by the Seine, a demarcation which is significant for at least three different reasons (each of which, ultimately, can be linked to the narrator's view that 'la réalité était plus fuyante que je ne le pensais' – p.83). First, the bisection of the capital adds to the *dédoublements* already mentioned above, all the more so in that it is referred to repeatedly (cf. pp.91, 117) and is further reflected by the divided Île des Loups (p.35). Second, it consolidates the links back to the *œuvre* as a whole, reprising the *rive gauche/rive droite* disjunction already seen in *La Ronde de nuit* (cf. also *Une jeunesse*, p.106). Third, and finally, it ties in intertextually (and as ever) to the work of Scott Fitzgerald and Marcel Proust, evoking the two Eggs of *The Great Gatsby* (see *The Bodley Head Scott Fitzgerald* (cf Chapter 2, Note 62), volume I) and the 'deux côtés' of *A la recherche du temps perdu*. (For more on the banks of the Seine in Modiano's work, see Assouline, 'Lieux de mémoire', pp.37–9, or Guicharnaud, 'De la Rive gauche au-delà de la Concorde', pp.341–52.)

53. Note how this reaction to *l'enfance* contrasts with that expressed on p.180 above – further proof that almost everything in Modiano's work is intrinsically ambiguous (cf. Paris in the preceding note).

54. A further sign of this, of course, is the fact that, more and more, he is able to address his problems *directly*, in largely autobiographical works, rather than *indirectly* through fiction, as he had done previously.

55. See, e.g., pp.51, 57, 79, 88, 117, 122, 125, 135, 149. These silences might elucidate Modiano's choice of title – a possible variation of 'un ange passe', used when there is an awkward break in the conversation.

56. Note the typical ambiguity here – earlier in the *œuvre*, any diary entry was seen in positive terms, as a record of a past long gone; now such an entry is the source of trouble.

57. See, e.g., his implied love-making with Gisèle on pp.17–18. (This descriptive *pudeur*, like the narratorial romance which produces it, has, of course, been a feature of the *œuvre* since *Villa Triste* in 1975 – cf. e.g. *Dimanches d'août*, p.131 above.)

58. See e.g. p.119: 'La coupe élégant de son costume et sa voix détonnaient dans ce café. Etait-il vraiment le patron?'

59. See e.g. pp.54–5: 'J'ai souvent entendu ce nom dans sa bouche: Jacques de Bavière. Est-ce que j'entendais mal? Et ne

s'agissait-il pas d'un nom plus prosaïque comme: de Bavier ou Debaviaire? Ou simplement d'un pseudonyme?'

60. Regarding this general lack of forthcomingness, cf., say, pp.69, 111 and 150 above, and note how this further gives the *œuvre* a distinct relevance to the modern world, where communication is similarly a problem.

61. We might also note in this respect that, if Gisèle is far from being the traditional whore-with-the-heart-of-gold who crops up endlessly in the *série noire*, she is arguably as close to this stereotype as Modiano is likely to get. (This parodic side to her role might be further suggested by the clichéd 'mysterious cases' that she possesses – see pp.12–13, 30.)

62. The character who has seen better days is, of course, a staple of Modiano's *œuvre* – cf. Note 60 to Chapter 6 above.

63. See e.g. pp.100–2. The influence of Proust can, as ever, further be seen in the evocative nature of certain words – see p.103: 'La sonorité du mot "tomate" avait quelque chose de bon enfant et de rassurant.'

64. Note the theme of the journey again.

65. This should not really surprise us – the importance of the *drame* in Modiano's work has already been underlined (in Note 61 to Chapter 6 above). Note also how this loss of Gisèle adds to the novel's uncertain, dream-like feel, as the author himself points out: 'Le roman est un peu [. . .] onirique. [. . .] Par exemple, pour tout ce qui concerne Gisèle, comme le récit est postérieur à ce qui s'est passé, on a l'impression somnambulique d'une présence et d'une absence à la fois' (Maury, 'Patrick Modiano', p.103).

66. Except, of course, that, in retrospect, Jean, like so many of his predecessors, will now have cause for nostalgia – cf. Franck Salaün: 'Le fait d'avoir eu un avenir condamne certains individus à la nostalgie d'un âge d'or, de ce temps où ils étaient pleins d'avenir' ('La Suisse du cœur', in Bedner (ed.), *Patrick Modiano*, p.34).

67. For further illustration of this (typical) presence of Fate in the work, see pp.49, 62, 110, 118, 122, where Jean's eventual loss is to some extent forecast – as if it had again been 'in the stars' from the outset. For more detailed analysis of the use of contrast, see Breut, *'Un cirque passe*: Un tour de passe-passe romanesque', in Bedner (ed.), *Patrick Modiano*, pp.103–17.

68. Amongst the many examples of this is the familiar refrain –

albeit in a variety of forms – of 'aucune importance' (pp.35, 64, 111, 119, 122, 142, 145, 150).

69. See e.g. the 'bleu pâle' of Gisèle's eyes (pp.31, 40, 76, 110), the 'bleu ciel' of the wall panelling (pp. 16, 83) and the prominent touches of 'bleu marine' (pp.20, 21, 40, 96, 97, 106, 118, 120, 121, 141, 153). Needless to say, perhaps, these colours further highlight the binary aspect of the text, their common basis of blue acting *associatively*, while their light/dark, sky/sea elements serve to form a *contrast*.

70. As has been seen, most of Modiano's novels, like so many *nouveaux romans*, defy the attempt at linear rewriting, being founded on contradiction rather than on logic. Yet we do not realize this until we try such a line of attack.

71. Modiano might well, for example, have chosen Gisèle's real name (Suzanne Kraay) on the basis that the *nom de famille* has, quite fittingly, connotations of the underworld – the Kray twins were notorious London gangsters, jailed for murder in 1969. (That the novelist is familiar with at least some of Britain's black sheep is demonstrated by his reference to Guy Burgess in *Une jeunesse*.) Note also that, as a man religious enough to attend mass on Sunday mornings (pp.22, 23) and yet still partake of life's more sensual offerings – champagne (p.86), pornography (p.15), strip-tease (pp.87–8), all-night binges (pp.21–2), etc. – Grabley, in name and in deed, evokes that other, better-known *bon viveur*, François Rabelais (1494?–1553).

72. This use of recurrent motifs as an alternative ordering device is, of course, yet another feature of the *nouveau roman*.

73. Note also the policeman's view that 'Il s'est passé quelque chose de très grave' (p.138) and cf. *Remise de peine*, pp.145, 162.

74. Others include: Jean's double status as criminal–detective; his sitting on a bench in 'un grand square avec un kiosque à musique' (p.151); and his 'betrayal' of the stranger near the Bois de Boulogne – Gestapo country *par excellence* (pp.98–100).

75. For details of this canine mirroring in *Un cirque passe*, see Breut, '*Un cirque passe*: Un tour de passe-passe romanesque', in Bedner (ed.), *Patrick Modiano*, pp.114–15. Cf. Note 14 to Chapter 3, Note 44 to Chapter 5 and *Fleurs de ruine*, p.142.

76. See also the visit to the nightclub in Rome (p.107) and the

menacing wartime phone call (p.143), both of which have similarly been foreshadowed in *Livret de famille* (pp.121–2 and p.174 respectively).

77. We also learn that Jean was engaged in 'du courtage en librairie' (p.12), and while Modiano himself has not broadcast this (possible) aspect of his past, the frequency with which his narrators are involved (in one way or another) in the book trade suggests that the trait might just be authorial in origin (cf. *Les Boulevards de ceinture*, pp.94–6, *Villa Triste*, pp.167–8, *Livret de famille*, p.121, *Voyage de noces*, p.95, and *Fleurs de ruine*, pp.32, 63).

78. This parcelling out of revelations applies to fictional characters as well, as the ever more detailed descriptions of Pacheco demonstrate. (See p.182 above. See also Note 50 to Chapter 3 above.)

79. See e.g. the aforementioned contradictions relating to Albert's wartime arrest (Note 8 to Chapter 6 above). Note also the inconsistencies surrounding many of Modiano's fictional creations: Pacheco is dark-haired in *Fleurs de ruine* (p.109), but blonde in *Voyage de noces* (p.129); Gay spells her name Orloff in the 1960s in *Villa Triste*, but is called Orlow and died in 1950 in *Rue des Boutiques Obscures* (pp.43–4); and so we could go on. Not that these incongruities should surprise us – they (deliberately) offset the element of unity bred by familiarity, and so ensure that, like everything else in the *œuvre*, the retention of characters from one book to the next is fraught with *ambiguity*. (For the added implications regarding identity here, see Bedner, 'Modiano ou l'identité introuvable', pp.51–2.)

80. The allusion here is to Robert Graves (1895–1985), whose autobiography, *Goodbye to All That*, was published in 1929.

81. Note that this physical flight/disappearance (the theme of the journey again!) acts as the concrete reaffirmation of his *permanent* isolation from his son – see his (typical) lack of communication when present (pp.20–1), and cf. his elusiveness once he has gone (pp.57, 90).

82. Regarding the father-figure and the game of cat and mouse, cf. *Livret de famille*, pp.49–71, or Note 72 to Chapter 2 above.

83. Note that this, in turn, further illustrates the novel's binary nature, Geneva and Rome being identical (both being seen as *asiles*) and yet entirely different (the former is reachable, the

latter is not). Note also that Switzerland, with its famed neutrality, is a fitting *pays d'élection* for a man who, as ever, is seen to arrange (business?) meetings 'dans des halls d'hôtels ou des cafés' (p.141) – neutral ground *par excellence*.

84. Note that, predictably, this past is extended to include the Occupation – see pp.143 or 148. (For more allusive references to the *années noires* in the work, see Note 73 above or, *passim*, Montfrans, 'Rêveries d'un riverain', in Bedner (ed.), *Patrick Modiano*, pp.85–101.) Note also that, in real life, Modiano *père*'s departure did not see the family abandon 15, quai Conti (his wife and his son were, according to Jean Chalon ('Le Dernier promeneur', p.10), still living there when *La Ronde de nuit* was published) – further proof that the flat is being used symbolically here, to emphasize the sense of completion and, ultimately, to suggest that a line is being drawn beneath the past.

Conclusion

Les choses, en effet, sont pour le moins doubles.

Marcel Proust

Si Patrick Modiano est écrivain, c'est aussi parce qu'il est le frère du mort.

Pierre Assouline

Looking back over the preceding chapters, the picture that now emerges is a clear one: Modiano is an author who, through his fiction, has pursued a lengthy – and largely successful – quest for personal exorcism. At the start of his career, feeling himself to be an orphan, he uses his work as a means of self-definition, a way of securing the roots that he lacks but desperately needs. Not for nothing, at this early stage, does he resort to false autobiography, using the pasts and the memories of other people to forge alternative family ties for himself; and not for nothing, either, does he evoke the time when his real parents first met, the troubled and troublesome age of the *années noires* – both tendencies, quite visibly, reflect his obsessive pursuit of his origins. As the *œuvre* progresses, though, this cathartic impulse plainly diminishes, albeit without ever disappearing completely. More and more – in his texts as well as in interviews – he feels able to talk about his childhood, a sure sign, no doubt, that his former anxieties and uncertainties are receding. And understandably so. Engagement, marriage and fatherhood, added, of course, to fame in his chosen profession, have all bolstered his once fragile identity, and so lastingly that the old, emotional soul-searching can henceforth be discarded.

This changed mental outlook filters into the later novels quite noticeably, in the form of more contemporary settings, increased linearity and narrators who are discernibly much less anguished than their predecessors.[1] Yet despite this evolution, there remains an immense consistency about the *œuvre*. The key themes of remembrance, identity, time and the past are maintained, unerringly, as one book gives way to the next, and the author's universe varies little in matters of substance either: it is for ever a place where *l'usure du temps*, absence and death are predominant, and where history and memory can never be complete; a place where feelings of nostalgia linger; where the byword is 'aucune importance', and where the characters are all shadowy and ghost-like; a place where the décors are mere *lieux de passage*, and where chance transforms choice into Fate; a place where reality is oneiric, where the self is unstable, and where alienation is rife. In short, it is a place which, for all its dashes of humour, is essentially bleak in conception.

Conceptually sombre it may be, but it is also, and above all, a world which is intrinsically ambiguous, for as we have seen, almost every feature of it is decidedly double-edged. Identity is viewed as something to aspire to, but is often a source of danger, and so has to be renounced. Memory is vital to the concept of the self, and insures against temporal decay, but sometimes retains things which would probably best be forgotten. The past is the seat of childhood, and the cause of a haunting nostalgia, but it also evokes immense suffering. Characters, settings and events are regularly real, but just as regularly not. People remain the same, but differ from their previous selves. *Documents* save precious moments, but prove that things have moved on. The Occupation is an ancestral bedrock, but suggestive of the Holocaust. Time can be a great healer, or a mean and heartless destroyer. Paris will always be Paris, but it is split right down the middle. The text can be autobiographical, or the product of sheer invention. The narrative can carry us along, yet at the same time self-destruct . . . And so the list goes on, culminating, eventually, in an overall, macro-level cult of ambiguity, for just as these examples combine, quite naturally, to form a *system* of antithesis within any one text (or, indeed, within the *œuvre*), so, too, is the exact opposite the case. The echoing of different epochs, the circle as a structuring device, the constant use of leitmotifs – these are just some of the *associative* ploys that are generally exploited, and they are exploited not just in the aim of conjunction, but, additionally, when systematized in turn, as a *contrast* to the disjunctive thrust that exists alongside them. 'Chez [Modiano]', Pierre Assouline has said, 'la vérité est toujours duelle.'[2] We can now affirm that he was not mistaken.[3]

The reason for this omnipresent dualism can, as we may again now readily concede, be traced back primarily to Modiano's formative years, to the time when he, himself, became aware not only of the dichotomy of his own identity, but also of another fundamental contrast, that of before and after, of presence and absence, with the turning point here being the death of his brother Rudy. 'Le choc de sa mort a été déterminant', the novelist has recently confessed. 'Ma recherche perpétuelle de quelque chose de perdu, la quête d'un passé brouillé qu'on ne peut élucider, l'enfance brusquement cassée, tout cela participe d'une même névrose qui est devenue mon état d'esprit.'[4] The subsequent loss of Albert (when he walked out on the family) served simply to increase this sense of rupture, and to eternalize the personal here/gone conflict from which, as from the uncertainties of self, the literary antagonisms would flow.

Yet despite this private impulse behind his writing, Modiano is anything but an author with little external relevance. On the contrary, his work is decidedly universal, whatever our focal point in it may be. His principal themes (identity, time, memory, etc.) embody abiding problems; the questions he constantly raises (for example, what is the relationship between life and art?) will always be burningly pertinent; the universe he portrays (with, say, its contingency, uncertainty, and ultimate lack of values) is broadly in tune with our own (and with that of the Twentieth Century in general), while his overt cult of polarity (presence/absence, fact/fiction, reality/fantasy, present/past, remembrance/oblivion) plainly derives from the one single opposition that totally preoccupies us all – that of life and death, or as Jean-Paul Sartre would say, that of *l'être et le néant*.

This final reference to Sartre, like the various points which precede it, leads us on, felicitously, to the subject of Modiano's debt to his predecessors, and here as elsewhere, ambiguity abounds. Is our author a sort of neo-classicist, whose models lie not in the 'experimental' post-war period, but way back beyond it, in a so-called golden age of the novel? Or are we dealing with a modernist, formed in the specific mould of the *nouveau roman* and other innovatory tendencies? Such, in broad terms, is the dilemma formulated, often only implicitly, by critics who still tend to see literature as the battleground of *anciens* and *modernes*. Yet in neither case is the epithet fully merited.

From the classical tradition, Modiano has obviously borrowed much. His confessed masters are, amongst others, Marcel Proust, Paul Morand and Scott Fitzgerald. Other influences, although not always recognized, include André Gide, Albert Camus and Gérard de Nerval.[5] There are even strong echoes of that kingpin of the literary canon, Honoré de Balzac.[6] Yet none of these mentors is imitated slavishly, or, for that matter, all-embracingly.

What is more, hand in hand with this use of the classic goes a frequent recourse to the modern. For what does Modiano's initial objective – a false autobiography – represent if not a project in line with one of the basic tenets of Structuralism: the ability of language to create (a whole new) reality by itself? And what do his works regularly evoke – through, say, their uncertainty, circularity and exploitation of the *polar* – if not the teachings and the practice of the *nouveau roman*?[7] However, just as his classicism is lacking in certain respects, so too is his modernism rather incomplete. 'Il y avait certaines choses auxquelles je n'étais pas imperméable', he has admitted of the New Novel and the avant-garde in general, but only 'quand c'était vraiment du domaine romanesque';[8] for the most part, as we saw in Chapter 1, he tends to pooh-pooh 'ce byzantinisme pour chaires et colloques'.[9]

As Jacques Bersani has remarked, then, 'Patrick Modiano [. . .] trahit les Modernes avec les Anciens et les Anciens avec les Modernes.'[10] But does this mean that he is so ambiguous a writer as to be almost unclassifiable? Not entirely. In his grasp of his whole cultural heritage and his constant allusions to it; in his recourse to a considerable number of prose formats (auto-biography, the war novel, the love story, the *polar*, etc.) and to 'borrowing' from what are often deemed to be less important genres (the cinema, popular music, or the comic-book); in his 'scepticism about identity, causality and meaning';[11] in his use of the *mise en abyme* and blatant contradiction; in his antipathy for any form of closure; in his ever-present irony, ludism and pastiching; and in much, much more besides, he most clearly (if unwittingly) invites us to link him to the trend which is still on virtually all commentators' lips today: postmodernism.[12]

To dub Modiano a postmodernist, though, is perhaps to give grounds for confusion, for as we have seen, the author himself would deny that he belongs to any 'new-fangled movement'. Furthermore, to subsume him into a mass would be to ignore his undoubted *uniqueness* on the contemporary literary scene.

'Modiano est un des seuls romanciers contemporains qui ait réussi à délimiter un univers qui lui soit propre', Francine de Martinoir has said,[13] and most, if not all readers would instantly agree, for the very good reason that, from the word go (witness the pastiches in *La Place de l'Étoile*), the novelist has displayed an absolute mastery in the realm of style, and has used this great talent to forge his own, unrivalled literary 'atmosphère'. Short, often verbless, sentences; a lack of (causal) conjunctions; striking symbols and leitmotifs; passages of pure poetry; a refusal to comment or analyse; the influence of the cinema – such are the fundamentals of Modiano's use of language, fundamentals which, when generalized, translate into the keywords regularly used to describe his style: immediacy, simplicity, concision, allusion, sobriety, neutrality and, above all, suggestiveness and rhythm.

Many of these words, of course, relate to long-established classical qualities, and Modiano himself accepts this traditional aspect of his prose, stressing – revealingly – that no other formal approach was possible for him. 'J'écris dans la langue française la plus classique', he insists,

> non par une insolence droitière, non plus par un goût des effets surannées, mais parce que cette forme est nécessaire à mes romans: pour traduire l'atmosphère trouble, flottante, étrange que je voulais leur donner, il me fallait bien la discipliner dans la langue la plus claire, la plus traditionnelle possible. Sinon, tout se serait éparpillé dans une bouillie confuse.[14]

An 'atmosphère trouble, flottante, étrange' combined with 'la langue la plus claire [...] possible' – decidedly, there are contrasts to be found everywhere in Modiano.[15] He really is the king of ambiguity.

This return to a point already made suggests, conveniently, a question that can now be addressed, as the French would say, *en guise de conclusion*: will Modiano, like his readers, forever go round and round in circles, or will he stop writing the same basic novel and break new ground in the future? On the strength of the evidence available, the former would seem the more likely occurrence, and this for three obvious reasons at least. First, common sense dictates that a formula that has proved, and is still proving, successful should not be changed – 'if it ain't broke, don't fix it', it might be said. Second, given the close links between the novelist's life and his fiction, he could well be incapable of writing differently, even if he actually wanted to. Finally, and perhaps most important of all, the current vein worked is not, as yet, deemed to have surrendered its ultimate treasure. 'Chaque livre me sert à déblayer', the author has readily confessed, 'pour essayer d'aller vers quelque chose de plus essentiel [. . .] Mais à chaque fois, j'ai le sentiment désagréable de ne pas y être parvenu.'[16] So, until he arrives at this 'quelque chose de plus essentiel' (if, indeed, it ever can be achieved), we can expect to remain on familiar ground. Yet we can also expect, somewhat paradoxically (that notion again!), to be constantly surprised and enchanted, for Modiano will, no doubt, continue to refresh his 'variations on a theme'.[17] Furthermore, as he does this, he will surely maintain what is, perhaps, his greatest paradox of all: he will carry on updating an age-old genre, a genre which, as we saw in Chapter 1, he himself considers 'anachronique'. In short, and to conclude, he will persist in that task which, despite all his other intentions, he has implicitly – and long since – taken to be his own: to fashion and refine a novel for his day.

Notes

1. Note also the more detached painting of the Occupation, reflected in the author's admission (in 1989) that 'L'Occupation m'a hanté parce que j'avais l'impression d'y puiser mes origines' (Montaudon, 'Patrick Modiano', p.16) – the past tenses here contrast vividly with the use of the present in earlier comments on the subject (see e.g. pp.13, 42 above).
2. 'Lieux de mémoire', p.39.
3. Further evidence of this is the way in which each individual text, although entirely self-standing, constantly refers to previous texts (whether by Modiano or by others) – it is as if while reading a new book we re-read an old one.
4. Assouline, 'Lieux de mémoire', p.37.
5. The *clins d'œil* to the first two of these authors have already been indicated in footnotes and epigraphs above. For Modiano's links to Nerval, see e.g. Gellings, 'Souvenirs de Nerval', pp.173–4, or Vercaemer, 'Ville et mémoire chez Patrick Modiano: *Quartier perdu*', pp.220–1.

6. In addition to the links articulated already (the reappearance of characters from book to book, for instance), note that, according to Gustave Lanson (*Histoire de la Littérature Française*, seventeenth edition (Paris, Hachette, 1922), p.1003), rather like Modiano walking the streets of Paris or consulting old telephone directories, Balzac would wander round Père Lachaise cemetery, looking for expressive names on the headstones.

7. For fuller, first-hand insights into the New Novel, see Alain Robbe-Grillet, *Pour un nouveau roman* (Paris, Minuit, 1963) or Nathalie Sarraute, *L'Ere du soupçon* (Paris, Gallimard, 1956).

8. Maury, 'Patrick Modiano', p.104.

9. Ezine, 'Sur la sellette', p.5.

10. 'Patrick Modiano, agent double', p.78.

11. Lodge, *The Art of Fiction* (London, Penguin, 1992), p.38.

12. Although there is no agreement on precisely what this term means, most of the definitions put forward would appear to embrace Modiano. Edmund Smyth, for example, admits as postmodern 'any creative endeavour which exhibits some element of self-consciousness and reflexivity', and stresses the importance of 'fragmentation, discontinuity, indeterminacy, plurality, metafictionality, heterogeneity, intertextuality, decentring, dislocation, ludism' (Smyth (ed.), *Postmodernism and Contemporary Fiction* (London, Batsford, 1991), p.9). For more on Modiano's place in this (fittingly) ambiguous 'movement', see Scherman, 'Translating from Memory: Patrick Modiano in Postmodern Context'.

13. 'Patrick Modiano: *Villa Triste* (II)', p.13.

14. Ezine, 'Sur la sellette', p.5.

15. Cf. another aspect of the author's technique, the fact that 'pour parvenir à leur forme finale (concision, sobriété, minceur), ses livres ont besoin de s'appuyer au départ sur une masse d'informations qui se situent aux antipodes de son style' (Assouline, 'Lieux de mémoire', p.46).

16. Montaudon, 'Patrick Modiano', p.17. This dissatisfaction has recently been restated (Maury, 'Patrick Modiano', p.103).

17. This has indeed proved to be the case – since these words were written, Modiano has published *Chien de printemps* (Paris, Seuil, 1993), another example of his 'same but different' approach.

Select Bibliography

To list every text consulted during the preparation of this book would result in a Bibliography which was inordinately long, so details will only be given here of those works by and on Modiano which have been directly referred to. (To complement the present selection, see Richie van Rossum, 'Bibliographie de Modiano', in Bedner (ed.), *Patrick Modiano*, pp.125–34.)

Unless otherwise stated, the place of publication in all cases below is Paris.

Works by Modiano

Novels and Longer 'Récits'

La Place de l'Étoile, Gallimard, 1968
La Ronde de nuit, Gallimard, 1969
Les Boulevards de ceinture, Gallimard, 1972
Villa Triste, Gallimard, 1975
Livret de famille, Gallimard, 1977
Rue des Boutiques Obscures, Gallimard, 1978
Une jeunesse, Gallimard, 1981
De si braves garçons, Gallimard, 1982
Quartier perdu, Gallimard, 1984
Dimanches d'août, Gallimard, 1986
Remise de peine, Seuil, 1988
Vestiaire de l'enfance, Gallimard, 1989
Voyage de noces, Gallimard, 1990
Fleurs de ruine, Seuil, 1991
Un cirque passe, Gallimard, 1992

Shorter Fiction

'Courrier du cœur', *Les Cahiers du chemin*, 20 (January 1974), pp.35–40

'Johnny', *NRF*, 307 (1 August 1978), pp.1–5

'Soir de Paris', *Le Figaro*, 21 November 1978, p.32

'Lettre d'amour', *Paris-Match*, 1 December 1978, pp.78–81

'1, rue Lord-Byron', *Le Nouvel Observateur*, 23 December 1978, pp.56–7

'Docteur Weiszt', *Le Monde Dimanche*, 16 September 1979, p.XX

'Memory Lane', *NRF*, 334 (1 November 1980), pp.[1]–30

'La Seine', *NRF*, 341 (1 June 1981), pp.1–17

Memory Lane, with drawings by Pierre Le-Tan, POL/Hachette, 1981

Poupée blonde [with Pierre Le-Tan], POL, 1983

'Mes Vingt ans', *Vogue*, 642 (December 1983), pp.188–93

Children's Books

Une aventure de Choura, with illustrations by Dominique Zehrfuss, Gallimard, 1986

Une fiancée pour Choura, with illustrations by Dominique Zehrfuss, Gallimard, 1987

Catherine Certitude [with Sempé], Gallimard, 1988

Prefaces

Rilke, Rainer Maria, *Les Cahiers de Malte Laurids Brigge*, Seuil (Points), 1980

Cocteau, Jean, *Le Livre blanc*, Messine, 1983

Le-Tan, Pierre, *Paris de ma jeunesse*, Aubier, 1988

Articles, Criticism, etc.

'Je me sens proche de lui', *Les Nouvelles Littéraires*, 1 January 1970, p.7

'Hervé Bazin vu par Patrick Modiano', *Magazine Littéraire*, 40 (May 1970), pp.21–2

'L'Anti-Frank', *Contrepoint*, 2 (October 1970), pp.178–80

'Un roman sur Paris en été . . .', in Patrick Modiano, *La Ronde de nuit*, Tallandier (Cercle du nouveau livre), 1970, *postface*, pp.3–5

'Un martyr des lettres', *Les Nouvelles Littéraires*, 11 June 1971, p.13

'Vingt ans après', *Le Figaro Littéraire*, 18 November 1972, pp.I, IV [pp.13, 17]

'*Les Écrivains de la nuit*, de Pierre de Boisdeffre', *La Nouvelle Revue*

des Deux Mondes, October–December 1973, pp.350–2
'Au temps de Lacombe Lucien', *Elle*, 11 February 1974, pp.6–7
'Les Livres de Julien Gracq . . .', in *Qui vive? autour de Julien Gracq*, Corti, 1989, pp.165–7

Other Works

'Patrick Modiano répond au questionnaire Marcel Proust', in Patrick Modiano, *La Ronde de nuit*, Tallandier (Cercle du nouveau livre), 1970, *postface*, pp.24–6
Lacombe Lucien (filmscript) [with Louis Malle], Gallimard, 1974
Berl, Emmanuel, *'Interrogatoire par Patrick Modiano' suivi de 'il fait beau, allons au cimetière'*, Gallimard, 1976
Morel, Jean-Pierre, 'Une Dissertation de Modiano', *Les Nouvelles Littéraires*, 18 November 1982, pp.37–8
Paris, Fixot, 1987
Paris Tendresse [with photographs by Brassaï], Hoëbeke, 1990
'Polar à huit mains: "L'Angle mort": Chapitre 3', *L'Evénement du jeudi*, 18–24 July 1991, pp.84–6

Interviews

'A bout portant . . . Patrick Modiano', *Paris-Match*, 13 March 1981, pp.28–9
Bosselet, Dominique, 'Patrick Modiano: "J'ai un petit talent d'amateur"', *France-Soir*, 12 September 1975, p.17
Brunn, Julien, 'Patrick Modiano: Exilé de quelque chose', *Libération*, 22 September 1975, p.10
Cau, Jean, 'Patrick Modiano marié, un enfant et un livret de famille de 180 pages', *Paris-Match*, 12 August 1977, p.13
Chalon, Jean, 'Patrick Modiano: Le Dernier promeneur solitaire', in Patrick Modiano, *La Ronde de nuit*, Tallandier (Cercle du nouveau livre), 1970, *postface*, pp.6–23
Chapsal, Madeleine, '10 ans après: Patrick Modiano', *Lire*, 120 (September 1985), pp.56–8, 61–2
D[ucout], F[rançoise], 'Patrick Modiano: on est toujours prisonnier de son temps', *Elle*, 22 September 1986, p.47
Duranteau, Josane, 'L'Obsession de l'anti-héros', *Le Monde*, 11 November 1972, p.13
Ezine, Jean-Louis, 'Sur la sellette: Patrick Modiano ou le passé antérieur', *Les Nouvelles Littéraires*, 6–12 October 1975, p.5
Geille, Annick, 'Patrick Modiano m'intimide!', *Playboy*, IX, 5 (May

1981), pp.64–6, 127–8, 130

Jamet, Dominique, 'Patrick Modiano s'explique', *Lire*, 1 (October 1975), pp.23–5, 27, 29, 31–2, 35–6

Jaudel, Françoise, 'Quête d'identité', *L'Arche*, October–November 1972, p.61

Josselin, Jean-François, 'Mondo Modiano', *Le Nouvel Observateur*, 8–14 January 1988, pp.59–61

Leclère, Marie-Françoise, 'Il a vingt-deux ans et il méritait le Goncourt', *Elle*, 8 December 1969, p.139

Libermann, Jean, 'Patrick Modiano: *Lacombe Lucien* n'est pas le portrait du fascisme mais celui de sa piétaille', *Presse Nouvelle Hebdo*, 8 March 1974, pp.3, 9

M., J.-C., 'Patrick Modiano: "Non, je ne suis pas un auteur rétro"', *Le Journal du Dimanche*, 26 May 1974, p.11

Malka, Victor, 'Patrick Modiano: un homme sur du sable mouvant', *Les Nouvelles Littéraires*, 30 October–5 November 1972, p.2

Maury, Pierre, 'Patrick Modiano: travaux de déblaiement', *Magazine Littéraire*, September 1992, pp.100–4

Modiano, Patrick, 'Patrick Modiano', *Paris-Match*, 1 December 1978, p.79

Montalbetti, Jean, 'La Haine des professeurs: Instantané Patrick Modiano', *Les Nouvelles Littéraires*, 13 June 1968, p.2

——, 'Patrick Modiano ou l'esprit de fuite', *Magazine Littéraire*, 34 (November 1969), pp.42–3

Montaudon, Dominique, 'Patrick Modiano: le plus agréable c'est la rêverie', *Quoi Lire Magazine*, 8 (March 1989), pp.15–18

Pivot, Bernard, 'Demi-juif, Patrick Modiano affirme: "Céline était un véritable écrivain juif"', *Le Figaro Littéraire*, 29 April 1968, p.16

Pudlowski, Gilles, 'Modiano le magnifique', *Les Nouvelles Littéraires*, 12–19 February 1981, p.28

Rambures, Jean-Louis de, 'Comment travaillent les écrivains: Patrick Modiano: "apprendre à mentir"', *Le Monde*, 24 May 1973, p.24

Rolin, Gabrielle, 'Patrick Modiano: le dernier enfant du siècle', *Le Point*, 3–9 January 1983, pp.63–4

Rondeau, Daniel, 'Des Sixties au Goncourt', *Libération*, 30 September 1982, p.23

Savigneau, Josyane, 'Les Chemins de leur carrière', *Le Monde*, 4 January 1985, pp.11, 13

Texier, Jean-C., 'Rencontre avec un jeune romancier: Patrick Modiano', *La Croix*, 9–10 November 1969, p.8

Critical Texts on Modiano

Alhau, Max, 'Patrick Modiano: *Vestiaire de l'enfance*', *NRF*, 437 (June 1989), pp.102–3

Assouline, Pierre, 'Modiano, lieux de mémoire', *Lire*, 176 (May 1990), pp.34–46

Audiard, Michel, 'Le Bal des anciens', *Le Figaro*, 19 October 1982, p.29

Audouard, Antoine, 'Modiano: Il n'y a pas beaucoup d'écrivains de sa hauteur...', *Le Figaro Magazine*, 20 September 1986, pp.52–3

Bedner, Jules, 'Modiano ou l'identité introuvable', *Rapports: Het Franse Boek*, Amsterdam, 2 (1988), pp.49–67

—— (ed.), *Patrick Modiano*, Amsterdam/Atlanta, Rodopi, 1993

Bersani, Jacques, 'Patrick Modiano, agent double', *NRF*, 298 (November 1977), pp.78–84

Besson, Ferny, '*Les Boulevards de ceinture*, par Patrick Modiano', *L'Echo de la Bourse*, Brussels, 8, 9, 10 December 1972, p.17

Bologne, Jean-Claude, 'Le nouveau piège de Modiano', *Magazine Littéraire*, 264 (April 1989), p.102

Bona, Dominique, 'Géographie du passé', *Le Figaro Littéraire*, 8 April 1991, p.4

Bony, Alain, 'Suite en blanc', *Critique*, 469–70 (June–July 1986), pp.653–67

Brenner, Jacques, *Histoire de la littérature française de 1940 à nos jours*, Fayard, 1978, pp.537–43

Brouwer, Anneke, 'L'Emploi des temps verbaux chez Patrick Modiano', *Rapports: Het Franse Boek*, Amsterdam, 2 (1988), pp.68–73

Buss, Robin, 'Fresh, familiar trail', *TLS*, London, 9–15 November 1990, p.1215

Chasseguet-Smirgel, Janine, *Pour une psychanalyse de l'art et de la créativité*, Payot, 1971, pp.217–55

Clerval, Alain, 'Patrick Modiano: *Dimanches d'août* (Gallimard)', *NRF*, 407 (1 December 1986), pp.89–90

Côté, Paul Raymond, 'Aux rives du Léthé: Mnémosyne et la quête des origines chez Patrick Modiano', *Symposium*,

Washington, XLV (Spring 1991), pp.315–28

Coward, David, 'What might have been', *TLS*, London, 5–11 May 1989, p.482

Czarny, Norbert, 'Un livre pour rien', *Les Nouveaux Cahiers*, 64 (Spring 1981), pp.60–2

——, 'Patrick Modiano: *Dimanches d'août*', *Les Nouveaux Cahiers*, 86 (Autumn 1986), pp.76–7

——, '*Memory Lane*, de Patrick Modiano', *L'École des Lettres II*, 7 (1989–90), pp.13–20

——, 'La Trace douloureuse', *L'École des Lettres II*, 14 (1990–1), pp.171–8

Daprini, Pierre, 'Patrick Modiano: le temps de l'Occupation', *Australian Journal of French Studies*, Clayton, XXVI, 2 (May–August 1989), pp.194–205

Delbourg, Patrice, 'Dans le saint des cintres', *Les Nouvelles*, 8–14 December 1983, p.36

Dormann, Geneviève, 'Modiano apprivoisé', *Le Point*, 16 October 1972, p.100

Doucey, Bruno, *'La Ronde de nuit': Modiano*, Hatier, 1992

Duranteau, Josane, 'Un début exceptionnel: *La Place de l'Étoile*, de Patrick Modiano', *Le Monde*, 11 May 1968, p.II

Ezine, Jean-Louis, 'La Légende Modiano', *Le Nouvel Observateur*, 4–10 April 1991, international edition, pp.65–7

Galey, Matthieu, 'Roman: Modiano, l'Hoffmann des villes', *L'Express*, 7 February 1981, pp.30–1

Gaudemar, Antoine de, 'Une inépuisable nostalgie', *Magazine Littéraire*, 192 (February 1983), p.65

——, 'Modiano le prisonnier', *Libération*, 7 January 1988, p.34

Gellings, Paul, 'Souvenirs de Nerval', *Rapports: Het Franse Boek*, Amsterdam, LXI (1991), pp.173–4

Golsan, Joseph, 'Author, Identity and the Voice of History in Patrick Modiano's *La Ronde de nuit* and *Les Boulevards de ceinture*', *Romance Notes*, Chapel Hill, XXXI, 3 (Spring 1991), pp.187–96

Golsan, Richard J., 'Collaboration, Alienation and the Crisis of Identity in the Film and Fiction of Patrick Modiano', in Wendell Aycock and Michael Schoenecke (eds), *Film and Literature: A Comparative Approach to Adaptation*, Lubbock, Texas Tech University Press, 1988, pp.107–21

Grainville, Patrick, 'Patrick Modiano: retour aux sources', *Le Figaro Littéraire*, 1 February 1988, p.vii

Guicharnaud, Jacques, 'De la Rive gauche à l'au-delà de la Concorde: Remarques sur la topographie parisienne de Patrick Modiano', in Catherine Lafarge (ed.), *Essays in Honor of Georges May: Stanford French and Italian Studies 65*, Saratoga, Anma Libri, 1990, pp.341–52

Josselin, Jean-François, 'Méfiez-vous du Modiano qui dort', *Le Nouvel Observateur*, 22–28 August 1986, international edition, pp.56–7

——, 'Patrick tel qu'en Patoche', *Le Nouvel Observateur*, 8–14 January 1988, p.61

Joye, Jean-Claude, *Littérature immédiate: Cinq études sur Jeanne Bourin, Julien Green, Patrick Modiano, Yves Navarre, Françoise Sagan*, Berne/Frankfurt/New York/Paris, Lang, 1990, pp.89–116

Jutrin, Monique, 'A propos de *La Place de l'Étoile* de Patrick Modiano', in Louis Forestier (ed.), *Arthur Rimbaud 4: Autour de 'Ville(s)' et de 'Génie'*, Minard, 1980, pp.107–11

Kaminskas, Jurate, 'Quête/enquête – à la recherche du genre: *Voyage de noces*, de Patrick Modiano', *The French Review*, Champaign, LXVI, 6 (May 1993), pp.932–40

Kanters, Robert, 'La Nuit de Patrick Modiano', *Le Figaro Littéraire*, 27 October–2 November 1969, pp.23–4

Lambron, Marc, 'Modiano et la mélancolie française', *NRF*, 340 (1 May 1981), pp.90–4

Lévi-Valensi, Jacqueline and Valette-Fondo, Madeleine, 'Le Romanesque de l'Absurde en France après 1960 – essai de définition à partir de quelques exemples', in Jean Bessière (ed.), *L'Intersiècle: 1: Absurde et Renouveaux romanesques 1960–1980*, Minard, 1986, pp.55–106 (pp.97–101)

Magnan, Jean-Marie, 'Les Revenants de nulle part', *Sud*, Marseilles, 28/29 (1979), pp.181–6

Martinoir, Francine Ninane de, 'Patrick Modiano: *Villa Triste*', *L'École des Lettres II*, 1 (1984–5), pp.7–18

——, 'Patrick Modiano: *Villa Triste* (II)', *L'École des Lettres II*, 2 (1984–5), pp.3–13

——, 'Sur le cadastre de la fiction', *La Quinzaine Littéraire*, 1–15 February 1985, p.5

Nettelbeck, Colin, and Hueston, Penelope, *Patrick Modiano: pièces d'identité: écrire l'entretemps*, Minard, 1986

Nourissier, François, 'Modiano: souvenir d'en France, souvenir d'enfance', *Le Point*, 11 January 1988, pp.72–3

Pécheur, Jacques, '*De si braves garçons*', *Le Français dans le monde*, 175 (February–March 1983), p.9

——, 'Patrick Modiano: *Dimanches d'août*', *Le Français dans le monde*, 205 (November–December 1986), p.18

Petit, Susan, 'Modiano, Patrick, *Remise de peine*', *The French Review*, Champaign, LXIII, 2 (December 1989), pp.408–9

Poirot-Delpech, Bertrand, 'Un diamant gros comme le Négresco', *Le Monde*, 29 August 1986, pp.11, 14

——, 'Charmes de l'imprécision', *Le Monde*, 10 February 1989, pp.15, 17

Poirson, Alain, 'Le Malaise du passé', *France Nouvelle*, 6 November 1978, pp.41–2

Prince, Gerald, 'Re-Membering Modiano, or Something Happened', *Sub-stance*, Madison, 49 (1986), pp.35–43

——, 'Patrick Modiano (30 July 1945–)', in Catherine Savage Brosman (ed.), *French Novelists since 1960* [= *Dictionary of Literary Biography*, vol. 83], Detroit, Gale Research, 1989, pp.147–53

——, *Narrative as Theme: Studies in French Fiction*, Lincoln/London, University of Nebraska Press, 1992, pp.121–32, 147–8

Pudlowski, Gilles, 'Tout Modiano en 60 pages', *Les Nouvelles Littéraires*, 19–26 November 1981, p.48

Scherman, Timothy H., 'Translating from Memory: Patrick Modiano in Postmodern Context', *Studies in Twentieth-Century Literature*, Manhattan, XVI, 2 (Summer 1992), pp.289–303

Sénart, Philippe, 'Revue théâtrale', *La Revue des deux Mondes*, July 1974, pp.180–1

Sturrock, John, 'Past Possibilities', *TLS*, London, 3 May 1981, p.506

Vercaemer, Philippe, 'Ville et Mémoire chez Patrick Modiano: *Quartier perdu*', *Eidôlon*, Talence, Université de Bordeaux III, 27 (February 1986), pp.209–22

Vercier, Bruno and Lecarme, Jacques, *La Littérature en France depuis 1968*, Bordas, 1982, pp.130, 293–9

Wardi, Charlotte, 'Mémoire et écriture dans l'œuvre de Patrick Modiano', *Les Nouveaux Cahiers*, 80 (Spring 1985), pp.40–8

Warehime, Marja, 'Originality and Narrative Nostalgia: Shadows in Modiano's *Rue des Boutiques Obscures*', *French Forum*, Lexington, XII, 3 (September 1987), pp.335–45

Index